MEMBERS
ONLY

*Bestselling titles by the same author*

Another Bloody Tour
Cricket XXXX Cricket

# MEMBERS ONLY

FRANCES EDMONDS

HEINEMANN : LONDON

William Heinemann Ltd
Michelin House, 81 Fulham Road, London SW3 6RB
LONDON   MELBOURNE   AUCKLAND

First published 1989
Copyright © 1989 Frances Edmonds

British Library Cataloguing in Publication Data

Edmonds, Frances, *1952–*
Members only.
1. Great Britain. Politics. Humour
I. Title
320.941'0207

ISBN 0 434 22184 8

Printed and bound in Great Britain by
Richard Clay Ltd, Bungay, Suffolk

*To my husband, Philippe-Henri Edmonds*

# Contents

| | |
|---|---:|
| Acknowledgements | ix |
| 1 A parliamentary affair | 1 |
| 2 Intruder in the palace | 7 |
| 3 Up the greasy pole | 27 |
| 4 The power, the glory, or just better than working? | 58 |
| 5 Rule Margarita! | 111 |
| 6 The brothers at Blackpool | 143 |
| 7 Brighton flock | 171 |
| 8 1992 and all that | 203 |
| 9 The next steps: a Thatcherite solution to the Houses of Parliament | 226 |

# Acknowledgements

I should like to thank the many people who have given so generously of their time and knowledge in helping me on this project. It is unfortunate that the more interesting information has often been gleaned from contributors whose political prospects would not be enhanced by any open acknowledgement. I shall therefore refrain from mentioning them by name. They know who they are and I thank them nevertheless. I must also take this opportunity to insist that those specifically named here cannot be held responsible for any of the opinions I express.

My greatest debt of gratitude is to Stewart Steven, editor of the *Mail on Sunday*, without whom this book could never have been written. (Sorry about the knighthood, Stewart!) There are a further four members of the *Mail on Sunday* staff whose assistance over the year has been invaluable to me: Alan Cochrane (assistant editor); Jenny Cowley (editorial assistant); Peter Dobbie (political editor) and Richard Heller (staff writer). On the publishing side, Helen Fraser (publisher, Heinemann) has provided unflagging enthusiasm and encouragement and I have been much comforted by her presence. I am grateful, too, to Derek Wyatt, my erstwhile editor at Heinemann, who commissioned this book and, with an uncanny degree of prescience, resigned immediately for a job in television. I should also like to thank David Hooper (Biddle & Co.), Heinemann's legal eagle, who has so far managed to steer me away from litigation; Hilary Davies (Pan Books), whose friendship has been much appreciated; Leo and Jilly Cooper who, amongst myriad other kindnesses, dreamt up the title of this book whilst I drank them dry of sloe gin; Tony Brooks, for the brilliant cartoons; my literary and business manager, Desmond Elliott (Arlington Books), who has made my life so much more fun; and my mother, family and friends who have tolerated my many neuroses during the gestation of this book. Most particularly I should like to thank my brother, Dr Kieran Moriarty, whose dissection of the original manuscript was the most meticulous of all.

London, November 1988

# 1 / A parliamentary affair

SHE HAD NEVER BEEN ONE
TO WORK WITH DISTRACTIONS.

The seduction was a push-over, though Heaven knows she should have seen it coming. She couldn't even claim naïveté as an excuse. Come off it, a woman in her thirties, she was no longer an impressionable, empty-headed *ingénue*, if she'd ever been that in the first place. Besides, she was no newcomer to the game. She'd been involved before – twice before, in fact – and knew the consequences. It would be wonderful at the beginning, of course – it always was: the excitement of novelty, the thrill of the unknown, the sense of exhilaration tempered only occasionally by that twinge of treacherous duplicity. But she didn't need the confusion of this added emotional commitment. Not now, of all times. Not now that she was finally beginning to get things sorted out. All right, so their twelve years of marriage had never been exactly harmonious, always more Schoenberg than Schubert, but things had been improving lately. As consorts went, Phil was not a bad lad. He left home early and he came home late: an ideal husband, really – out of the way all day. He seemed much happier since he'd dumped that fearful crowd he'd been hanging around with for far too long.

What a bunch of bruisers! Boozing, swearing, fighting, gambling, womanizing, getting stoned and stirring up racial strife wherever they went – she wondered whether the Home Secretary had outlawed them yet – the England Cricket Team. Anyway, he didn't appear to be missing them now. If the new, ice-blue Rolls was anything to go by, he was already carving himself a comfortable little niche in the City. As what, precisely, she never cared to enquire. Financial adviser to Lester Piggott, for all she knew.

No, it wasn't his fault her life was beginning to feel so dull, so meaningless and boring. Poor Phil. He had worked his spinning fingers to the bone to give her everything a woman could possibly want: a Schedule 'D' lifestyle; a joint overdraft; regular visits from the VAT man; total, gilt-edged insecurity and much, much more. But somehow all this was no longer enough. True, three interviews on *Wogan*, a choice of *Desert Island Discs*, *A Question of Sport* with Bernard Manning, and an appearance on *Daytime Live* with her childhood hero, Sooty, left little to strive for. And yet, from somewhere in her innermost being, a nagging void cried out to be filled, an increasingly urgent need just begged to be answered. The day that voice from the past enticed her to lunch, she knew that she could never resist, that in the end, she was bound to succumb. He had even booked a table at their favourite place . . .

The *maître d'* welcomed her like a long-lost child. He asked no questions, refused to probe, ignored her lengthy and unexplained absence. At Greek Street's Gay Hussar discretion was of the essence, for there was nothing that Victor, the Hungarian from Barrow-in-Furness, had not heard or seen in his forty years as keeper of the Houses of Parliament's best-loved restaurant. It was there in the days of the post-war Labour government that firebrands such as Gaitskell and Attlee had redesigned the nation over bowls of boiling leek-and-potato soup. His list of clients contained a formidable line-up of Prime Ministers and cabinet ministers, of personalities who had all left their hallmark on British policy-making. But of the whole bunch it was one of the earliest regulars, Michael Foot, who still ranked in Victor's esteem as the greatest man he had ever known: 'Absolutely pure, straight and decent, never able to see the bad in anyone, only the good.' How such a person could have prospered in politics remained one of those imponderable mysteries, like where Mrs Thatcher found time to have the tint; how Roy Hattersley's tongue fitted into his mouth; whether Neil Kinnock's mind had been irretrievably lost in the labyrinths of its own subordinate clauses; and who on earth was Robert Maclennan. Towards the kitchen, the shelves heaved with the weighty tomes of many appreciative patrons; *The Diaries of Barbara Castle*; *The Diaries of Lord Longford*; and a copy of *Savages* – the intimate reminiscences, no doubt, of the Transport and General Workers' Union.

Things had not changed since last she was there. It was no surprise to see Lord Donoughue (former policy adviser to both Harold Wilson and James Callaghan) ensconced as usual. He even listed the Gay Hussar among his recreations in *Who's Who*. 'It's the only private club in London where they don't charge the members,' he had told her on a previous occasion. 'It's got everything: the best value, the best food, and Victor.' In another corner, ITN's diplomatic correspondent, Jon Snow, was lunching with the kindly, avuncular Lord Longford. She noticed former Defence Secretary, Michael Heseltine, leaving in a hurry of hair and hubris, not entirely dissimilar to his departure from the cabinet, really. Elsewhere, that most articulate of Tory renegades, Mr Julian Critchley, was swapping scurrilous tales with a well-known publisher of military history. 'She'll only go,' wafted one intriguing snippet of conversation, 'if they send her to the Lords as Archbishop of Canterbury . . .'

She made her way to the room upstairs where he was waiting impatiently. The legendary Albert, unobtrusively efficient, showed her to her seat and left them alone. It was far more cosy and intimate there, hidden away from the inquisitive gaze of half a dozen rubber-necking journos and a goodly contingent from *Private Eye*. Their organ lived a mere step away, conveniently situated on the other side of Soho Square.

'Abandon hope all ye who enter here.' The warning flashed suddenly across her mind, a vague memory of sunny student days long gone, of hours spent one eye on the prescribed texts, watching agile young cricketers at play on Fenner's. She smiled wryly to herself. She was already too far in, she realized, to extricate herself from this one now.

Of course, she could have said no at the outset, but he was not the sort of man to take no for an answer. Besides, she was ripe for it. The seed had fallen on fertile soil. She was in the mood for mischief and he knew it. But where would it all lead to this time? Illicit midnight trysts in dark, seedy bars. Snatched lunches of whispered conversations in quiet corners. The odd, eagerly anticipated assignation cancelled at a moment's notice. And, of course, the constant threat of discovery. She could hear her more censorious friends already: 'Why waste your life like that? ... Why throw yourself away? ... Isn't it high time you just settled down and had some kids?' And what would her husband make of all the odd and implausible late-night absences? No, on second thoughts, no danger there. She'd just returned from a month's book promotion tour to Australia. Good old Phil. It had taken him three weeks even to notice she'd gone, and only then when the contents of the deep freeze had eventually run out.

He came on very heavy. It was all far too fast. She must have time to think things over, she countered, weigh the pros and cons. Her rash and impetuous nature had spelt trouble before, lost her friends, made her enemies, filled her wardrobe full of disastrous designer mistakes, and the bathroom cabinet with congealed cosmetics.

'No,' she insisted, getting up to leave. Not for the first time, she had eaten too little, and had had too much to drink. 'You know you can't expect a decision just like that. What you're suggesting is a major upheaval. It's all right for you, your life goes on the same. But I'm the one who'll end up all alone. I'm the one who'll spend the sleepless nights agonizing over what to do next. At least give me some breathing space, will you? And please, in the meantime, don't call me at home.'

He knew even then that he could afford to hang on. She'd taken the bait. All he had to do now was reel her in.

Back home in Notting Hill Gate, that Caribbean end of Kensington, the full enormity of his proposal began to dawn on her. As usual she sought solace in the solitude of her study, *incomunicada* but for two separate telephone lines, a fax machine, a television, an environmentally apposite ghetto-blaster, a video of *Gone with the Wind* and a radio tuned into BBC's Radio 4. No, she had never been one to work with distractions. It was only there that she felt comfortable, surrounded by her prized possessions: an autographed poster of her role-model, Mike Gatting, recently returned from Pakistan and soon, so she'd heard, to be appointed Emeritus Urdu Professor of Wit, Repartee and Race Relations; the personalized, bicentennial Fabergé egg, brought all the way from Australia by doting members of the Test and County Cricket Board and movingly inscribed: 'To Frances, in gratitude for her outstanding contribution to English cricket.' There were mementoes, too, for her fifteen years as an international conference interpreter: a commemorative coin of the 1984 World Economic Summit, a token of the Foreign and Commonwealth Office's legendary munificence, it looked like a krugerrand and depicted London's Lancaster House. Once it had been burgled from her flat in Brussels, only to be restored through the mail box with an impertinent explanation in impeccable English: 'This is not gold, it is only copper. It is what we Europeans have come to expect from your Mrs Thatcher's government!' And, of course, she had her hoard of happy memories: of the Akasaka Palace in Tokyo, where a forward posse of President Reagan's heavies had flattened her and colleague, Jennifer, flush with the ornamental stucco-work, leaving interesting ormolu-encrusted imprints all over their cleavage. The dear President had been so embarrassed. 'Sorry, girls,' he called out jovially. Oh, how unbelievably handsome he was. So incredibly tall. So improbably dark. So astoundingly clever and well briefed. It was easy to see how nothing escaped him . . .

Was she prepared to throw all this up for the sake of one man's passing whim? True, she had reached a watershed in her linguistic career. She could no longer listen to anything any politician had left to say, let alone repeat it. For a conference interpreter this clearly had its drawbacks. And she would miss that previous incarnation as a cricket widow, too – or at least a few of the characters: the golden-haired Gower, the extrovert Lamb, and even the irrepressible I. T. Botham. Why, 'Beefy', so she'd heard, had recently claimed yet another brace of victims. And that was only in Economy Class! Ah, yes. Happy days while they lasted. But when all was said and done it was now time to move on. She turned on her new word-processor as if looking for an omen. What temporary aberration had induced her to buy the wretched thing in the first place? A Luddite with even the simplest of consumer durables, she stared hopelessly at its green screen in advanced catatonic trance. 'Hello, Frances,' it winked at her in its own inimitable, user-friendly way. 'How are you today?' Sycophantic machine, but at least it was more communicative than her preoccupied husband. No, there was no denying it. She needed the buzz of something else, some new, extra-marital excitement. But was she about to make the most dreadful mistake?

She picked up the telephone and dialled that old familiar number. Now she'd made up her mind, she wanted to let him know straightaway. She wondered whether Angela, his secretary, had recognized her voice as she tried unsuccessfully for some time to connect them. The line was engaged for hours, it seemed, but for once he was actually there at his desk.

'You win,' she conceded, when she finally got through. 'I'll sign the contract. A book, if you insist, on the Houses of Parliament.'

The satisfaction in his voice was clearly audible. 'I knew you'd see it my way in the end,' he replied. 'It was either that, you understand, or another bloody XXXX tour . . .'

# 2 / Intruder in the palace

CHILDREN NEVER TIRE OF ANIMALS IN THEIR
NATURAL, PRIMEVAL STATE.

I remember my first visit to the Houses of Parliament as if it were yesterday. I must have been about eleven or twelve, and it was Upper III Alpha's annual class outing. Even under normal circumstances, the young ladies of Upper III Alpha were hardly of the 'sugar and spice' variety, and a day trip to London meant mischief in spades. For weeks beforehand we plotted suitable revenge on Mother Mary Paul, who was steadfastly refusing to allow us out in civvies. Ursuline convents, of course, believe in penance, but to us the pain of stigmata seemed infinitely preferable to the ignominy of being seen out in those lurid green gymslips and unspeakable velour hats. Mother Mary Paul was unyielding, however. Uniform, she felt, would give the Metropolitan Police Force a better chance of locating any 'runners' and, besides, she added meaningfully, after the major school scandal of Linda Brewer's illicit red suspender belt, our parents would want us to look 'decent' for the local MP.

The day release was to be a two-centre affair: Parliament followed by London Zoo. It is wonderful how children, despite abundant television exposure, never tire of animals in their natural, unspoilt, primeval state. We spent a fascinating few hours watching them jumping up and down, chattering mindlessly, straining like children on potties, dribbling at the mouth, whining, shrieking, laughing and fighting, ganging together in packs and observing strange, pre-ordained pecking orders. It was all great fun, and we were bitterly disappointed when it was time for the zoo.

And so it was with a fair dose of nostalgia for friends and times long gone that I revisited the Palace of Westminster some two decades later, this time in somewhat more purposeful mood. Resplendent once again with its recently scrubbed and gilded Gothic curlicues, this great secular cathedral rarely fails to impress the casual sightseer. Of all our national monuments, it must surely rank as one of the most evocative. I still think of the many Christmases spent far away from home on tour, when the mere chimes of Big Ben tolling London time over the BBC World Service airwaves could reduce the most hardened of cricketers to a sentimental blub; and of country clubs in Madras and Kingston, where the familiar image on a well-known sauce bottle would engender stirrings of home-sickness in even the toughest of tourists. But these are sentiments for popular consumption only. The view of the working inmate of the Houses of Parliament is consistently more jaundiced: 'No air, little natural light and few bathrooms,' complained one newly arrived MP. 'No wonder the place is ridden with halitosis, BO and scurf!'

Undeterred by such prospects of malodorous dandruff, I wandered once again along St Stephen's Hall to Central Lobby. The place was full of American cellulite-sufferers, chewing low-calorie gum and ransacking the book-stand for soft-focus postcards of places unknown. Is there any other national assembly in the world which enjoys – or rather *endures* – such liberal access? It is difficult to imagine the natives of Capitol Hill, for instance, allowing themselves to be similarly besieged by 'Kiss-me-quick/Here-we-go' mobs of holidaying Brits. Most of our Transatlantic cousins were after icons of the Prime Minister – 'Your lurvely lady,' as one gentleman in a 'Love You, Las Vegas' sweatshirt put it so neatly. But another had heard that a different kiosk further inside the building purveyed a far better class of memento: tote bags, bottles of Scotch, table mats and after-dinner mints.

'All in green and gold,' he promised. 'Just like Harrods, only much more prestigious.'

'Yessir,' drawled one delightful, Southern octogenarian belle who, judging by the twinkle in her eye, might well have been related to Miss Joan Rivers. 'And the guide on the bus told me they were thinking of selling ladies' lingerie there too. Real silk French camiknickers. Hasn't come to anything yet, though. Just can't decide where to put that there portcullis logo.'

The group ruminated this one for a minute in silence. Flogging ladies' underwear, of all places, *here*? They had heard of Mrs Thatcher's soft spot for Marks and Spencer, for both its shops and their keepers. But who would have dreamt that the 'Mother of Parliaments' was so fast degenerating into the PM's local Westminster branch?

Further along the corridor, a well-heeled French couple were studying the sweep of arrestingly poor pictures.

'They're supposed to depict the "Building of Britain",' remarked madame, heavily caparisoned in Gianfranco Ferre costume jewellery, and decidedly unimpressed.

'No wonder they're so bad,' replied monsieur, chauvinist *par excellence* and equally unmoved.

On behalf of the nation I felt suitably aggrieved, but on further inspection was obliged to admit that *les Français* really did have a point. For have we not, to paraphrase Wordsworth on Westminster, 'anything to show more fair'? Or could we not, with nearly 90 per cent of the Tate Gallery's pictures rotting away in some long-forgotten cellar, find a few better exhibits to grace the corridors of power? How odd that none other than Sir Henry Newbolt himself, he of 'play up, play up, and play the game' celebrity, should have selected these second-rate daubs to hang there in the first place. And how ominous that the mediocre manifestations of his suspect taste in art, together with the noble aspirations of his hearty line in poetry, should end so abruptly at Central Lobby.

Of all the vantage-points in the Houses of Parliament, Central Lobby is the ideal place to sit and stare, to watch the comings and goings of many of the rich, famous, powerful, influential, bright, admirable, impressive and even Mr David Steel. It is a constant source of wonderment how so many people manage to become members of this place without losing one jot of their insignificance. The atmosphere here always bears more than a passing resemblance to a stint in church. Muffled voices mingle, rise and reverberate against the sparkling Venetian mosaics of the great vaulted roof, eventually bouncing back in an unintelligible continuum of sound, like a bad attack of tinnitus, or President Mitterrand before he had his teeth fixed. The place is full of petrified Gothic gargoyles, not all of whom belong to the House of Lords, and ornate wood carvings, impregnated with Pledge. From above the four exits, the patron saints of England, Ireland, Scotland and Wales seem to view proceedings with celestial indifference, though perhaps deep down, like members of the Barbarians' selection committee, they retain an abiding interest in the performance of their own lot. How many happy hours I've since managed to clock up there, at least three of them waiting for 'Citizen' Ken Livingstone to fail to materialize for a twice-confirmed interview. Perhaps on reflection I should have suggested an expensive lunch at Monsieur Thompson's trendy French restaurant in Kensington Park Road. Older, more cynical members of the dreaded 'capitalist press' confirm that 'Red' Ken always manages to pitch up for those. But an evening spent slouched on one of the green leather-upholstered seats need not be time completely wasted. It is always interesting to speculate which politician's cerebral qualities might most be enhanced by an unexpected crowning with the great brass Hardman chandelier, or to try and decipher the meaning of the Latin inscription embedded in the Minton tiled floor. Another decade of comprehensive education, combined with Mr Kenneth Baker's ideas on core curricula, will doubtless ensure that the classical motto, along with everything else in Westminster, remains a mystery to most.

To the south of Central Lobby lies the House of Lords, where my first excursion was sponsored by Lord Elwyn-Jones, the much loved former Lord High Chancellor, now in his eighties. But such considerations of *gravitas* and status appear to cut little mustard with the boyos back home in the valleys: 'So Jones the High Chancellor did well for himself in London,' they concede. 'But the other brother, Idris . . . Ah, the other brother played *international rugby for Wales!*'

For the alternative person, the sort of person concerned about equal rights for gay whales or one-parent organic vegetable growers, and suddenly overwhelmed by a terrible urge to abseil in on their Lordships from the Visitors' Gallery, then Lord Monkswell, sometime labourer and factory worker, might prove the most useful friend at court. As it is, my swinging, revolutionary days evaporated in 1968 with *Paris Match* pin-ups of 'Danny the Red', and I took tea instead with the utmost gentility and Baroness Hooper, erstwhile Conservative Member of the European Parliament, and now one of the new young breed of 'working peers'. For those Lords in search of stronger liquid refreshment, she informed me, the Bishops' Room was the place to go, though no one ever talks of being as drunk as a bishop. It had certainly not taken the government long to rope in a hard-working, legal eagle like Gloria. A Whip after a mere six weeks, and soon responsible for steering the controversial Great Education Reform Bill (GERBIL) through the Lords, she will do well if only because it is impossible not to like her. Judging by the style of a different lady in 'the other place', this approach has yet to be espoused as official party policy.

This glorious Upper Chamber, ironically enough, has for years been more familiar to us than its drab green, directly elected counterpart down the corridor. It is perhaps the ritziest example of the work of Augustus Pugin, the inspired Gothic interior designer who, together with architect Charles Barry, recreated the place after the disastrous fire of 1834. Like Kenny, the couturier son of that remarkable Australian, Dame Edna Everidge, neither partner in this talented duo had any time for understatement, believing instead that 'tawdriness' was only ever the result of 'half measures'. Consequently, there is more gold-leaf in evidence here than anywhere barring President Bokassa's bedroom – though, one fondly assumes, less hanky-panky. At the far end of the chamber sits a squat, red, bulging pouffe – not another opponent of the Local Authorities Bill's notorious Clause 28, but the Lord Chancellor's Woolsack, stuffed with balls of wool from every country of the Commonwealth. To some, this may serve as a reminder of the pastoral nature of our economy; to others, of the bits of fluff collected on the more successful interparliamentary delegations.

Our better acquaintance with the House of Lords is due, in large measure, to the earlier intrusion of the television cameras. Just how little people know about the workings of Westminster was underlined by early complaints from disappointed TV viewers. Some even bewailed the fact that their Lordships appeared to be wearing ordinary clothes, not ermine-trimmed robes and the family fender! But the Lords rightly refuse to bow to any plebeian pressures, and have gone to great lengths to ensure that the solemnity of their station shall not be trivialized by any of the small screen's usual shenanigans. The strict ground rules laid down for all broadcasts are similar to those sought for the televising of the Commons: no focusing on somnolent or congenitally bewildered members; no undue attention to surreptitious scratchings of the private parts, pickings of the nose, or rehoistings of the bra-strap; no coverage of demonstrations of any sort . . . like the Blackpool of Stanley Holloway's *Albert and the Lion*, in fact, 'nothing to laugh at at all'.

Not that the place is as ludicrous as people commonly care to think. True, the level of debate is very uneven. It may, on occasion, sound unutterably inane and irrelevant, but more often, of course, it is not quite that good. For all that, the quality of discussion is still far higher than in the Commons, and much less partisan. Peers of the Realm cannot be threatened into toeing a party line by fear of constituency reprisal, nor seduced into acquiescence by promises of political preferment as Keeper of the Cabinet Hairspray. Indeed, after their apotheosis to 'the other place', there is really very little left with which to tempt or intimidate them. Neither do their Lordships appear to be falling over one another for the dubious distinction of leading on radical, difficult and unpopular third-term Thatcher legislation. And yet, with a majority of over 100 seats in the Commons, it is from the Lords that the government has been expecting its fiercest opposition. True, it is not difficult to poke fun at this somewhat remote and archaic institution, especially after lunch, when the vision of noble Lords following proceedings through amplifiers in their headrests generates that unfortunate and widely held impression of a twilight home of geriatrics slumped in dazed post-prandial torpor. This, however, is far from the whole story. It is received wisdom that many peers are so old they have to be carbon-dated. But it is precisely this combination of great age and experience which provides the House of Lords with its strongest suit. Former ministers and Prime Ministers, captains of industry, people who have all excelled in their own individual fields, clearly still have a valuable contribution to make to national debate and such folk are only too happy to invest their authority in the occasional well-timed speech.

In the Upper House, however, as opposed to the Commons, it is now often down to the 'youngsters' to man the government's barricades and to do much of the major slog. It was positively endearing, for instance, to watch the boyish Lord Beaverbrook in early 1988, nowhere near as alarming as his illustrious ancestor but already a junior minister, trying to fend off awkward questions from a far more seasoned Opposition. On one occasion, fielding a few real nasties on European Community draft toy safety and unit-pricing directives (hardly the sort of stuff of which impassioned debate is made), his efforts to stonewall met with polite ripples of mirth. 'My Lords,' he concluded in apology for the Consumer Ministers' slow progress on the matter, 'in Europe, nothing ever happens overnight.' Older members, chaps with aeons of Council of Europe, European Parliament and Western European Union sessions under their belts, awoke to guffaw at such disarming naïveté. *Overnight*, as statesmen of their greater understanding had long since learned, is the *only* time anything worth while *ever* happens in Europe . . .

The real cockpit of the nation, however, is to be found to the north of Central Lobby, far more restrained than its patrician counterpart in every facet, apart from that of behaviour. The House of Commons, like the rest of the palace, has had its fair share of setbacks over the centuries. Badly damaged during the Second World War, the original Barry's Chamber was later lovingly and punctiliously restored to all its former shabby glory. Too bad that architect Barry genuinely loathed it to begin with. Apart from on set-piece occasions, such as the State Opening of Parliament, the Budget, or Prime Minister's Question Time, most visitors are struck by the preponderance of decidedly empty benches. Clearly, like the rest of us, MPs have better things to do than to listen to other MPs. On the other hand, for the major events, the Lower Chamber can only accommodate around 450 of the 650 members comfortably, leaving latecomers to push and jostle as if for *Phantom of the Opera* returns. It is this, according to the late Sir Winston Churchill, which gives Parliament that indefinable 'sense of crowd and urgency', hardly the overwhelming impression derived from the average afternoon spent listening to, say, Mr Peter Bottomley, minister for Belisha beacons, 'stop' signs, zebra crossings, breathalyser tests and clampers. Not that he in particular is any worse – indeed, he is often quite a lot better – than many of his colleagues. On occasion, however, he does show a distressing tendency to obfuscate himself into complete incomprehensibility. 'Poor Bottomley,' one sympathetic yet cynical Tory backbencher was heard to aver on that uncomfortable occasion. 'She's got him talking through his surname!' For those who want to prosper in politics, a soul, it appears, is the average subscription.

The very layout of the chamber lends itself to our confrontational style of politics. MPs recall their first few days in Parliament, finally facing the lifelong foe in the class struggle, and trying to size up the competition across the floor: 'Don't worry about those bastards opposite,' old hands are wont to advise them. 'Watch out for the *real* enemies right behind your back!'

It must all be completely overwhelming for the average raw recruit. The Houses of Parliament cover an area of some eight acres, and the entire building is an endless maze of cubby-holes, committee rooms, staircases and corridors. Much of it is incredibly grubby, though perhaps not quite so noxious as must have been the case in earlier times. Quaint old traditions still persist, as vestigial as a brain in a Young Conservative. Even today, in memory of days when the chamber itself, and not merely the level of discussion in it, made strong men heave, members are entitled to a free pinch of snuff from the principal doorkeeper, guardian of the snuffbox. Requests for ground amphetamines whenever Sir Geoffrey 'Verbal Valium' Howe is at the Dispatch Box have thus far been resisted.

But finally the great day dawned when I might no longer share the joys of the Visitors' Gallery, savoured over the months with convivial sausage-makers from Schleswig-Holstein and luminescent nuclear waste disposal experts from places such as Mol. Possession of a press pass means instant elevation to the rarefied heights of the Press Gallery, where egregious political commentators only *look* like convivial sausage-makers from Schleswig-Holstein. The atmosphere there, with its super-abundance of men, booze and gossip, is more than vaguely redolent of a Test Match press box, abiding as it does by similar, unspoken rules on who sits where and for how long. I wonder, as the benefits of television coverage are gradually rumbled, whether the political journos will go the same way as their cricketing colleagues and base their reports on the day's periodic edited highlights, forsaking neither bed nor the twenty-tog duvet. There are about 300 of these accredited journalists in the Houses of Parliament, about eighty or so of whom have lobby passes. These intrepid souls, undaunted by twentieth-century tales of communicable disease, hang around in the Members' Lobby, trying hard to get stories. Failing that, and gaunt with the pressures of imminent deadlines, they hang around in Annie's Bar, trying hard to get sloshed. Annie's Bar, the recurrent leitmotif of many a poor lobby correspondent's life, is a dingy room in the bowels of the building. A place where correspondents, members, and men described as the 'usual channels' all congregate to swap tales and scandalous titbits, it operates on the basis of an unspoken deal. Indeed, the entire establishment seems to be run on such arrangements. For any comments made here are non-attributable and strictly 'off the record' – an admirable convention which makes a virtue of necessity. The usual fifteen rounds of double Scotch and soda and no one can remember who said what to start with anyway.

Far more insidious, of course, is the controversial system of unattributable lobby briefings, secretive sessions orchestrated to devastating effect by the Prime Minister's Press Secretary, the Prince of Propaganda, Mr Bernard Ingham. A craggy man with improbable carrot-hued eyebrows, this increasingly politicized civil servant presides with impunity over these, the government's own systematic breaches of the Official Secrets Act. It really is the most intriguing phenomenon. Nowadays, we hear much sanctimonious clap-trap about ministerial 'leaks', the most priggish, quite amazingly, perpetrated by one protagonist of the Westland scandal, the Prime Minister herself. But the most damaging leaks of all are rarely 'accidents', those few cases of civil servant mutants developing consciences or similar failures in the system. On the contrary, most leaks are plots carefully organized by ministers themselves, specifically designed to cause maximum embarrassment to a political 'friend'. (Witness the treatment of Michael Heseltine during the Westland affair.) In Ingham, the Prime Minister has a direct, yet officially unrecognized conduit for nicely processed 'information'. Whilst the entire lobby knows what Mr Ingham says, no one will ever admit that it was he who actually said it. It seems an extraordinary way to run a railway and, to their credit, papers like the *Independent* have always refused to play the game. Not that it has ever been a particularly honourable game to play. It is the sort of game whereby a former Leader of the House of Commons, John Biffen, wakes up to read in the morning papers that he is about to become surplus to Prime Ministerial requirements, that he is already, in effect, 'semi-detached'. More disturbing still, it is the sort of game whereby even Her Majesty the Queen must be apprised via the national press, that she would not be encouraged to visit the USSR should the opportunity ever arise.

From up in the Press Gallery eyrie, there is a fairly good view of Mrs Thatcher and her troops of Roundheads. From my occasional position, in the cheap seats, I may look down on the bobbing wave of conical crania, often disturbingly bereft of any sign of individual cerebral activity. What a life of terrible tedium, that of the average backbencher! Seldom asked for his opinion, merely his vote, he can rely only on the eternal hope of promotion to sustain him through those desperate hours as lobby fodder. Many of us now quite genuinely believe that a genetic engineer has been appointed to Conservative Central Office. How else could the new generation of Tory MPs appear so virtually interchangeable? White, male, middle-class, middle-aged, sober-suited, sporting a blue silk tie, married to a sweet young thing with sensible, Maggie-lookalike Aquascutum suits and 2.4 kids – for all the world, just like that ghastly UHT long-life milk now on offer from the Continent: sanitized, sterilised and absolutely homogenized.

'Where on earth do they find these extraordinary young men?' one German ex-general asked veteran Scottish Nationalist, Winnie Ewing, when a similar influx of blue-rosetted clones arrived in the European Parliament after the first direct elections of 1979. In vain, he looked for the usual quota of British 'characters' –

politicians in the robustly aggressive John Prescott/Tam Dalyell mould – and was visibly disappointed with the anonymous job lot which was delivered instead.

'All from Harrods,' replied Winnie, adding that Harrods is sadly no longer *quite* what it was.

To be fair, there are growing signs of dissent emerging from the 'damper' reaches of the Tory backbenches, but the majority of ambitious Young Turks still nod, boo, cheer and laugh at all the appropriate moments in the House, and generally do precisely what the parliamentary Whips tell them to do. Perhaps they ought to think of taking the Right Honourable Sir Joseph Porter, KCB, and First Lord of the Admiralty aboard Gilbert and Sullivan's *HMS Pinafore*, as their patron. For his was the sort of philosophy with which the clones could readily identify:

> I always voted at my party's call,
> And I never thought of thinking for myself at all.

And perhaps, with apologies to Sir Joseph, there might have been a message there for a certain someone sitting on the Opposition benches too:

> I thought so little they rewarded me
> By making me the leader of the SLD.

The Opposition benches, of course, tend to field a more mixed social bag of representatives. They range from public-school boys, like Mr Michael Meacher, intent on living it down, to chaps like Leith's left-wing mace-basher, Mr Ron Brown, intent on living it up. But in today's Filofax-generation Parliamentary Labour Party, there are fewer genuinely working-class members in evidence, a growing majority being drawn from the ranks of teachers, lecturers, journalists, and the 'yap' professions in general. Such bourgeois considerations are rarely allowed to inhibit the many atavistic flights of nostalgia about the jolly, fraternal old days 'down the pit' – the best originated by that most professional of sons-of-toil, Mr Dennis 'Beast of Bolsover' Skinner. And yet even this honorary court heckler's antecedents are not that ideologically sound. Despite twenty years in the coal industry, there is a blot on his otherwise impeccable proletarian credentials. As former Tory cabinet minister,

Mr John Biffen, was once obliged to remind him: 'We grammar-school boys must stick together.' Nevertheless, socially stigmatized by a grammar school and Oxford education though he may be, Mr Skinner would still be forgiven almost anything by the residents of the Press Gallery. Nervously sitting on the edge of his seat, diagonally opposite the government's Dispatch Box, he always looks within a whisker of marmalizing any minister improvident enough to offend him. A mere hop, skip, and jump, we all cheerfully imagine, and the beleaguered Social Services Secretary could well be trying out the joys of NHS Intensive Care for himself. There is never a dull moment when Dennis the Menace is around, which, incidentally, is almost always. Even his most implacable enemies would be obliged to admit that his attendance record is second to none (he steadfastly refuses to 'pair'), and that he is scrupulously incorruptible (he will never, for instance, accept a drink from a journalist, a self-denying ordinance which is almost extinct). Far from gaining opprobrium for his bumptious behaviour, he is held in the greatest of affection by many of the House, even on the Conservative side. There are few MPs who fail to respond with glee to the deflation of pomp and self-importance, especially in their Right Honourable Friends. Immured with fawning civil servants in their ivory towers, Ministers of the Crown may get away with murder in their own departments but not in the House of Commons. Parliamentary democracy needs the relentless iconoclasm of members such as Skinner. If nothing else, they provide a healthy antidote to an arrogant third-term government of increasing remoteness.

The House of Commons is, of course, a club, and a male-dominated club at that. The unprecedented phenomenon of a woman Prime Minister often tends to obscure the fact that only forty-one of our 650 MPs are female, and even that feeble statistic is an all-time record. The most basic women's facilities are therefore virtually non-existent. It took me over a month, for instance, to discover a ladies' lavatory, which may well explain the shrill edge the Prime Minister's voice acquires late on in the week during Thursday afternoon's Question Time. MPs' lavatories are marked, rather ambiguously, just 'Members', a generic form of nomenclature which has led to no end of embarrassing incidents. When, for instance, newly arrived Labour MP, Ann Clwyd, opened one such door, she was shocked to find the Serjeant-at-Arms in full flood, so to speak. Truly traumatized and sword unsheathed, the poor man has never been quite the same since.

But any moves to change this clubby, macho atmosphere are resolutely hindered by a hard core of the old brigade. Catering arrangements at the House of Commons are another fine example. For years, MPs would eat stodgy, nursery food with clapped-out cutlery in dingy dining-rooms and love every minute of it. Perhaps it reminded them of happy days being flogged and buggered at public school, or of their own misanthropic men-only clubs further down the road. Things started to change for the better when Mr Charles Irving, the drily amusing Tory MP for Cheltenham, took over the chairmanship of the Select Committee on Catering in 1979. By that stage, the House's valuable wine cellar had already been disposed of, to the distress of genuine oenophiles and dedicated dipsos alike. It was the classic, short-term solution of selling off capital assets to finance current expenditure; to this day, the sacrifice remains unforgiven by the grander 'vintage' type of Tory. Despite such economies, however, Mr Irving still inherited a £3m. deficit in 1979, which imaginative husbandry turned into a £1m. gross profit by 1988. He kicked off by putting a stop to the scandalously feudal staff conditions, and insisted that a pension scheme be introduced. He then created further uproar by bringing in the Westminster Environmental Health Department in order to sniff out any real or metaphorical rats. Many MPs are still horrified at this unprecedented invasion of their secret squalor, but at least it has inhibited those outbreaks of salmonella poisoning to which members of the Upper House have been so painfully subjected. To cap it all, Mr Irving introduced a harpist into the Harcourt Visitors' Dining-room, precipitating virtual apoplexy in Mr Enoch Powell, an odd reaction since no one could recall his ever going in there anyway. He opened the kiosk of which our American friends had heard, and which, like the rest of the House of Commons, is full of humbug and fudge. This bright entrepreneurial idea generates a turnover of some £600,000 a year, originally helped by the sales of packets of cigarettes. These, incidentally, have subsequently been stopped. Clearly, it was felt, the influence of the government's statutory health warning should at least extend to its own front door!

But of all the improvements Mr Irving has wrought for the welfare of his fellow-sufferers, his greatest contribution is to the quality of the cuisine. Trained in catering and hotel management, he rooted out the stodgy fare of yesteryear as fast as Mistress Maggie checked the rising damp in her cabinet. His lean and keen approach has not always been met with the unequivocal approval of the calorie/cholesterol crusaders, but he battles on regardless with 'this miserable job'. Let's face it, if healthy minds come in healthy bodies, we do well to wonder how the ship of state has not already sunk. One only has to think of Numbers 2 and 3 in the Conservative batting line-up. World Economic Summit watchers have often witnessed the worried wobbles of much collegiate adipose tissue when either Nigel or Sir Geoffrey falls foul of the boss on such occasions. But despite the 'sausages and plum duff' ravings of Tory MP Teresa Gorman and her ilk, the average member has no reason to pile on the pounds eating House of Commons fare. A dietitian's advice has been enlisted, and now low-calorie and vegetarian menus are always on offer. Mr Irving's name is always to be found on Early Day Motions criticizing unnecessary cruelty to animals, and he insists on humanely killed meat and organically grown vegetables wherever possible. Menus change every day, and for a period would contain one recipe submitted by an accommodating MP. Unfortunately, however, this convivial little practice sometimes backfired. On one occasion, upon discovery that his chosen dish was 'Maggie's Chicken', one well-known Labour MP felt obliged to send it back! For all that, when MPs are heard to whinge about dining facilities in the House of Commons, take it all with a pinch of salt. The secret delights of a Thames-side lunch on the terrace in summer is one of the best-kept, all-party conspiracies ever.

In the Members' Dining-room, strict segregation is the order of the day: Tories at one end, Socialists at the other, with the clerks and the rest in the middle. The Prime Minister herself occasionally drops in, though such visitations are preceded by a careful positive-vetting by her Parliamentary Private Secretary. A table full of cabinet casualties might make small talk over the 'couilles flambées à la façon Jacques Chirac' excessively hard going. Only the most ill-advised of Tories would put things on the slate with Mrs T. around. The prospect of a lunchtime lecture on the evils of consumer credit is enough to encourage even the worst improvident to come clean with the readies. She is even known to visit the Tea Room when rumblings of backbench rebellion percolate as far as Number 10, and potential poll-tax and social-security-cuts refusniks have been made to feel very uncomfortable over the lapsang suchong and rock cakes. In the Tea Room also, the favoured haunt of the Labour Party, ideologically sound soul-mates tend to stick together, whilst the Smoking Room attracts mainly Tories and the odd Socialist grandee. The Houses of Parliament also sport a plethora of bars, one of the least attractive of which must surely be the Press Bar. With its crushed puce wallpaper and indigo carpet, it has been known to make even inveterate Malvern Water tipplers feel queasy. All in all, however, there are some thirteen watering-holes throughout the palace, although journalists who dare mention a casual relationship between such a statistic and an empty Commons chamber may find themselves in trouble with the Privileges Committee.

The chamber itself, it must be said, is a great disappointment, with its frightful mess of ugly radio microphones hanging down from the ceiling on long, thin wires. Viewed from the galleries, our Honourable Members seem what so many actually are: mindless puppets being manipulated on strings. And the sound of Mrs 'That's-the-way-to-do-it' Thatcher and Mr Kinnock busily haranguing each other from their separate Dispatch Boxes, often bears a risible resemblance to a seaside Punch and Judy show. Each of these microphones covers a clutch of members sitting in close physical proximity, hence the good Dr David Owen's gracious contributions are often submerged by the background barracking of Mr Dennis Skinner operating in fine *basso profondo* counterpoint. Supporters of the televising of the Commons have always maintained that a visual image would do much to improve the public's perception of the place. At least TV viewers would understand where all the noise is coming from and why, a phenomenon mere radio coverage can never explain. Television should also encourage better attendance for everyday debates in the House, and ensure that viewers become more familiar with the characters and institution for which they vote and pay. Indeed, with some healthy hype, the plots that proliferate in the House of Commons might even start to rival those conceived in the Old Vic, and jostle *EastEnders* in the popularity ratings.

Gradually, we shall all become accustomed to the well-loved old stage-props, too, for (like the better class of Oxfam shop in Kensington) there are contributions here from all over the world. The table comes from Canada, the Dispatch Boxes from New Zealand and Mr Speaker's chair, in black bean wood, represents 'The Gift of Australia'. That *ex cathedra* pronouncements on British parliamentary procedure should emanate from a chair which comes from, of all places, *Queensland*, always strikes me as vaguely incongruous. The Queenslander's own state government is elected on the basis of a gerrymander system so disgracefully unfair it could have been dreamt up by the architects of the community charge. When ditched as party leader, their former Premier, Sir Joh Bjelke-Petersen, initially refused to quit, precipitating justifiable fears of a constitutional crisis. And yet this is the state which has provided our Speaker's chair; the one state in Australia which refuses to go on summer time because the ex-Premier's wife, Senator Flo, maintains that, 'it rots the curtains'; and the one state in Australia where such sentiments as these are liable to pass for informed opinion! Of the other bits of furniture on display, we may also notice the clerks' chairs. These hail, incidentally, from that other great parliamentary democracy: South Africa.

Casual observers are always struck by the contrast between the ritualistic, deferential forms of address and the barrage of party political vitriol which tends to ensue. Every member here is 'Honourable'; while Privy Councillors are 'Right Honourable' (as the old joke goes, never right and seldom honourable). No member may refer to any other member by name, only by constituency. Vituperative forms of address such as 'that pathetic, little creature' (Australian Prime Minister, Bob Hawke on Opposition leader, John Howard), are certainly not encouraged.

The bible of parliamentary procedure, *Erskine May* (no relation to the former chairman of the England cricket selectors, Peter, but almost as uninspiring), even lists expressions which have been banned in the past as 'unparliamentary'. Bounder, dog, puppy, liar, cheat, rat, swine, jackass, and stool-pigeon – they all seem fairly moderate by current standards. But despite such valiant efforts at verbal abuse, the British fail signally to rank alongside the big boys of innovative parliamentary invective. The House of Commons at its berating best has never come anywhere close to the imaginative imagery of a certain Caribbean Parliament, for instance, where one Honourable Member was recently described as 'a big-bellied, fat-nosed, Yankee-speaking pilot fish'.

Certain basic rules of behaviour must also be observed, some more redolent of the Third Form than others: sit down whenever Mr Speaker tells you to sit down; shut up whenever Mr Speaker tells you to shut up; no eating, drinking, or smoking in the chamber; no lingering in the Division Lobbies; and, more abstruse, when making a point of order during a vote, always remember to remain seated and wear a hat. The Serjeant-at-Arms always keeps two collapsible toppers available for the purpose. Of course, Mr Speaker may always 'name' unruly MPs who fail to conform, and have them suspended, the ultimate sanction, which occurs with almost monotonous regularity nowadays. There are those who would blame this on Mr Speaker Weatherill's inability to control the House, but that is not entirely fair. An amiable ex-cavalry officer, Bernard 'Jack' Weatherill does his scrupulous best to balance the rights and demands of all sides of the Commons, and likens the precarious procedure to 'riding a horse'. His is an almost impossibly thankless task. He was never the Prime Minister's favourite for the job, a point which clinched it for him with the entire House's backbenchers. And now government managers are constantly complaining about his failure to protect her sufficiently during Question Time, a concern akin to worrying about Mr Ian Botham's being mugged by fellow-airline passengers. At the same time, Mr Kinnock and his Whips have not helped by their singular inability to control their own supporters, some of whom have even branded the eminently fair-minded Speaker a 'Tory stooge'. The son of a crippled journeyman tailor, the poor man seems insufficiently bespoke to suit anyone. Not that such a consideration should be allowed to detract from his many attractive qualities. To remind him of his humble origins, for instance, Mr Speaker Weatherill still carries the thimble his mother gave him underneath his fine robes. Indeed, the increasingly rowdy behaviour in the Commons must often make him wish he had joined the family firm instead, making wildly expensive suits for the likes of Sir Nicholas Fairbairn. But the disruptive tactics employed by certain MPs are surely more the product of ten years of frustrated opposition than any fault of his. He is not, perhaps, in quite the same unforgettable mould as that of his predecessor, Viscount Tonypandy, formerly Mr George Thomas, and a man whose quick wit and mellifluous Welsh tones endeared him to all. And yet it is to Mr Speaker Weatherill that the unenviable job of quelling the star-struck TV show-offs will inevitably fall.

On either side of the chamber run the Division Lobbies, through which members must physically pass to register their 'Aye' or 'No' votes. The Lords, in contrast, clearly capable of far subtler emotions, vote 'Content' or 'Not Content'. In most other Parliaments, this mindless form of physical exercise has long since been obviated by electronic voting systems, but even these are not without their problems. In the European Parliament in Strasbourg, for example, an Italian voting system was installed, though nobody, and especially not the Honourable Members for whom it was designed, could ever remember voting for it in the first place. In the early days, it used to operate very much *all'italiano*, soon becoming temperamental, overheated, overwrought, and frequently refusing to work at all. Strangely enough, it involved a lot of thrusting of personal credentials into recalcitrant holes, a department in which many members were thought to be remarkably proficient, but for some reason not in this particular instance. Eventually, everybody got the hang of it, an Italian analyst was brought in at vast expense to convince the machine that it wasn't really overworked, but probably only thought it was, and now the place could hardly function without it. But British MPs still prefer their antiquated system of countless hours of unalloyed boredom, marching again and again through their 'Aye' and 'No' lobbies, often blissfully unaware of what they are voting for or against, but ever in the hope, one suspects, of rubbing up against the powder-blue shoulder-pads of power.

One other notable feature has its roots in days gone by. Running down the chamber, the length of two swords apart, are two red stripes. No member may 'overstep the mark' or address the House from beyond a red line. It is a tacit reminder that jaw-jaw is better than war-war, though MPs are now supposed to leave their swords in the cloakroom, dangling from the pink loops of ribbon supplied. For members of more modest requirements, wire coat-hangers are provided.

To the east of Central Lobby runs a staircase to the committee rooms, whence more whimsical members may gaze out over the Thames to St Thomas's Hospital, and contemplate the eternally imminent collapse of the National Health Service. The corridors are carpeted with acre upon acre of alarmingly aggressive Axminster, bright green, yellow and red – all in all, not the sort of place to rest a weary head with a hangover. Members' offices are scattered hither and thither, depending on seniority and contacts, and the shortage of proper accommodation is a constant gripe among less fortunate backbenchers. Some of them do not even rate the privilege of a shared office, but have to make do instead with a mere desk down in the dungeons of St Stephen's cloisters. Huddled together unhappily in the half-light, they look like the tortured souls of Dante's *Purgatory*, all doing their penance in hope and perseverance, and all waiting to be moved onward and upward to the divine intervention of the 'Blessed Margaret', the Whips' office or the Serjeant-at-Arms. Older or more unpopular members eventually acquire rooms of their own, some of the best in the Norman Shaw building, the Old Scotland Yard, situated on the Embankment. Across the river, smugly grand, sits the vast mausoleum of the dear departed Greater London Council. That short stretch of river can make such a terrible difference, as Mr Ken Livingstone, Labour member for Brent East, soon found out to his cost. Ejected from his million-square-metre Lambeth pad, not even a broom cupboard could be found to house him for his first year in the Palace of Westminster.

So this then, is the Mother of Parliaments – for sentimentalists, the greatest forum of the land; for Rochdale's Sir Cyril Smith, 'the longest-running farce in the West End'.

'Don't waste your time down there,' advised Tony Benn early on in my research. 'Nothing important ever happens there. It's just an hotel. Lots of people come and go and different people make it to the presidential suite. But in the end, whatever happens, the management remains exactly the same.'

The cockpit of the nation, a bad chat show or just another rubber-stamping outfit – which best describes the Houses of Parliament? What sort of characters would strive to belong? And, more intriguing still, what Faustian deals do our Members of Parliament strike, in order to clamber upwards on Westminster's greasy pole?

# 3 / Up the greasy pole

*"VOTE FOR ME — I'M INTERESTED IN PEOPLE."*

'Gadzooks!' exclaimed the nice clean-shaven young man standing there on the doorstep. Sporting a very professional-looking clipboard, a sheaf of 'Vote for Dudley Fishburn' posters and an outsize blue rosette, the poor boy looked demonstrably shaken. Not half as much as I was! Extracted from the Badedas bath by a shrill, persistent doorbell, I was not exactly expecting the Alain Delon lookalike as suggested by the advert ... well, not really. Such adolescent day-dreams tend to die along with hopes of SAS paratroopers dropping in with the chocs; or of besotted strangers on the Underground thrusting flowers in your hands. Sadly, the reality of my life is somewhat more banal. It was far more likely, I surmised, to be the chronic key-mislaying husband.

But the chap confronting me with the Trumper-type haircut was certainly not the sweetly anticipated Philippe-Henri. Swathed only in a towel the size of a loin cloth, I was uncomfortably aware of the growing red flush of my exquisite embarrassment. Glowing visibly in the half-light, it crept stealthily down, eventually merging with that filigree of pulsating blue veins that passes for my legs. For the first time in years, and to put it quite crudely, I was gob-smacked. Fortunately, however, we were dealing with a member of the local Conservative Association. Such excellent fellows learn enterprise at the knee of Lord Young, and taking the initiative is part of their creed.

'Good evening, madam,' he volunteered swiftly, pulling himself together and looking me straight in the eye. 'I take it you're one of us!'

Even under the circumstances, such a conclusion seemed odd. Was it only Tory ladies who, thus skimpily clad, would open their doors to complete strangers around eight o'clock at night? Surely, on the contrary, such behaviour might suggest affiliations with an entirely different sort of crowd: the Rainbow Alliance Payne and Pleasure Party, perhaps, a group led by Madam Cyn herself, the tea, sympathy and nooky hostess with aspirations to Chief Whip?

But whatever their allegiances, for the first fortnight of July 1988, the good burghers of Kensington would be given no peace. Precipitated by the death of the constituency's Conservative member, Sir Brandon Rhys Williams, the first by-election of this parliament was being billed as a litmus test for the country at large. For the Conservatives, whose majority in the 1987 election was 4,447, it was of the utmost importance to hang on to the seat. To begin with, such a victory must have seemed like a cinch. But that was before the electorate met Dudley Fishburn, Esq. A self-proclaimed 'dry as dust man', Mr Fishburn would be standing firm on the government's track record. Firm, that was, until the dust, along with Dudley, started to shift mid-election. Fortunately for the Tories, however, the Labour Party was playing true to form. Almost, though not completely, devastated by a leadership struggle and a controversial policy review, what better time to launch its secret weapon, Mr Neil Kinnock, on the unsuspecting front-line states? What with well-publicized scoops of South African wine in Zambia, detention under armed guard in ideologically sound Zimbabwe and poor jokes about the demise of the leaderene in Botswana, the Right Honourable Member for Islwyn was looking every inch an electable alternative ... for membership of the Kalahari County Council, at least.

Doing her admirable best in the face of such adversity, Labour's friendly pretender, Ms Ann Holmes, was being heavily punted as 'right up your street'. An amiable lady, it seemed that only a trip down the notorious drug-trafficking All Saints Road could wipe the smile off her face. But the poor woman had other problems apart from the smirk. The unceremonious dumping of the previous candidate, Mr Ben Bousquet, raised awkward, ugly questions in the putative People's Party. A black councillor, Mr Bousquet had been allowed to run for Kensington 'the Hopeless'. So why the heave-ho, people asked, as soon as Kensington became 'the Marginal'? Like West Indian strike bowlers on the English county circuit, Ben had been encouraged to dislodge all the openers. But wrapping up the tail, as usual, would be left to someone else.

Hustling for the middle ground, the SDP and SLD boys were busily battling it out, their new-look, fratricidal configuration second only to Labour's. And, of course, just to brighten things up, there was the usual alternative spectrum of deposit-dropping daft. Never, since the seventeen candidates fielded in 1984 at Chesterfield, the by-election which returned a victorious Tony Benn to Westminster, had the electorate been treated to such a hotchpotch of hopefuls. On that occasion Benn had seen off challenges from quite a selection of folk: the Four Wheel Drive, No Dental Increases, Spare the Earth, Death off the Roads, Yoga, Acne, Elvis Presley and Reclassify the *Sun* as a Comic parties. Throughout this event, too, a similar line-up of flamboyant self-publicists would be heavily in evidence: the ubiquitous Cynthia Payne; the veteran Screaming Lord Sutch (Monster Raving Loony Rock Music); candidates from the Greens, London Class War, Free Trade, Anti-Left Fascists, Fair Wealth, Levellers, Anti-Yuppies, Peace and Independent Juanta parties; not to mention a certain Dr David Owen (Voice from the Past). In fact, all over the constituency, for the first week at least, we all thought the good doctor himself might be fighting the seat. Almost to the end, the circulating bumf did little to dispel the impression of the SDP as David Owen's personal fan club. Here, for example, is a picture of me, Dr David Owen, with Mr Mikhail Gorbachev. Here is another picture of me, Dr David Owen, with Mr Ronald Reagan. And, finally, here is an altogether much better picture of me, Dr David Owen, completely on my own.

'Hello, we're from the SDP,' the canvassers would explain. 'David Owen's party.'

Ms Holmes's workers, of course, could never be so sure.

After a few weeks, however, the SDP candidate actually acquired a name of his own. In the mould of his leader, Mr John Martin was in favour of everything good and against everything bad. His programme included a better-funded NHS; sound defence; higher standards in schools; more help for the elderly; greater choice in housing – yes, it all seemed very sound. Alone among the contenders, Mr Martin also came out strongly against the annual Notting Hill Carnival. A constituency event which stirs up old prejudices, fosters ill-will, creates a lot of unwanted noise and litter and is detested by many local residents, it is a jamboree not unlike a by-election, really, but without Mr Vincent Hanna. But in by-elections, local issues often loom larger than cosmic questions, such as the nuclear deterrent, and Mr Martin had certainly found a very sore point. Besieged Notting Hillites were all ready to regale him with personal testimonies of Carnival carnage. What about all those front gardens littered with half-empty hypodermics and half-full Durex? The three days of ersatz bonhomie founded exclusively on Crucial Brew, ganja and Soaca music, that potent amalgam always liable to erupt into something really nasty, like a Lawson/Thatcher conversation on exchange rates, perhaps, or a friendly football match in the city of Glasgow. All tied up, of course, with the muggings and stabbings perpetrated on purveyors of Coca Cola at £3 a can, the sort of free-marketeers so beloved of Professor Milton Friedman and the New Tory Right.

On every side the party big guns were out in full force. Labour's Trade and Industry spokesman, Kiwi whizz kid, Bryan Gould, was particularly impressive. It was the same Gould who had helped mastermind Labour's 1987 election strategy, a campaign based almost exclusively on a soft-focus, Mateus Rosé-type advert of the happy Kinnock couple. Unfortunately, as indeed with the dreaded Mateus itself, the packaging struck many of us as more impressive than the product. Château Kinnock, people felt, was distinctly too sweet, lacking in body, insufficiently mature and with an alarming tendency on occasion to go popping its cork. A nice try, but Labour's admen had succeeded in converting no one to the cause. Still, at least they had put the frighteners on Conservative Central Office, driving an irrevocable wedge between the PM and Party

Chairman Tebbit. Perhaps that, on reflection, had been their greatest success.

But back at the by-election the Conservatives were certainly not being outdone. The costers of Portobello Road had rarely been so flattered. Bearing an uncanny resemblance to the candidate himself, ex-Deputy Chairman Jeffrey Archer pumped flesh all day with indefatigable enthusiasm. If his name had been on the ballot paper, he would have cantered home a cert.

'He is perfectly brilliant at it,' new Tory MP Hugo Summerson told me during a Lords and Commons cricket match against an Old Westminster XI. A charmingly self-deprecating man, Mills and Boon's 'most romantic MP', Hugo had already observed the Archer effect in his own marginal Walthamstow seat. 'He marshals everyone together and sends them off in pairs. "Remember," he tells them, "Jeffrey Archer/Hugo Summerson. Jeffrey Archer/Hugo Summerson." The shop girls think it's wonderful. They hang out of the windows and wave. Then people come up all day and ask him for autographs. The only trouble is, at the end of the day, I think everyone has completely forgotten about Hugo Summerson.'

Ah, yes. The British public are a fickle lot. In Kensington they had even forgotten the Chingford Strangler himself. But there he was – dark, spindly and lethal, the funnelweb spider of Ponder's End – out stalking as well. Sooner or later, it seemed, some incident was bound to occur. Sure enough, our local butcher mistook him for dreary, dry-as-dust Dudley. Oh, dear! The faithful froze as Terrible Tebbit started to eye the kebabs, all horribly impaled on skewers and showing few signs of life. 'Nice fish stall you've got here, mate,' observed Norman meaningfully, and continued his rounds. Strong men in the entourage heaved a sigh of relief.

Elsewhere, breezing along graciously like a galleon under full sail, Lord Whitelaw was doing his bit to rally the troops. Trailing his clouds of charisma behind him, his progress was regal, his feet barely stopping to make contact with the ground. What joy to find former Prime Minister, Lord Home, buying a bunch of bananas! Hello to a French diplomat here and a German attaché there. Winning the hearts and minds of every person he met, it was unfortunate that none of them was entitled to vote. But still Willie remains in a class of his own. His retirement from the cabinet due to ill-health has been sorely felt, for his reputation as 'the usual channels in spades' kept successive Conservative governments on course. Nevertheless, for all his genius as Mr Fixit *extraordinaire*, he often seemed to revel in the image of upper-class buffoon. Once, whilst delivering a prepared statement, he read the same page out twice but carried on regardless, despite shouts of Opposition abuse. Of course, he explained, he was aware of repeating himself. But surely such important matters were always worth a reprise! Then there were the classic Whitelawisms – concepts such as 'stirring up apathy' – which raised many a laugh. And yet, for all that, Willie always found a way of gaining people's genuine affection. Even the toughest members of BBC's *Newsnight* team, a crew not known to slaver over politicians in general, had nothing but kind words for the deputy PM. On one occasion, a female producer recalls, whilst electioneering in Bakewell, Willie was invited to sample the local confectionery. Obliging as ever, he took a large mouthful of Bakewell 'pie'. (Not 'tart', he was informed: beware of cheap imitations!) Immediately he was accosted by the most dreadful old harridan. What was today's Conservative Party coming to? she cried, working herself into a state. How dare he just stand there, openly eating in the street! In his own mellifluous and accommodating way, Willie tried to explain. 'And don't speak to me with your mouth full!' came the fulminating response. 'You know Mrs Thatcher wouldn't like that at all!'

But in politics it takes more than genial good humour to deliver the goods. More than anything, it was Willie's own-brand man-management which saved many a day. 'Whenever anything here went wrong,' explained one of Westminster's most influential business managers, 'Willie would race around, saying: "All my fault. All my fault." Of course, everybody knew very well that it wasn't. But once he'd taken the blame, then they could all get on with the job. It was that sort of attitude which made him such an effective operator.'

But Lord Whitelaw was not the only political heavyweight out there stealing the show. On the SLD side, old 'Woy' himself, Lord Jenkins of Hillhead, was keeping everyone amused. Their candidate, Mr William Goodhart, he explained, had been a genuine resident for some twenty-eight years or more. Their party, you see, did not believe in putting up big stars for important by-elections, mere carpet-baggers who knew nothing about the local constituency. A shadow of self-recognition suddenly clouded Woy's face. 'Well, not at the beginning, anyway,' he trailed off, quite sheepishly, we thought. Dear Woy, whilst he has raised a minor speech defect into a perfected art form, it has certainly resulted in the odd fiasco. As President of the European Commission, for instance, his introduction of 'high-ranking officials' would render us English interpreters all utterly helpless. And at one press conference, his attempts to unveil the new blueprint for European integration almost ended in tears. A beleaguered host of French, German, Italian, Danish and Dutch linguists downed tools and converged hysterically on us. What the hell, they asked, was meant by this concept of a *Euwopean Fwesco?*

Far removed from the glamour surrounding the big shots, the ranks of poor, wind-swept canvassers were still plying their trade. Some, future prospective candidates themselves, were ostentatiously accumulating credit in the bank. Eventually, they knew, their own hour would be nigh. Others, more idealistic, were just doing what they felt to be right. But whatever their motives, their beliefs or their pressures, it was difficult not to admire each one's stoic persistence. For a start, the weather was unconscionably bad. Rarely had the country seen such rain in July. With a sixty-minute respite, it must have poured the whole campaign – quite enough time, however, for Malcolm Marshall to rout England five times in a row. The Labour leader criticized the national media for an apparent want of enthusiasm. But it was hard to get wound up about such a lacklustre fight. In a half-hearted effort to broaden the interest, Kensington was projected as a template for the great North–South divide. But the truth, as ever, was more complicated than that. It has always been an area where rich and poor have coexisted in cheek-by-jowl proximity. In the end, it was inevitable that the great poll tax fight should erupt.

The majority of electors, I am convinced, have little sustained interest in issues other than those economic. Apart from the tiny, self-selecting group of those genuinely fascinated by politics, most people's concerns revolve entirely around the wallet. Of course, folk will start worrying about the state of the NHS, but only when a relative of theirs is taken seriously ill. And then suddenly education becomes so terribly important, but only when their own appalling little ankle-biters go to school and prove dyslexic. No, in the final analysis, most people cast their vote on the basis of their own feeling of prosperity and individual well-being. Indeed, an extraordinary MORI poll conducted in early 1988 tends to bear this theory out. Whilst the majority of respondents declared their opposition to the government's policies, 60 per cent of them still maintained they would continue to vote Conservative. 'The English,' I was told by one despairing Welsh MP, 'are the most politically ignorant nation in the civilized world. Promise them cheaper beer, longer chips and bigger tits and they're absolutely guaranteed to vote for you.' Indeed, Mr Rupert Murdoch has made billions out of similar market research.

Yet there is, perhaps, one exception to the self-interest rule. People do get a trifle twitchy on the subject of defence. That is more a gut reaction, however, than any rational evaluation of policy: the stock I-didn't-win-a-world-war-to-take-orders-from-those-Russians response. In the 1987 election, the Conservatives exploited such feelings at Labour's unilateralist expense, and early-evening images of trundling tanks proved irresistible indeed. Under a Labour government, we were told, we would never feel safe. And the British nation, whilst dining, likes its fish fingers secure.

But of all the many issues raised in the by-election, problems of inner-city neglect, unemployment, race relations, poverty, drugs, law and order, housing, education and health, none attracted more attention than the controversial community charge. In this respect, Kensington's voters were indicative of the entire country's feelings. Was it fair, people everywhere were asking, that a duke in his mansion should pay the same as the dustman? Indeed, to reinforce the point, the SLD showed shots of the Duke of Buccleuch and Queensbury's handsome house, and poignantly compared it to a certain Fred's little home. Both, claimed the SLD candidate, would be paying the same charge. Could that, we all wondered, be morally right?

Since most of us fell somewhere between the duke and the dustman, however, what we needed to know was what *our* tax would be. Only then could most people decide whether they supported it or not. Of course, those who had never previously paid rates were bound to find the new system completely iniquitous. Other householders, resentful of high rates based on local services they did not use, thought the *per capita* charge a much fairer approach. What confused the issue was that everyone was spinning us a different tale. Like the Utilitarian Mr Gradgrind of Dickens's *Hard Times*, all we wanted was facts. But facts are to politicians what mineral water is to journalists: completely alien. And so began the saga of the spurious statistics.

With statistics, so the old adage runs, you can prove almost anything and governments everywhere are adept at rigging numbers to make their own performance look good. Unemployment figures, inflation rates, monies spent on education and health care ... our own Prime Minister is a past mistress at churning the numbers out and dressing them up to best advantage. The rub, of course, is that Mr Average rarely takes the blindest bit of notice. Our emotions and impressions are seldom influenced by figures. If, for example, on the basis of personal experience, people genuinely *feel* the NHS is going down the pan, then no amount of claims about increased spending will persuade them otherwise. Similarly, for the masses of Liverpudlians unemployed since the demise of the docks, the number of computer-programming vacancies in Milton Keynes is of zero concern. Such general cynicism, perhaps, stems from the one incontrovertible law of basic street creed: Politician plus statistic equals credibility gap.

But in Kensington, the gap was developing into a veritable abyss. People can hardly be expected to cast an informed vote when at least one of the candidates is patently lying through his teeth. The community charge, claimed the Conservatives, would be a snip at £122 a head. Cobblers, said Labour: more like £384. Don't be silly, countered the Conservatives: you're including the current cost of the soon-to-be abolished Inner London Education Authority in that. Nonsense, retorted Labour: your own Environment Secretary, Nasty Nick, has quoted our figure as being correct ... Bogus, shouted the ones. Dishonest, cried the others. Couldn't trust any of these blighters to run a ruddy whelk stall, concluded the rest of us. Even by polling day, not one of us had managed to discover the real truth of the matter. But whatever it was, and it still remains to be seen, in a very close contest Ann Holmes went down to Dudley Fishburn by a mere 816 votes.

'Thanks to Labour,' she had reminded us only a few days prior to polling day, 'new 52A bus stops are being installed in Barlby Road.'

A few more in Elgin Crescent, I swear, and Ann Holmes would have won. For it is of such things as bus stops that Members of Parliament are made.

Kensington, of course, is merely one constituency out of 650, but it is nevertheless an interesting microcosm for the World of Westminster. For a start, the entire exercise gives us some indication of the sort of persons who put themselves up to become our elected representatives. Certainly, with all the indignity, the abuse, the hustling, bustling, begging, cajoling and convincing involved in winning over the man in the street, it takes a certain sort of character to believe that the carrot at the end of the stick is worth while. What is more, after all the hassle, the winner of the glittering prize, our new Member of Parliament, has not even acceded to a particularly admired or respected profession. In 1985, for example, a MORI poll conducted for *The Economist* showed that the House of Commons was 'declining in public esteem' and 'doing a poor job in controlling the work of the government'. In the same year, another MORI poll disclosed that, only just ahead of journalists and door-to-door salesmen, MPs ranked third from bottom in public esteem. In early 1988, the Market Research Society showed that only 18 per cent of the population believed MPs' standards of honesty to be 'very' or even 'fairly' high. One earlier and very detailed Granada survey discovered that 40 per cent of people thought that 'most politicians were in it for what they could get out of it'. And less than half the population could name a single thing that their Member of Parliament did. All in all, the research does not paint a particularly pretty picture of our Honourable Members. And what is worse, especially for the more self-important amongst them, is the revelation that fewer than 50 per cent of us even know the name of our local MP! Happily, however, this does not inhibit most of them from speaking on behalf of us all. How many MPs, for example, preface their every comment by a resounding 'Now what this country wants/thinks/needs'? Despite our overwhelming indifference, or so it would seem, some siren song of fame keeps ever ringing in their ears.

And yet, outside the Westminster cocoon, I doubt whether so many as a dozen MPs have made the slightest impression on the general public's consciousness. The cabinet itself, with Tebbit and Heseltine comfortably out of the way, is now distressingly monochrome and short on political flair. Would anyone, for instance, recognize Defence Secretary George Younger, even if they were to fall over him in the street? It is not that the cabinet's present incumbents are not all highly competent and intelligent administrators in their way. But the Empress has made sure that there is now no obvious competition around. With the outstanding exception of Chancellor Lawson, who resolutely refuses to tug the forelock, even the top boys seem hopelessly neutered, grey and anonymous. What chance, under those circumstances, do the rest of them stand?

One evening, in the early summer of 1988, I had dinner with television presenter Vivian White. A few weeks earlier, during an extraordinary interview with Vivian on BBC's *This Week, Next Week* programme, Neil Kinnock had decided, unilaterally, to rewrite Labour's entire defence policy. Gone for ever, claimed the Labour leader on that inauspicious occasion, were the days of 'something for nothing unilateralism'. A stunned nation left its lunch burning on Regulo 3. Staggered were the semantics experts. Something for nothing, they had always thought, was precisely what unilateralism meant. Amazed were Labour's CND supporters. Good old Neil, they had always believed, was supposed to be one of them. But more pole-axed than anyone was a certain Mr Denzil Davies. As Labour's Shadow Defence Secretary, Denzil felt that if unguided Kinnock missiles were going to be dropped, then he of all people should at least have been warned. In the fall-out, Mr Davies felt obliged to resign, avenging himself by informing the press, not his leader, in the middle of the night. Yes, even Labour shadow ministers are allowed their fifteen minutes of fame. But the entire episode, apart from providing further evidence of Mr Kinnock's own extraordinary deathwish, was an object lesson for our more hubristic Members of Parliament. It was only in his valiant efforts to call it a day that anyone had even heard of Denzil Davies MP.

But apart from the high spot of watching Neil Kinnock trying to garrotte himself on camera, Vivian has spent a professional lifetime observing the antics of politicians. If anyone, then surely someone as objective as he might understand their basic motivation. If fortune and certainly fame were to be reserved for the few, then weren't at least some MPs interested in helping their fellow-citizens? I thought the poor man might choke on his Mee Goreng Thai wheat noodles. 'Interested in *helping* people?' he finally spluttered incredulously. 'Whatever you do, don't trust any MP who tells you he's there because he's interested in helping people. The only reason they're there is because they're interested in *politics*. Politics and, of course, themselves. And that has absolutely nothing to do with helping people.'

Far more cynical today, I am still not entirely convinced. A few laudable exceptions, such as Birkenhead's Labour MP, Frank Field, spring readily to mind. The scourge of the Social Services Department, Field is relentless in his crusade for the poor and underprivileged. Successful claims on behalf of his hard-done-by constituents have even set legal precedents, and his 'surgery' is a highly professional advice bureau, second to none. It is precisely this sort of Labour MP whom 'hard-left' constituency caucuses try persistently to oust. Nevertheless, despite decent MPs such as Field and his ilk, there is no shortage of Honourable Members capable of selling their own mothers for the sake of the most minor preferment. To thrive in politics, it would appear, self-interest, stamina and ambition are the basic prerequisites. Intelligence and competence come much farther down the list. And, in the drier regions of the Conservative Party at least, any concept of caring or compassion has disappeared altogether. Yes, unfortunately, in order to prosper in that menagerie which is the House of Commons, politicians must develop a very thick skin. If nothing else, the parliamentary selection procedure helps the callous along.

'Being elected,' claims Trade Minister Robert Atkins, 'is the easy part to becoming an MP. It's being *selected* that is difficult.' There speaks the voice of bitter experience. Having lost his Preston North seat in 1983, Robert was obliged to run the usual gauntlet of selection committees. Rejected at first by South-west Cambridgeshire, Mid-Kent and Mid-Norfolk, he was finally selected for the staunchly Conservative seat of South Ribble. Now he is considered a safe pair of hands at the Department of Trade and Industry, and far more important, according to my husband, when fielding at third slip. At all events, Atkins seems to have put the job entirely in perspective. It was essential early on, he realized, to put conniving officials in their place. At the end of his first day in government, for instance, he was presented with the usual ministerial red box crammed to bursting with bumf.

'And, Minister,' intoned the retreating cohorts of civil servants, about to clock off, 'these are terribly important. They all need an answer by first thing tomorrow morning.'

It was the classic ploy of well-ensconced functionaries trying to bamboozle the newcomer: keep him so busy with bits of paper that he won't have a clue what's going on; make sure he won't ever have time to interfere with the department; and by the time he's sussed the system he'll have been replaced by someone else. It is along these lines that the Civil Service has run this country for years. And so Atkins dutifully picked up his documents, the first an eighteen-page memo on the rational allocation of departmental waste-paper baskets.

'OK,' he conceded, mock-ingenuously. 'Since these are clearly so terribly important, I do think we had *all* better stay here tonight and go through them together.'

Shock! Horror! The department had never seen such a flurry of activity. Officials ran hither and thither making alternative plans: the dinner invitation to Putney cancelled abruptly; the long-awaited Covent Garden evening with the loved one, in some cases even the wife, shelved for ever, perhaps. Obliged to stay on, they dealt with every single paper in turn. Finally, by about 3a.m. it was time to go home. 'And do you know something?' says Robert, with a disarming smile. 'The odd thing is it never happened again.'

But in his selection, at least, Robert Atkins was a lucky man. His minor Odyssey round the constituencies was even under par for the course. Indeed, most MPs will happily tell you the most harrowing tales, but with frantic follow-up requests not to mention their names. They, after all, have to live with these people. Some of the worst shockers stem from the belief, shared by most Tory selection committees, that a candidate's wife comes included in the package. The local Tory doyennes do not want to end up with some Mandy Rice-Davies lookalike pulling first the AGM raffle and then their midlife crisis husbands. 'Stand up and turn around,' one poor, prospective candidate's wife was ordered. 'We all want to see what you look like from behind.' Any suggestion of a backless little halter-neck number and, you can bet, the dear husband would have found himself doomed.

Another prospective Tory candidate was rather pleased with himself after a particularly brilliant speech on the state of the economy. 'That was good,' said the chairman of the rural Yorkshire selection committee. 'But what we want to know is do you, or do you not, approve of fox hunting?'

By far the worst experience, however, was that endured by Environment Minister John Selwyn Gummer. Now, the public perception of Mr Gummer is not of a man blessed with the greatest sense of humour. But close friends and associates all maintain he is one of the cleverest and wittiest speakers around. In one constituency, whilst still seeking a seat, his sparkling contribution was acclaimed with thunderous applause. The next hopeful, a far less inspiring contender, only managed to elicit a very lukewarm response. It looked like the decision was cut and dried when suddenly the other fellow was called in and given the job. A gracious man, the lesser luminary admitted to being pleasantly surprised. 'Oh, that's all right,' some old dear started to explain. 'We just felt sorry for you. Selwyn Gummer is so brilliant, we know he'll soon find another seat. But you probably won't stand any chance at all!'

But even selection as a prospective candidate carries with it no guarantee of success. Most aspiring MPs cut their teeth on at least one hopeless seat. What a demoralizing prospect for those poor unfortunates pitted against, say, Labour's Allan Rogers in the Rhondda. There, with the largest UK majority (30,754), the returning officer virtually *weighs* the Labour vote. But occasionally even the best-laid plans have been known to go awry. Sometimes, even putatively safe seats are at the mercy of external influences. In the Ryedale by-election of 1986, for example, a Conservative majority of 16,142 was overnight transformed into almost a 5,000 loss. The reason had nothing to do with the Tory candidate, Mr Neil Balfour, a friend of mine and therefore clearly an excellent chap. But a few days before polling day, American F111 bombers had taken off from British shores with Mrs Thatcher's blessing. The idea, we were told, was to give Colonel Gaddafi and his terrorists a taste of their own medicine. The plan backfired, however, and the resultant newsreels of scores of innocent women and children, dead and wounded, did little to enhance the Conservative government's popularity. 'It was the only time ever,' said Neil, no stranger to canvassing 'that I actually had people slam doors in my face.'

General elections, however, are less likely to produce such maverick results. Candidates with safe seats generally do get elected. But even blissfully immured in Westminster, no member can be sure of security for life. Labour MPs, in particular, are constantly being obliged to jump through hoops. For, whatever their performance or their majority, they are all subjected to mandatory reselection by the constituency party between general elections. These strictures have created problems, even for the most assiduous MPs, especially when a hard core of unrepresentative left-wing activists, such as Militant Tendency, have been allowed to take over. The Tories, on the other hand, are far more genteel. The greatest rascal, once successfully returned, is rarely deselected and, general elections permitting, retains a sinecure for life. Why, even Billericay's disgraced former MP was allowed the privilege of resignation. Arraigned for spanking young gentlemen above and beyond the call, Mr Harvey Procter is now carving out a new career for himself, running a shirt shop – what else? The Conservatives, it seems, can be a forgiving brotherhood when they want. Much of the financial backing for Procter's venture has come from former Westminster colleagues. Indeed, as one informed source reports, 'There are now at least half a dozen Tory members right behind Harvey.'

And yet, for all the hoop-jumping, there is no shortage of people who dream of the magic codicil, MP, to their name. Every general election draws at leat 2,500 hopefuls, not to mention the countless numbers of those fallen earlier at the selection fence. Bob Worcester, the personable American chairman of MORI, gives the same words of advice to all prospective Labour candidates: 'Let me talk you out of it,' he suggests. 'It's a miserable, mean job. And the chances of anyone ever making it to cabinet minister are infinitesimal.'

Now, when a man like Bob Worcester talks chances, you know

he is not speaking off the top of his head. The official Labour pollster since 1970, his forecasts have proved remarkably accurate over the last six general elections. His list of clients is endless, for he does, after all, lead the field in market research. But the enthusiasm of the average political aspirant still refuses to be tempered. 'And so then I ask them,' explains Bob, 'what newspaper they read. And they all say: the *Guardian*. And I say: well, that's fine. It's one of the best. But who reads the *Guardian*? Most of the people you will be out talking to read either the *Mirror* or the *Sun*. So if you want to know what the man in the street is thinking, start taking the down-market tabloids. And then remember, on top of that, that one in four adults does not even read a newspaper at all. They get their opinions from the small screen in the corner.'

And not, one may confidently assume, from programmes like *World in Action*. But at least Bob leaves the idealists and political theorists in no shadow of doubt. Perhaps free bread and circuses is all the masses really crave. And, if so, the Socialist struggle will be uphill all the way.

But for those 'lucky' ones who finally make it to Westminster, the real battle has only just begun. Certainly, life in the chamber is nothing if not confrontational. Imagine, if you will, an eternal series of weekly Test Matches against the West Indies and you begin to get the picture of the House of Commons at play. Unfortunately, despite protests, the Ashdown and Owen teams have yet to qualify for first-class status and still only count as minor league. At least this simplifies the competition for the average spectator. On the one hand, then, with their numerical supremacy, the Tories, like the West Indians, seem completely invincible. On the other side, Labour, like England, is searching for a captain worth his place in the team. And there to ensure fair play, is a supposedly neutral umpire, Mr 'God help me *Erskine May*' Speaker. Recently, this poor fellow has come in for a lot of stick from both sides. First of all, he has given an extraordinary number of the Opposition out, usually on the basis of controversial lbw (Louts, Bullies and Wallies) decisions. But observers feel there have been plenty of blatant lbw's on the other side, too. And yet not a single one of them has ever been called. The highlight of each Test is always the dominant captain's two innings. Mrs T., like Viv Richards, is one of the few players around still capable of emptying the bars. Looking supremely confident, she takes guard in the middle, and immediately starts smashing opening bowler Kinnock's sad long hops to all parts of the park. Why on earth, we all wonder, does he still insist on hogging the action? Surely it's high time the party changed its attack? Why not bring on Labour's more penetrating bowlers, men whose spot-on line and length have beaten the bat on many an occasion? Smith, Cook, Brown, Gould and even golden oldies Hattersley and Healey have all had her stumped, exploiting that recognized flaw in her technique, an inability to turn. But perhaps, deep down, Neil is frightened of letting the other boys shine. And so again and again he keeps trundling on – 'Just taking them lashes,' as West Indians say. Of course, struggling as he is, he must justify his own inclusion to the board of selectors. But, with his record, it is surely just a matter of time before he finds himself dropped.

In fact, the cricket analogy is not really such a ridiculous one. In the House of Commons, as in cricket, both sides naturally yearn to win. But each team is also fraught with its own internal conflicts, with the internecine struggles of ambitious individuals striving to dominate. Indeed, both in sport and in politics, a colleague's misfortune is often welcomed by his team mates. For it may be precisely his downfall which affords them the long-awaited opportunity to excel. And then, in the final analysis, there is really only one job which everybody wants. Was there ever a cricketer or politician born who did not long to lead the team?

The ascent of the greasy pole, however, is a long, frustrating climb. And for those in opposition the prospect is even grimmer. All they can do, as yet another expedition gets under way without them, is languish in the foothills, praying for disaster to occur. But if you are the 'right sort' of Conservative MP, vote the right way and do as you are told, initial salvation from the backbenches will soon come in the form of a Parliamentary Private Secretary appointment. The job of the PPS is somewhat ill-defined. But, in a nutshell, he is supposed to act as the eyes and ears of his minister in the House. Cushioned from the asperities of backbench existence, it is easy for any government minister gradually to lose the plot. Speeches and answers are drafted for him. Diaries are filled to account for every minute of his day. Chauffeur-driven limousines ferry him around. He soon starts to feel quite unbelievably important, more seduced by the symbols of power than by any actual use of it. Indeed, over time, closeted in his department, with hoards of civil servants alternately backing him up and bogging him down, he is in danger of becoming remote from the cut and thrust of Westminster life. He therefore needs some form of liaison officer to keep him in touch. In days gone by, only the most senior ministers had a PPS, and it was then a far more equal relationship. A PPS would probably be a friend of long standing, a man who would not mince his words if his minister performed badly at the Dispatch Box. But nowadays virtually every minister has one of these glorified fags and, as Nicholas Soames, Nicholas Ridley's PPS, has been moved to admit, such a preponderance has tended to devalue the currency. The grandson of Sir Winston Churchill, Soames is often to be glimpsed in the chamber seated just behind his boss, sucking sweets and furiously scribbling notes to all and sundry around. A genial, Bunteresque character, he seems to be Nasty Nick's only positive attribute. Surely Ridley cannot be *so* bad, I often think, if someone like Soames can put up with him each day?

The job of PPS is not a paid one, but it nevertheless makes the lucky beneficiary one of the government's 'payroll vote'. This group comprises the government's hundred or so ministers, all of whom are obliged to vote with the government or else resign. But, having tasted the fruits of 'success', such as they are, few show any inclination of wanting to be cashiered back to the ranks. The PPS ploy is a cheap wheeze for 'fixing' another hundred Tory MPs, for a PPS also is expected to behave like 'one of us'. Government Whips, if nothing else, are adept at doing their sums and the current residents of Number 12 Downing Street have got it all well worked out:

From 375 Conservative MPs, take around 100 ministers.
That leaves you with 275.
From 275, take anything up to 100 Parliamentary Private Secretaries.
That leaves you with 175.
From the 175, take the new, ambitious Young Turks, straining to scramble on to the first part of that old, greasy pole.

And what you have left, in today's Tory Party, is a mere clutch of potential rebels: ex-ministers, free-minded MPs and independent thinkers who cannot, or can no longer, be successfully 'nobbled'.

Depressing, isn't it? Especially since the supposed role of Parliament, as we were all taught at school, is to keep a constant check on government. And the role of an MP, as we learned at the same time from Edmund Burke, the eighteenth-century political philosopher, is to bring his own individual judgement to bear on any issue. Indeed, in the House of Commons guide, a pamphlet distributed to all visitors to the galleries, there is a touching, little personal message from the Speaker to the same effect: 'The strength of the House of Commons,' writes Bernard Weatherill, 'is that it possesses the right to argue for or against any proposal, the right to question, to debate and to speak out.' Quite so, Mr Speaker, but *not*, if you want to get on in the ruling party, the right to exercise your own judgement and vote against anything the government wants to do. 'We have all been warned by the Whips,' says one Tory MP, 'that if we step out of line just once, then that's it. No job. Consigned to the backbenches for ever, or at least until there is a change in the leadership. The only thing they don't seem to mind our voting against is any sort of funding for the EEC!'

Of course, any government will argue that such manifest railroading is justified; that its legislative programme was always there in the party manifesto for all to see; and that it was on the basis of that manifesto that it was returned to power by the 'country' (i.e. 43 per cent of the country). But these are specious arguments. First of all, most of the electorate have never even read a manifesto, let alone agreed to one (though, in my view, culpable ignorance forfeits the right to complaint). But, more important, a manifesto is a composite creature – like the curate's egg, it is good in parts. Any candidate, whilst agreeing with the basic guidelines, may be implacably opposed to one individual aspect of it – the poll tax, for instance. But the discipline of the party machine does not allow for such nuances of conviction. In Mrs Thatcher's party, quite simply, either you are for us, or you are against us. And it is the job of Tory Chief Whip, Mr David Waddington, to know precisely where everyone stands. It is on that basis that the good boys may be put up for a PPS, or even a junior ministerial job, and the bad boys will receive a black mark by their name. It is not for nothing that the Chief

Whip is feared and revered throughout Westminster as the Patronage Secretary.

So much, then, for all the sentimentalists' wash about British parliamentary sovereignty. With an unassailable government majority, Parliament is effectively sovereign to nod its head and say 'Aye'. And virtually nothing the Opposition and a few unfixable rebels can do will prevent such a government from doing precisely what it wants. In Britain, we like to call this system democratic. But it is, as Lord Hailsham – albeit in Opposition – averred, merely an 'elective dictatorship'. Whether or not we agree with His Lordship, let us at least concede that this is a system designed to produce *strong* government. Its major disadvantage, of course, is that strong government does not necessarily mean good government. But it is, at least, government capable of getting things done. Our first-past-the-post electoral method does tend to result in an outright majority and, with that, a clear mandate for one party to rule. The suggested alternative of both the SDP and SLD parties, proportional representation, generally produces a far more blurred scenario. It is a picture which often leads to coalition governments, sometimes to arrangements where small minorities hold disproportionate sway. Witness the constant horse-trading in places such as Italy, Israel and Belgium. In this country, it is true, a large-majority government is virtually unstoppable. But every five years, the British people is in theory free to axe the lot and select an entirely new team. It is for that one fleeting minute at the ballot box that democracy truly rules. Our tragedy is that we consistently fail to grasp it. Jean-Jacques Rousseau noticed the same phenomenon way back in the eighteenth century:

The English people believes itself to be free; it is gravely mistaken; it is free only during election of Members of Parliament; as soon as the members are elected, the people are enslaved . . . In the brief moment of its freedom, the English people makes such a use of its freedom that it deserves to lose it.

Considering some of the dubious creatures gracing the benches of today's House of Commons, I cannot help believing that old Jean-Jacques had us sussed.

Under the Westminster system it is therefore much easier for parties to win elections outright, though overwhelming success may bring its own attendant problems. The last Conservative landslide, for instance, has even conferred a degree of licence on backbench revolts and matters as diverse as the Official Secrets Act, the poll tax, social security cuts and health charges have all met with well-orchestrated Conservative opposition. Guaranteed a comfortable buffer zone of pro-government votes, it is always possible for any dissident Tory MP to throw caution – and his short-term career – to the winds and try his hand at independence. With a smaller majority he could never contemplate such a luxury, since even the greatest of dissenters would balk at the risk of bringing his own government down. For in the final analysis, when it comes to the crunch, keeping your own lot in power is the name of the game. And the strength of the Conservative Party, above all the others, is the unshakeable belief in its own divine right to rule. Of course, the physiognomy of the Tory beast has changed dramatically since the war. It is doubtless true, if you listen to veteran MP, Julian Critchley, at least, that in twenty years the party has gone from the estate owners to the estate agents. But nowadays, that is the case in all walks of life. Everywhere it is the players rather than the gentlemen who are calling the shots. In politics particularly, those genteel days of Prime Ministers who did their economics by matchsticks are gone for ever. And, quite frankly, so what? The degentrification of the House of Commons is not the problem which keeps me awake at night. On the contrary. With an indexed salary of some £23,000 per annum, a similar secretarial allowance, not to mention generous travelling and accommodation concessions, we no longer expect or deserve mere interested amateurs as our Members of Parliament. As always, however, there is another, less desirable side to the parliamentary coin. The growing professionalization of the MP's job has fostered a different set of concerns. Today, the abiding characteristic of the new genre of career politician is his blatant ambition. Not that there is anything wrong with ambition *per se*. But it is the prevalence of ambition and arrogance without scruple or ability which bothers me far more. And especially in those persons who would presume to rule our lives.

Touring Jamaica in 1986, I was introduced to a black, Marxist lawyer, a lifelong friend, supporter and close associate of former Prime Minister, Michael Manley. Of course, he admitted, third-world politics were riddled with corruption and everybody knew it. But there again, he argued, so were first-world politics, only in an infinity of more sophisticated ways. 'And I would go even further,' he continued. 'With very few exceptions, I would say that for any politician anywhere to be really straight he has *got to be* independently rich. And even then, there's only a fifty–fifty chance. The temptations for "graft" [corruption] are always so great. We know, by their very nature, that all politicians have a price. But what saddens me the most is that their price is so low.'

I have pondered that conversation long and hard ever since. Coming from a self-proclaimed Marxist, the argument of wealth as a vague guarantee for political probity seemed odd to say the least. But after studying the village of Westminster for some time now, I think I am beginning to understand more clearly what he meant. Certainly, if we look back over the past ten years, the only cabinet resignation on a genuine point of principle has been that of the aristocratic Lord Carrington. Similarly, Richard Shepherd, the MP whose Private Member's Bill on the Official Secrets Act met with unprecedented government opposition, and perhaps the most outstanding Tory rebel during Parliament's first session, is a man of independent means. Principles are so much easier without the dependent blue-rinsed wife, the 2.4 kids and the mortgage to consider. And looking over to the Opposition benches, who is the man who most despises 'the pollsters and the admen' with their pragmatic policies for 'making the Labour Party electable at any cost'? Why, none other than the former Lord Stansgate, aka Anthony Wedgewood-Benn, aka Tony Benn himself. Such fortunate folk, however, are in the minority. Like self-made millionaire, Michael Heseltine, they can actually *afford* the luxury of not being in office. So many of their more miserable colleagues, however, are obliged to be political trimmers. They have boarded the ship of state, nailed their futures to its mast, and now must tack with prevailing winds wherever their captain shall decide. Such people hanker after office, and what they perceive as power, at almost any price. They worry me. For what sort of political system have we managed to achieve, where autonomy is gladly traded for a lousy PPS job?

From the laager-formation of the House of Commons, that inbred Ambridge of SW1, it is easy for values and principles to start looking different. Here, the humble PPS is positively envied as having made it 'over the wall'. He has thrown his two sixes and may now embark on the game of Snakes and Ladders, Westminster-style. Progress upwards may indeed be swift. Take the case of Mrs Virginia Bottomley, for instance. Elected for Surrey South-west in a 1984 by-election, she toted bags cheerfully and efficiently, first for former Education Minister, Chris Patten, and then for Foreign Secretary, Sir Geoffrey Howe. In the surprise pre-recess shuffle of summer 1988, she was duly rewarded with the job of Parliamentary Under-Secretary at the Department of the Environment and was immediately confronted with the PR nightmare of British shores awash with dying seals. But it is some comfort that so-called 'nice' people do still manage to flourish at Westminster and la Bottomley now is manifestly on her way. Of rather more concern, if perceived as any index of the direction of the Conservative Party is taking, was the simultaneous promotion of Mr Eric Forth to the position of Junior Trade Minister. Now, many of you may not, as yet, have even heard of Mr Forth. Rest assured of one thing: very soon you will. A parliamentarian of the New Right, he has been described as a younger version of Mr Norman Tebbit, but without quite the finesse or IQ. Indeed, his controversial appointment raised many an eyebrow even within the party. But it evoked outright protest from the Conservative MP for Cambridge, Mr Robert Rhodes James, who was even moved to threaten withdrawl of his support from the government for that session.

But what sort of fellow could provoke such a vehement reaction? What could possibly be so wrong with Mr Forth, apart from his tailor? In any event, surely we need a sprinkling of such people in the Commons if only for parliamentary sketch writers' copy. Oddly enough, I have always felt a strange degree of affection for the poor man. Initially, I had assumed he was suffering from some advanced form of jaundice. Happily, it transpired, the vaguely sallow complexion – framed, incidentally, by the most alarming Elvis sideburns – was merely a reflection of his jewellery. Quite a collection, all told. Indeed, it occurs to me in my more whimsical moments, only a Corocraft-sponsored Christmas tree could out-twinkle Mr Forth.

Now, as everybody who has ever listened to him knows, our Eric comes from Glasgow. He does not speak with any hint of an American accent. Neither is he black. He does not weigh in at eighteen stone. Neither does he shave his head into one of those fetching little last-of-the-Mohikans tufts. Nor does he go around duffing up the good people of his mid-Worcestershire constituency. But, to my lights, in the drab sameness of the Tory Party, Eric would seem the nearest thing they have got to a Mr T. lookalike. Perhaps you are beginning to get the idea of Mr Rhodes James's *bête noire*.

Of course, none of this would have mattered in the slightest had Mrs Thatcher left Eric sparkling incandescently on the backbenches. But his promotion to the government, albeit to a junior post, raised a few disturbing points. For, if his sort of talents are to be swiftly and ostentatiously rewarded, then what sort of example does that set for other aspiring politicians? The fact that a man decides to devote his maiden speech to opposing the Sex Equality Bill is hardly going to endear him to me. But that is his right. It is when he starts discoursing on Rodin's *The Kiss* during debates on page-three girls that I really start to worry about his grasp of feminist issues. Similarly, Mr Forth is perfectly entitled to be as obnoxious as he wants to members of the Labour Party. It is his chosen task. But to oppose extra 'Short Money' funding for Opposition parties on the basis of *his* assessment of their value, seems to exhibit a rather tenuous understanding of the concept of opposition. Let us, for the present, pass over his genius as PR man to the PM. (His questions to Mr Tony Nelson during the televising of the Commons debate were an eloquent example: 'Will my Hon. Friend concede that my Right Hon. Friend the Prime Minister has two unique contributions to make to the debate? One is her considerable length of service in the House, and the comparison she can make on that basis; but more important is her experience at the Dispatch Box during Prime Minister's Questions, about which she can express a concern that probably cannot be felt by any other Hon. Member.' *Hansard*, incidentally, does not report the muffled sounds of gagging from various quarters of the Press Gallery.) No, let us in charity forgive Mr Forth the odd verbal grovel. So many of them are at it nowadays. Instead, let us focus on the extraordinary help and advice meted out to members of his own constituency. Concerned about your children not being able to afford decent housing? No worries, says Uncle Eric. Just go out and buy up property in 'the grotty part' of town! It is truly amazing, isn't it, that, even in third-term Thatcher Britain, some people have still not managed to figure these things out for themselves?

But the greasy pole of politics is equipped with no fail-safe ratchet system. Young meteors may rise vertiginously all right, but their sudden descent back to earth is equally probable. For ministers come and ministers go, and often on the PM's passing whim. Sometimes, however, even the Prime Minister cannot 'fix' things to her fancy. The occasional glittering prize is taken out of her gift. Take the classic case of Mrs Lynda Chalker, for instance, elected for Wallasey in 1974, and subsequently promoted to Minister of State at the Foreign Office. 'It is the job I always wanted,' says Mrs Chalker. 'I could not ask for anything more.'

She peers at you kindly over her spectacles, exuding that indefinable *gravitas* all FO folk contract. The glorious ghosts of empire fill every cranny of her office. Wykehamists with double-firsts drop in with sheaves of notes. True, there are hostages in Tehran, a famine in Ethiopia and a host of awkward bastards in the European Community to deal with. But compared with her previous incarnation at the DHSS, it is not half bad. In fact, inspired by the *manes* of a thousand imperial forebears, life at the Foreign Office can seem really rather swell. And yet, buried at the back of her mind, a constant niggle reminds the minister that all is not well. With an insomnia-creating majority of 279, Mrs Chalker knows that the slightest anti-government swing at the next election will leave her without a seat. Gone overnight the gilded glamour of office! Just the prospect of gruesome selection committees all over again!

The more usual fall from grace, however, is generally precipitated not by the electorate, but by the PM herself. Once stripped of their epaulettes by She Who Must Be Obeyed, ex-ministers hold out little hope of rehabilitation. Peter Walker, however, is an obvious exception. Vehemently opposed to Mrs Thatcher during her leadership struggle, he was subsequently dropped from the shadow cabinet – hardly surprising, under the circumstances. Nevertheless, despite his dripping wet, middle-of-the-road attitudes, he has since clambered his way back into the cabinet and is now Secretary of State for Wales. Major potential troublemakers, it is often assumed, are more easily controlled from the *inside* and the same ploy was tried on the newly radicalized Tony Benn Mark II in Harold Wilson's time. A less dramatic case of survival, however, is that of John Selwyn Gummer, a meteor whose trajectory was also temporarily arrested. Axed as Conservative Party chairman back in 1985, his prospects then might well have looked bleak. For, despite the maternal instincts of the Tory ladies' faction, a resemblance to the Milky Bar Kid had not proved sufficient qualification for the job. But fortunately, in Selwyn Gummer's case, the set-back proved surmountable. He now rides senior hit-man in Nasty Nick's 'Wreck the Environment' squad.

But of all the career reversals witnessed under Mrs Thatcher's regime, surely those of Mr Cecil Parkinson must be the most amazing. Obliged to resign from the cabinet in 1983 after the well-publicized affair with his secretary Sara Keays, he is now again the apple of the PM's otherwise Victorian eye. Of course, the British attitude to the sex lives of its public figures has always been a trifle prissy. On the Continent, by contrast, people have always adopted a far more reasonable view of their politicians's peccadilloes: the 'What does it matter who the blighters screw so long as it's not the country?' approach. Certainly, in France at least, mistresses are to ministers what Citroën Deux Chevaux are to medical students: part of the deal. So it was hardly surprising when President Mitterrand failed to understand what the Cecil scandal was all about. If extra-marital relationships were to be banned from his cabinet, claimed *le président* gamely, then he would be left with forty homosexuals to choose from.

Not for the first time, however, old François chose to miss the point. Surely, despite the usual humbug of the popular press's moral outrage, Cecil's real weakness was never his adulterous affair. Indeed, without the birth of the unfortunate Flora, even the party's inner circle might have continued to turn a blind eye to that. Besides, the day infidelity becomes a reason for resignation, half the House of Commons will be lining up outside the Job Centre. For, despite lengthy editorials to the contrary, the British are no longer surprised when their politicians prove duplicitous and vain.

Indeed, I am even inclined to believe these are the only genuine prerequisites for the job. And Cecil, with his monogrammed shirts, his slicked-back hair, and his 1930s band-leader looks, has provided evidence of both. But what is far more disturbing about Mr Parkinson's character is the seeming evidence of his vacillating weakness. However understandable, irresolution is not the hallmark of a man fitted for high and ever-higher office. Twice at least he asked Miss Keays to marry him. Twice at least he later changed his mind. And yet, in the final analysis, Cecil is the one who has ended up smelling of roses. Sara, on the contrary, has had her reputation dragged wholesale through the mire. The whole sorry business is a fine example of the Tory Party closing ranks to protect its own. He, the married man and, if anything, the guiltier of the pair, was given a standing ovation at the 1983 party conference. She, the used and abused woman, became an immediate outcast from the Conservative fold. Today, you read a lot about Cecil, about his urbanity and his charm. But, as far as I can ascertain, these attributes seem to impress themselves almost exclusively on male correspondents. I have yet to meet the sensible woman who did not think the man's behaviour was that of a cad. And yet, even within the party confraternity, forgiven is not forgotten. Despite his salvation, teacher's pet still comes in for a lot of heavy sarcasm from his own parliamentary colleagues: 'Energy Questions' proclaimed the television monitor one afternoon in a Commons private dining-room.

'Cecil will be on his feet,' surmised my luncheon companion, glancing briefly up.

'Makes a change,' replied another. And just *everybody* laughed.

Now it may well be that, as Energy Secretary, Parkinson has done a passingly competent job in preparing the nation's assets for denationalization. But so what? There is no shortage of street-wise Tory barrow boys around who, as the scandalously undervalued sale of Royal Ordnance to British Aerospace was amply to demonstrate, are equally capable of organizing the scam of the century. But no matter. It is Cecil's star which is relentlessly in the ascendant. Not only, in 1988, was he appointed chairman of the prestigious Star Chamber – his task, mercifully redundant, to arbitrate between the various claims of all the major money-grabbing ministries – but now he is even being tipped to succeed Nigel Lawson as Chancellor of the Exchequer: Asti Spumante after Dom Perignon, if ever there was such a notion! Without a doubt, Cecil Parkinson must count himself the luckiest politician in the Commons today. Only rarely does the Omnipotent choose to raise a man from the dead.

By definition, of course, miracles are few and far between. Most MPs do not bask in the warmth of such overt favouritism, and wend their way more wearily up Westminster's slippery slopes. Gradually, however, aware that they are never going to make it right to the top, the more realistic set themselves more feasible objectives. 'I would be happy now,' claimed Mr Richard Needham, Junior Minister for Northern Ireland, 'if I could learn a foreign language and make it into the cabinet.'

For a life's ambitions, these seemed modest enough, though perhaps not quite so modest as many a junior minister's abilities. Of the two desiderata, however, I found the first distinctly more worth while. As Montaigne once confided to his diary: 'Another language is another soul.' And an extra soul could prove a useful attribute in a future cabinet minister. If nothing else, it might compensate for the one he lost in getting there to start with. But whatever his karma, Needham's overall sense of perspective will probably see him through. In some detail, he explained to me about Marks and Spencer's problems selling underwear in the Midlands. In this area, it would seem, atypically high proportions of Asians and West Indians are creating havoc with the system. West Indian ladies, apparently, have big busts and like bright colours. Asian ladies, on the contrary, have small hips and go for pastels. From time to time, the Marks and Spencer computer finds it all too much and springs an apoplectic anode. It was one of my more instructive conversations with a politician – odd, yet strangely comforting. At least one member of Her Majesty's government, I felt, has grasped the nation's knickers.

Aspiring politicians, however, can never rest from hustling, and the 1979 crop of 'Maggie's boys' has spawned some prime examples. Appointed Minister of State at the Department of Health in the 1988 reshuffle, David Mellor is perhaps one of the more obviously ambitious. A member of the 'Shock! Horror!' headline-grabbing school of international diplomacy, his controversial trip to Gaza as Foreign Office Minister earlier in the year created serious waves with the pro-Jewish lobby. But, if nothing else, it succeeded in upstaging Neil Kinnock's subsequent visit – a result which, according to Mellor's detractors at least, was not entirely secondary to his purpose. It seemed all the more ironic, therefore, when the nurses' pay settlement appeared to founder in the summer, that neither Mellor nor his boss, Kenneth Clarke, was physically available for comment. Of the new-look Department of Health's three arch-communicators, only the most junior member, Edwina Currie, was finally winkled out to try and calm things down. And of all her many and indubitable qualities, calming things down has never been considered Edwina's most outstanding, as the great egg débâcle was subsequently to show. Strange to relate, however, Mellor remained resolutely low-profile somewhere in Italy. And Clarke steadfastly refused to cut short his Spanish holiday on the Costa Nawfullotamoneytofundapayaward. All in all, not a very impressive performance on the public relations front, particularly as Labour's Shadow Social Services Secretary, Robin Cook, was busily making immense political capital out of their 'crisis, what crisis?' absence. Indeed, his letter to an 'empty' DHSS, addressed 'To whom it may concern', was an inspired example of understated criticism. A tiny leprechaun of a man, Cook continues to show an immense talent for nailing the government at every opportunity, as John Moore, the demoted Social Services Secretary, has learned to his cost. Once a premier-league high-flyer himself, the poor chap is now just half the man he was. Politics, stripped to basics, is just a sophisticated blood sport. The only difference is that no one knows when he might be the victim. *Caveat Mellor!*

But the finest example of the 1979 vintage is, arguably, John Patten. Currently Minister of State at the Home Office, he was the first of the bunch to be appointed a minister. Like Mellor, a highly intelligent, competent and articulate man, he shares with him one potentially fatal flaw. Even in today's profoundly bourgeois Tory Party, it really does not do to be so obviously on the make. Tall poppies have a tendency to find themselves mown down. Perhaps, to a certain extent at least, this explains the staying power of one of Westminster's greatest survivors, Sir Geoffrey Howe. A year younger than Mrs Thatcher, although nowadays he might pass for her grandad, he has still not given up hope of leading the party. And yet he has always taken care to hide that ambition behind a vaguely bumbling exterior. He is constantly, and to my lights, unfairly dismissed as an irretrievably boring speaker. And yet this apparently saturnine Welsh barrister has a fine mind and a little-appreciated line in self-deprecating humour. I remember one morning during the London Lancaster House World Summit, when the Foreign Ministers were dispatched to discuss their contribution to the final communiqué. They would report back to the assembled heads of state and government later that afternoon. 'Sit down, gentlemen, sit down,' said Sir Geoffrey wearily, as the Foreign Ministers of the world's seven most highly industrialized nations piled into the conference room. 'Let us try to make our modest input into their stratospheric thinking.' At least Sir Geoffrey has found the true measure of international jamborees.

But there is life in the old dog yet. Despite Mrs Thatcher's avowed intention of fighting the next election and handing over eventually to a much younger man, Sir Geoffrey stubbornly refuses to give up hope. He is even getting a trifle rebellious in his dotage, ganging up with Nigel against Margaret on matters such as the European Monetary System. But his long-term leadership strategy has taken some peculiar turnings. MPs do not expect the Foreign Secretary to forsake their lofty forum for a guest appearance on the *Wogan* show. And yet, how many one of them, given the opportunity, would not have done exactly the same. In their heart of hearts, and despite their nonsense, they know which of the two shows carries more clout in the country.

'Poor Geoffrey,' confided one ministerial colleague, well versed in the works of another populist, right-wing leader and trying to explain such frivolous antics. '"*Meglio vivere un giorno da leone che cent'anni da pecora,*" as *Il Duce* used to say.'

I mulled that one over carefully. Better to spend one day as a lion, than to live as a sheep for a hundred years – yes, Mussolini had a point. But for all Geoffrey's belated public relations efforts, will his day now ever come?

'If Margaret went tomorrow,' claimed one government colleague, 'he'd be trampled in the rush.'

Poor Geoffrey. At least as sometime Chancellor of the Exchequer and Foreign Secretary he has almost reached the summit – not a bad effort, by anybody's standards. But what of all those other ravening Westminster wolves condemned to be sheep for ever?

# 4 / The power, the glory, or just better than working?

*"WHAT DO YOU MEAN — **HOW** CAN I TELL SHE'S A POLITICIAN'S SECRETARY."*

I distinctly remember listening to Sue Lawley's interview with Arthur Scargill on *Desert Island Discs* one morning. Arthur Scargill, of course, the demagogic miners' leader who reportedly has three Shredded Wheat for breakfast: two to eat and the other to wear on top of his head. Anyway, the conversation progressed agreeably enough along the usual relaxed, spill-your-heart-out lines when suddenly, perhaps a touch *faux naïf*, Miss Lawley felt obliged to put the obvious question. Had Mr Scargill, she wondered, ever felt the urge to move over into mainstream politics? Now La Lawley, an intelligent woman, must have known what to expect, her self-answering enquiry not unlike those soft lobs at which the oleaginous wing of the Tory Pary so brilliantly excels. Even the most casual of observers must have noted that Prime Minister's Question Time has become increasingly peppered with them, all devastatingly uninspired variations on the original theme. You know the sort of thing: 'Will my Right Honourable Friend, the Prime Minister, agree with me that she is without doubt the best Prime Minister that this country, or indeed any country, has had this century, or indeed, if I'm reading the handwriting of my

Honourable Friend, the Prime Minister's Parliamentary Private Secretary – or does that say Ingham? – correctly, ever?' Sit down, pat on the head, wait for a job at the Department of Trade and Industry. It is a constant source of annoyance to many of us that such relentless probings for enlightenment and information are often interspersed with the Opposition's petty-minded irrelevances about funding the nurses' pay award; hospital closures; cuts in housing benefits; nuclear reactor safety; one, two or three million people out of work, etc. But for the Knights of the Crumbs from the Mistress's Round Table, such considerations must never interfere with the fearless Quest for Truth.

Back at *Desert Island Discs*, however, old Arthur could see the question coming for miles. He was waiting for it. No longer quite the force he once was before the defeat of the miners' strike in 1985, Scargill must still count as a major figure in Britain's industrial aristocracy. Of course, the TUC barons have had their wings clipped since 1979, the year which saw the end of the jolly concordat between a cabal of union leaders effectively running the country and a supine Labour government pretending hopelessly that it wasn't. By that stage, of course, the entire country was heartily sick of the unions' dominance, and thus psychologically primed for any future legislation, however draconian, to curb their by then excessive powers. No more cosy sessions over the beer and sandwiches with Margaret Thatcher in charge. And the man in the street was the first to rejoice.

Nevertheless, as Scargill was quick to point out, despite the undoubted diminution of union influence, the portals of St Stephen's Gate hold even less attraction. Everybody, he went on to explain, knows exactly who is the President of the National Union of Mineworkers. True, the membership of his union has been on the wane. Now that the number of affiliations has dropped below the magic 100,000 figure, the NUM is no longer entitled to an automatic seat on the TUC General Council, a bitter blow indeed. For all that, the NUM President's job still carries weight. The vast majority of MPs, on the contrary, argued Scargill, wield precious little power at all.

For once I found myself in total agreement with Mr Arthur Scargill. The representatives of both labour and industry have always exercised more influence over the nation's politics than mere politicians. But massive, long-term unemployment – a problem successive Tory governments seem conspicuously either unwilling or unable to solve – has gradually undermined the TUC. Nowadays, increasingly, it is big business which calls the shots, the extraordinary case of Australia proving particularly instructive. There, even with a Labour government in power, the ex-trade union boss turned Prime Minister, Bob Hawke, is loathe to sneeze before seeking the approval of Messrs Murdoch, Holmes à Court, Packer and Bond. In Thatcher's Britain, on the other hand, the government has not found itself obliged to kowtow to the demands of private industry, since there has never been any real possibility of conflict to begin with. The two have always been more or less happily in tune with each other, though what tensions will emerge if interest rates continue rising along the lines of late 1988 remain anybody's guess. Nevertheless, whatever other legacy she intends to leave to posterity, Mrs Thatcher will still go down in history as one of the entrepreneurs' best friends.

Almost on a par with big business in the contemporary power stakes are the media moguls and the newspaper magnates – all those opinion-formers who, far more than any politician, are adept at moulding the way we think and behave. In any democratic society, the concentration of such enormous influence into so few hands must be cause for concern. The virtual Maxdoch/Murwell duopoly, for all the well-hyped claims of individuality, continues to produce an astonishing sameness of pap. But that is not the worst of it, not by a long chalk. Far more significant is the general question of public accountability. For however minimal their clout, at every general election at least, MPs are made answerable for their own, or more usually, for their own party's performance. Newspaper and television channel proprietors, on the contrary, are subject to no such constraints. Not only do they enjoy the luxury of power but, as Stanley Baldwin, quoting his cousin, Kipling, once noted, 'Power without responsibility – the prerogative of the harlot throughout history.' As fellow-sufferers at party conferences will readily attest, they just don't make speech-writers like Kipling no more . . .

But the media, and access to it, is ever more important to those actors on the political stage. For increasingly it is a leader's TV image more than any other issue which wins elections. In the United States, the most powerful country in the world, the alarming superficiality and hype of the 1988 Presidential Election should serve as a warning to us all. It was there, after all, that a nonentity such as J. Danforth Quayle, an unknown, lightweight, alleged draft-dodger-turned-defence-hawk, could be selected as Republican George Bush's running-mate. No doubt Bush, whose personality – or the lack of it – has long been overshadowed by the showbiz glitz of Mr Teflon Man himself, was feeling in need of some youth and glamour on the ticket. Make no mistake about it: America is the sort of society where Samantha Fox could end up ensconced in the White House. But is a spurious resemblance to Robert Redford *really* sufficient qualification for the man potentially 'a heartbeat away from the President?' And is it any wonder that the most frightening words in the USA today are 'Dan, I'm not feeling very well'?

What is worse is the fact that we have already started on the same meretricious tack ourselves. Witness the first SLD leadership contest between Paddy Ashdown and Alan Beith, a case of two bald men fighting over a comb if ever there was one. But in a page-three society, what chance did the modest, intelligent, schoolmasterly type ever stand against the Ramboesque, ex-Special Boat Squadron marine commando? Ashdown was always going to win the battle hands down, as the party that mixed portable phones with yoghurt went overwhelmingly for matter over mind. Nor does Ashdown, the Arnold Schwarzenegger of the SLD, seem in any way afraid of exploiting his overt masculinity to best effect. People still remember when he first burst on to the scene at an Alliance conference a few years ago. It was, by all accounts, a virtuoso performance, vaguely redolent of Mr Tom Jones in his 'Why, Why, Why Delilah?' phase. The jacket soon came off to reveal a shirt with the sleeves rolled up, the top button undone and the tie already loosened. He then proceeded to wow his audience with an ostentatiously physical performance, far more impressive than anything he was actually saying. Suddenly, men all over the conference hall started to feel uneasily inadequate. SDP wimps, soon returning Porsche-bound to the living-module on the Isle of Dogs, would all be sending for Nautilus equipment brochures the very next day. Pasty-faced

Liberals, sickly from an excess of excessively healthy health food, wondered why *their* homemade primrose wine never produced quite the same results as Château Ashdown clearly did. The Liberal ladies looked despairingly at their own dear leader. A vaguely risible figure even at the best of times, David Steel looked more than ever like a kindergarten escapee, his striped shirt and bright-white collar only emphasizing the point. On the other side, with one obvious exception, the assembled SDP ranks looked very thin on what disco-land's Sharons and Tracys might refer to as 'talent'. And so, clearly, when it came to the leadership of the newly merged SLD party, Paddy Ashdown had it made. After such a bitterly traumatic birth, neither of the two caretaker leaders had the force left to fight. David Steel bowed out, a tired if not broken man. And poor Robert Maclennan, never resembling anything so much as a Taiwanese rip-off version of Dr David Owen himself, was only ever a sad reminiscence of the Man Who Might Have Been.

But the Social and Liberal Democrats are far from alone in their enthusiasm for the medium at the expense of the message. Eager for tips in summer 1988, the Labour and Conservative parties dispatched their own conference managers to the Democrat and Republican camps, their general remit to observe a few tricks of the trade. Frankly, the whole idea is enough to make all sensible folk shudder. For whatever else is necessary to capture the senior-citizen vote, I think we can live without the prospect of Maggie slobbering all over Denis on the party conference platform. Why should we give two hoots how our American cousins want to play it? Let British politicians at least maintain some vestiges of dignity. There is still more to British politics, one hopes, than a convention hall full of hysteria and helium-filled balloons . . .

But if politicians are becoming increasingly adept at media manipulation, how much more so the media folk themselves? For all MPs' wishful thinking about the influence they enjoy, there is not a single political commentator worth his salt, or even the slightest pinch of it, who does not direct more intelligent opinion than the vast majority of anonymous Westminster men. Hugo Young (*Guardian*), Ed Pearce (*Sunday Times*), and Gordon Greig (*Daily Mail*) are some of the best examples, or at least a few of the pressmen's most respected pressmen. And on the small screen, of course, the acid test for any politician is an ability to hold his own against the formidable Sir Robin Day, that Torquemada of televised political inquisition. Yet what is the idea of a career in politics if not to influence people and events? And, in the final analysis, how many politicians actually manage to do so? Even for those lucky MPs who make it into government, the potential sphere of influence remains severely limited. The input of junior ministers into policy-making has never been more than nugatory. And nowadays, according to former Defence Secretary John Nott, at least, even the full cabinet has degenerated into a mere rubber-stamping outfit. More and more, the cabinet college is expected to accept conclusions that have effectively been reached elsewhere, decisions already taken by restricted groups of people operating in *ad hoc* cabinet committees. Not to mention the alarming increase in the influence of the cabinet secretariat itself, a body which is not even staffed by ministers but by a body of appointed advisers unaccountable to the electorate. It makes much of our MPs' feverish parliamentary activity seem so patently pointless. For in the Westminster hotel, as you may recall, people come and people go and different individuals make it to the presidential suite. But in the end, whatever happens, somehow the management remains exactly the same . . .

Despite all the evidence, however, few MPs will ever openly admit to the overwhelming inanity of their House of Commons existence. It is a career of years spent wandering obediently in and out of 'Aye' and 'No' lobbies; of hours upon hours of redundant debate in a generally empty chamber; of contributions endlessly worked and reworked, yet destined to be neither heard nor read. It is a ton of wasted effort for the *Hansard* records alone, a *dialogue de sourds* in a class of its own. But to what end all the interminable argument if not to convince others, something very few Honourable Members seem capable of doing? Indeed, according to Mr Speaker Weatherill, a man who manages to stay awake by keeping notes on such matters, only five MPs during Parliament's first session actually managed to alter the course of a debate by their contributions: Michael Fallon (Conservative, Darlington), who argued brilliantly for the retention of Latin in schools; Terry Lewis (Labour, Worsley), who put the knife into OFTEL, purveyors of sexy telephone messages; Tony Nelson (Conservative, Chichester), who managed to convince waverers to join the pro-televising the House of Commons camp; and Norman Tebbit who, operating in unstoppable tandem with Michael Heseltine, hastened the abolition of the Inner London Education Authority. To these I personally would add Richard Shepherd (Conservative, Aldridge-Brownhills), whose spirited defence of his own Private Member's Bill to amend the Official Secrets Act was at once noble, touching and inspired. Admittedly, the unprecedented measure of a three-line government Whip against the bill eventually thwarted his efforts. Nevertheless, more than any other MP in this Parliament, Shepherd showed what one independently minded individual, what one single MP who refuses either to be bought off by his government or intimidated by the party Whips, can manage to do. For after such damaging controversy, the Home Secretary was obliged to draw up new Official Secrets legislation – a fudged and botched job, tailor-made to fuel yet more acrimonious debate as it wends its way to the statute book. But if nothing else, the episode taught us all one salutary lesson. Democracy should be grateful for its dwindling band of Shepherds. It is to those MPs with sufficient guts and principle to defy their own government on occasion that the feeble flame of British parliamentary control is currently entrusted.

As far as the fading art of Commons oratory is concerned, however, the undisputed maestro of them all must surely be Tony Benn. Members of every persuasion can be spotted flocking to the chamber for his performances, all agog at the mere prospect of hearing him speak. It is a rare pleasure indeed, though few Honourable Members have the same happy effect on their colleagues. Less engaging contributions are often drowned by the stampede of Hush Puppies heading for the exit. It must all be most disheartening for the average Cicero *manqué*. Of course, there is some solace in the thought that we all have different gifts. Sometimes it is merely a question of redirecting them along the right lines. I have often thought that the purple perorations of many of our MPs could empty Wembley Stadium in a flash. Perhaps their soporific talents might be better harnessed in some form of football crowd control.

Talking of hooligans, it was Benn's speech on MPs' behaviour in the House of Commons which was probably his finest effort in

1988. It was a beguiling piece of tongue-in-cheek mischief, delivered to a packed House in the aftermath of left-wing Ron Brown's disgraceful mace-bashing incident. Opprobrium was of the essence. Tempers were running high. There were suggestions of hanging and flogging again. Perhaps even crucifixion. And these were all proposals from the Labour backbenches! But Tony Benn has not spent a quarter of a century observing Commons Man and his shenanigans for nothing. Standards of behaviour now, he maintained, were no worse than they had been in the past. Why, he could even remember the youthful Irish firebrand, Bernadette Devlin, in her prime. Incensed on one occasion, she even crossed the floor to slap Reggie Maudling on the face 'and almost woke him up'.

But such entertaining speeches are sadly few and far between. Today, there is a distressing paucity of Benns, Foots, and Powells around, of politicians capable of moving us by great, well-argued debate. The predominance of television has put paid to the sort of oratory which could inflame men's passions. Indeed, televised oratory comes across as little more than demented raving. Today's goggle-box *aficionados* have developed minimal concentration spans of fifteen seconds or less, and communicators are obliged to pander to the phenomenon. And so it is that politicians everywhere have succumbed to the shorn language of adspeak: to those short, sharp, oft-reiterated tabloid sentences which the Prime Minister has mastered to such sonorous effect. But politics is a performing art. Its exponents should either speak well or shut up. It's high time someone told them so. Certainly, I'd rather a pair of Viv Richards's well-publicized piles than an average week in the chamber of the House of Commons.

Considering the row upon row of sparsely populated benches, most MPs must generally feel the same. But let any outside observer even mention the shortage of MPs gracing the cockpit of the nation and he is swiftly jumped upon. You see, we are all told, the reason so few Honourable Members are in the chamber making cosmic contributions to the affairs of state is quite simple. Everyone is so terribly occupied *upstairs*. All the important work that you, the cavilling public don't appreciate, all the *real*, *in-depth* scrutiny of policy and legislation, all the hauling over coals of recalcitrant and tight-lipped civil servants, all that and much, much more besides, is being effected quietly and efficiently in the committee rooms upstairs. By nature a sweet, ingenuous and trusting sort of person, I too believed that to begin with. Now I've simply added it to my ever-growing list of the world's best whoppers. In order of magnitude, they now run: 'The cheque's in the post'; 'Of course I'll still love you in the morning'; 'We are the Conservative Party and the National Health Service is safe in our hands'; and the new improved, 'This is the House of Commons and we're all very busy, beavering away upstairs.'

There is no doubt that much of an MP's Westminster life may be expended on meetings. Apart from myriad party and party-faction groups, not to mention the jolly junkets of the Inter-Parliamentary Union and trips to watch the odd Test Series with the Commonwealth Parliamentary Association, there are essentially two types of committee in the House of Commons. First of all, there are the standing committees which meet in the rooms on the riverside first floor of the Palace of Westminster. For this reason, bills dispatched in that direction are often referred to as being 'sent upstairs'. Established to deal with individual bills, standing committees are subsequently dissolved once the job has been done. Generally speaking, they meet in the mornings but, for more controversial measures such as the Finance Bill, they may go on until late at night. There is no doubt that such meetings do tend to be time-consuming, but often it is time sacrificed to no real purpose. Indeed, as Richard Crossman, a Labour cabinet minister during the 1960s, wrote in his celebrated diaries: 'The whole procedure of standing committees is insane . . . Under the present system there is no genuine committee work, just formal speech-making, mostly from written briefs.'

The testimony of many MPs seems to bear this allegation out. Elected in 1987 as the new Conservative MP for Skipton and Ripon, an old friend of mine, David Curry, soon found himself co-opted on to one such committee, its unhappy remit to scrutinize the contentious Health and Medicines Bill. It was this piece of legislation, incidentally, which sought to introduce charges for eye tests and dental check-ups, measures which precipitated a major backbench revolt amongst those Tories in both Houses who thought them both mean and paltry. Now, David has already made a name for himself as a bright boy in the European Parliament. Between 1986 and 1987 he acted as *rapporteur général* for the EEC budget, that annual tripartite blood-letting ritual where the European Parliament, Commission and Council of Ministers all flex their respective muscles and have a therapeutic go at one another. He also showed himself to be an extremely able chairman of the Parliament's influential Agriculture Committee, a remarkable feat of prestidigitation, involving the conciliation of interest groups as diverse as French Gaullist farmers, German Green environmentalists, Danish Conservative fishermen and a goodly quotient of British Labour anti-marketeers. Fluent in French, pro-EEC, clever with honours and a mordant line in wit, it is difficult to know which of Curry's many attributes will stitch him up first in the party of the GCSE. Anyway, David's first impressions of the Westminster committee system were not entirely euphoric. To begin with, any government's aim is to push its own legislative programme through with as little hassle as possible. It is the job of the Opposition to be obstructive, to slow things down and, in the process, to gain as many concessions as possible. So the last thing any government wants is MPs from its own side 'wasting' time by asking questions, tabling amendments, requesting further information and generally exhibiting any interest whatsoever in genuine examination of the legislation at hand. In fact, the profile of an ideal government committee man is one who keeps his head down and does the crossword puzzle all morning.

To begin with, Mr Curry was rather surprised by the fatuity of it all. Accustomed to tougher scrutiny and livelier debate even in committees of the much maligned EuroParl, he spent some time wondering what sort of positive contribution he could make to proceedings. His most positive contribution, he was duly given to understand, was to keep quiet and get on with his mail. He has never, he assured me, been so completely up to date with his private and constituency correspondence! And yet, what is the purpose of sticking hundreds of MPs into committees with neither the resources nor the encouragement to do a proper job? Even for members of the Opposition, those whose task it is to resist government legislation, the exercise must be totally dispiriting. Figures indicate that only about one in twenty amendments proposed by backbenchers in standing committees is ever passed, statistics which suggest a monumental waste of intelligent and capable manpower. Indeed, despite the many hours devoted to the health of the nation, the only issue Curry really recalls from the entire experience was an incident over the attendance register. Then Junior Health Minister, Edwina, she of homonymous surname, objected to the way in which their respective names were being called. She said it seemed to imply some sort of man and wife relationship. David countered that the feeling was entirely mutual and immediately commissioned a T-shirt bearing the legend 'No Relation'. And so it is that life goes on in the Ambridge of SW1. Just another episode in the series they call *The Tharchers*, an everyday tale of simple Westminster folk.

The House of Commons has also spawned a system of some fourteen departmental select committees, a vision of parliamentary perfection originally visited upon Mr Norman St John Stevas whilst he was still of this earth. As leader of the House, St John Stevas felt that only such a network could vet every aspect of government policy, administration and expenditure, and as such would be a tremendous step forward towards parliamentary reform. The view of his immediate predecessor, Labour's veteran parliamentarian, Michael Foot, was far less enthusiastic. Still sentimentally attached to a House of Commons, however discredited, Foot felt that the host of select committees would only detract even further from the focal point of Parliament: the chamber itself. But whatever the arguments for or against, the system has met with some degree of success. To some Honourable Members, it has given a vague feeling of *raison d'être*. To others, it has afforded a healthier alternative to the bars. Of course, in theory at least, select committees do enjoy extensive powers. They may, if they so wish, enlist the support of specialist advisers, and force ministers and civil servants to turn up and answer questions. Indeed, in 1982, the Energy Committee even got on its high horse and press-ganged an unwilling Arthur Scargill to come along and give evidence. But in practice, whilst the system excels at taking issue with relatively defenceless folk, it tends to leave the all-powerful Whitehall mandarinate alone to do precisely what it wants. Indeed, the defects in the system were made embarrassingly clear by the Zircon spy satellite fiasco. Thanks to the efforts of investigative journalism, the Public Accounts Committee – putatively the Commons most influential monitoring body – was shown to have voted millions of pounds for a project of which its members remained in total ignorance. And indeed, neither they, nor the rest of Parliament, had any idea what they had done until a certain journalist, Mr Duncan Campbell, apprised them of the fact. So much, then, for the efficiency of parliamentary scrutiny. For all Westminster's huffing and puffing, the inscrutable, in short, still never get scruted.

But despite their many defects, at least these myriad committees do serve the purpose of keeping some of our MPs off the streets. Not all of them, however, wish their Westminster days to be so drearily restricted. In the first session of Parliament, for example, thirty-two out of 374 Tory MPs failed to serve on either a select or standing committee. And out of 229 Labour MPs, eleven managed similarly to exclude themselves. And yet, although select committees are not normally the route to make a political name for yourself, their chairmen do enjoy considerable prestige within the House itself, a degree of status often manifested in the form of decent office accommodation – no mean privilege in the Palace of Westminster. In these committees, too, a broad cross-party consensus may often be reached which could never be achieved on the floor of the House. The problem is, however, that such happy coalitions may often degenerate into restricted coteries of experts talking to one another, the results of their labours too complicated for their less specialized colleagues to understand. More unfortunate still is the growing feeling that government is only happy to countenance a watchdog so long as the watchdog never bites. It is an impression which was more than borne out by the Westland affair of early 1986.

It is a truth universally recognized that all governments will readily tell you everything apart from anything you really want to know. During the Westland crisis, the major political scandal which resulted in the resignation of two cabinet ministers, the Defence Committee called for evidence from two senior civil servants. The Prime Minister, however, would have none of it, and the then cabinet secretary, Sir Robert Armstrong, head of the Civil Service, was sent along in their stead. Now, Sir Robert is doubtless a man of many fine qualities. But an ability to answer questions has never appeared to be one of them. Sadly, even at that late stage of his career, some sort of induction course might have saved him from making such an egregious fool of himself a few years later. For it was the same Sir Robert Armstrong who was subsequently to achieve notoriety in the *Spycatcher* trial, the distinguished civil servant reduced to little more than an international laughing-stock in a New South Wales courtroom. It was from Armstrong that the stiletto-sharp Sydney lawyer, Malcolm Turnbull, extracted the celebrated 'economical with the truth' confession. It was Armstrong who started the whole world asking whether the politicization of the job of cabinet secretary had not gone just a trifle too far. And it was Armstrong who, according to Turnbull himself, 'had become, in many eyes at least, a hired gun prepared to do anything in the service of his boss [Mrs Thatcher]'. Such a dextrous stonewaller, such an impeccably 'well-educated mushroom' was clearly the ideal man to deal with any awkward questions that might be raised in the Commons Defence Committee. Unfortunately, many of our friends Down Under have yet to learn about the amount of deference due to top civil servants. Certainly Mr Turnbull, a legal whizz kid who combines street-wise Sydney with double-first Oxford, was decidedly unimpressed with either Sir Robert or the quality of his testimony. But then again, neither had the Defence Committee been particularly overwhelmed by the co-operation it had received, and decided to say as much in a very critical report. The government's response came swiftly enough, complete with thinly veiled threats about the possibility of restricting committees' rights to examine civil servants in the future. At last, the watchdog had dared to bare its teeth. And immediately it was threatened with the prospect of having them pulled. Once again, so much for all the guff about in-depth parliamentary scrutiny! For, in the end, it was an Australian court case, more than any House of Commons committee, which revealed to an international audience how British government really works: in arrogance and in secrecy and through a permanent network effectively answerable to no one.

If, to the average outsider, life inside the House of Commons seems miserable and pointless, then so it would seem to most of the inmates as well. When, for instance, Tory MP Jonathan Aitken went to visit the House of Commons doctor for his annual check-up, he took the opportunity of asking him to identify our MPs' most common complaint. Various possible maladies had fleetingly suggested themselves to Jonathan: cirrhosis (surely an odds-on favourite amongst members of the Tory Party); prostatism (or was that more likely to be an Upper House indisposition?); monocular vision (certainly there was no shortage of that in parties across the entire political spectrum); or perhaps even stereotopy, a form of frontal-lobe dementia resulting in a repetition of the same thing over and over again. Common enough in Thatcherspeak, how Labour MPs must wish that their own leader might contract such a condition, at least for the duration of party defence debates. But no, the doctor assured Aitken: strangely enough, it was none of these disorders. According to his diagnosis, the most widespread affliction in the House of Commons was quite simply 'unhappiness'. And such a mournful conclusion is hardly surprising. There are far too many MPs around who are forced to spend long hours and late nights at Westminster with no genuinely satisfying job to do. Moreover, MPs who live outside London are often obliged to spend their weeks away from home. Divorce, 'House of Commons' style, has become an occupational hazard, as private secretaries and research assistants swiftly develop into surrogate spouses. And yet, despite all drawbacks, few MPs ever voluntarily relinquish their seats. For, despite all the dangers of despondency, the Westminster club still affords its members possible avenues of salvation. The secret of contentment simply lies in finding the right niche.

The French have an expression for it: *être bien dans sa peau*. It means something along the lines of feeling happy being precisely who and what you are. Yes, things often do tend to lose a little in the process of translation. Anyway, to be honest, I cannot lay claim to any personal experience of the state, though, oddly enough, at Westminster at least, the condition does seem to affect relatively more women than men. Who, in all honesty, could fathom the precise reasons why? It may lie in the traditional theory that the female is the less ambitious sex and therefore that much more easily satisfied. Or perhaps – and this is the explanation I would espouse – it is due to the fact that women are more realistic in their expectations, less liable to frustration and, all in all, far more 'together' individuals than their male counterparts. In today's House of Commons, few MPs exemplify that happy amalgam of balance and serenity more than Madam Deputy Speaker, Miss Betty Boothroyd.

Miss Boothroyd, to her eternal credit, represents an increasingly rare phenomenon – a Labour MP beloved by both sides of the House. Stranger still, even in the Commons Press Gallery, that hotbed of mischief whence few politicians emerge with their motives unscathed, rarely is any ill ever spoken of Betty. Intrigued by such generalized affection, I asked one veteran lobby correspondent if there was anyone around who had managed to conceive a dislike for her. His eyes misted over for a moment in that sentimental Celtic way. 'Yes,' he conceded eventually. 'I suppose there are a few. But those are just the sort of stupid bastards you don't need to waste your time on.' Indeed, Miss Boothroyd is held in such extraordinary regard all around that even the seemingly supercilious Environment Secretary, Mr Nicholas Ridley, is rumoured not to dislike her. If she possesses one failing, then that might conceivably be it.

But what makes Miss Boothroyd's popularity all the more incredible is that, since 7 July 1987, she has had the unenviable task of keeping order in an increasingly rowdy chamber. The second woman ever to be elected Deputy Speaker, she is the only woman currently capable of silencing the Prime Minister, something the combined manpower of Mr Neil Kinnock, Mr Jimmy Young, Sir Robin Day, the cabinet and the entire EEC has never managed to do. Given the invidious nature of her current position, she is particularly fortunate to be blessed with almost endless reserves of stamina, good humour and tolerance. With the growing hopelessness and anger of a frustrated Opposition, such qualities in a presiding officer are clearly without price.

More than anything else, however, it is undoubtedly her no-nonsense background which helps her to cope. Born in Yorkshire, 'over forty-five years ago', Betty still retains her friendly Northern ways. These include the endearing idiosyncrasy of calling everybody 'love'. The effect of such an epithet on the arch-Old Etonian Ridley may only be imagined. As a child, she always excelled in gymnastics and dancing, and even spent a short period as a professional dancer with the legendary Tiller Girls. 'I'm not that fit today though, love,' she adds hurriedly, thwarting any suggestion of a possible routine. 'I suppose if I tried a high kick in this dress I'd fall base over apex.'

But despite all her self-deprecating claims of being 'pleasantly plump', Miss Boothroyd is a handsome woman, well groomed and attractively turned out. Like the Commons other high-profile lady, she manages that look of brisk efficiency and femininity which many tumble-dried male colleagues find so utterly appealing. Neither is she afraid of indulging her twin loves of clothes and jewellery; for the past ten years, she has never been seen without a diamond-studded gold brooch in the form of a portcullis logo, the gift of Muslim friends in Sri Lanka. 'Of course, for stints in the chair, Mr Speaker has his robes,' she explains, 'and the other two Deputy Speakers wear frockcoats and pin-striped trousers. But I wear my own clothes, something different every day. I think if you look bright and cheerful, it makes everyone around you feel better.'

Certainly, despite her taxing regime of five hours' sleep a night, Miss Boothroyd exudes an infectious degree of verve and vitality. A naturally gregarious person, her elevation to an office on the 'Ways and Means Committee' corridor leaves her feeling rather cut off from the cut and thrust of everyday politicking. The much loved Viscount Tonypandy, George Thomas, the man who made the job what it is today, once suggested that 'Mr Speaker has no friends', and Betty half agrees. 'It is not that, as Deputy Speaker, you're above politics,' she maintains. 'But somehow you are sideways removed from it. On getting this job I resigned from Labour's National Executive Committee. I'd been there eight years and it was time for new faces. But I do miss not seeing people as regularly. Sometimes I pop into the cafeteria for a sandwich, a cup of tea and a chat. But since I have to spend long periods in the chair, I'm not around as much in the corridors to hear what's going on.'

Despite the hermetically sealed atmosphere of Westminster, an unhealthy environment designed to foster niggardliness and back-stabbing, Miss Boothroyd remains refreshingly straight and unpretentious. Elected to the House of Commons over fifteen years ago, she has always been a militant moderate, an advocate of 'sensible policies in the Labour Party' even before that nice Mr Gould started trying to make them so fashionable. 'There is only one thing I'm intolerant about,' she adds, smiling benignly as if to the favoured niece, 'and that's intolerance itself. People sometimes forget that *all* points of view must be allowed in this House. Some may well be unpopular. But everyone must have the right to speak and be heard. That's my job. To make sure everybody gets a fair chance.'

Deciding who shall catch Madam Deputy Speaker's eye is no easy business. MPs' constituencies, special interests and previous speaking time must all be scrupulously balanced. On her desk, Betty keeps an orange exercise book in which she has carefully affixed mug-shots of each of our 650 MPs (not a pretty sight!), together with their names in alphabetical order. Trying to learn them all at twenty-four hours' notice proved rather frantic in the beginning. 'Mr Speaker Weatherill always has someone there to help him,' she explains. 'But I have no help in trying to remember who is who. To start with, it was terrible. I sat in the chair and my mind went absolutely blank. Total amnesia. People I'd known for twenty years, I just couldn't remember their names. And then I thought, "Bet, just use your common sense." So I just leaned over to the Whips on either side and whispered, "Psst! Who's What's-his-name over there?"' Certainly, Betty seems to have put our Honourable Members in their proper perspective.

But despite the public's growing impression of the House of Commons as a home for hoorahs and hooligans, Miss Boothroyd has not as yet been obliged to 'name' anyone for bad behaviour. None the less, on several occasions, she has had to ask MPs to 'withdraw' unparliamentary expressions. She does not believe that MPs behave any better or worse because they see a woman in the chair. 'And I wouldn't want them to!' she adds emphatically. 'We're all equal here, you know. I don't want any special deference.'

Of all her many attributes, however, the greatest – so she claims, rather modestly – is God-given health. Like many other MPs, she maintains a punishing schedule. With them, she seems to share the stamina of Daley Thompson combined with the recovery rate of Eddie Merckx. Such qualities, more than any others, appear to be the essential ingredients in the career of any long-haul MP. Often Betty will take an early-morning train for a constituency meeting in West Bromwich, and be back in the chair by 4p.m. I cannot help thinking that the three male incumbents often seem to leave her with more than her fair share of late-night sessions, but that, she insists, is merely a figment of my fevered, feminist imagination.

But what Betty specifically brings to the job is any woman's most precious asset: common sense. Combined with an innate showbiz sense of the grand occasion, this may sometimes prove theatrical. One evening, with a couple of hundred hysterical MPs hammering on prematurely locked Division Lobby doors, Madam Deputy Speaker made an unprecedented announcement. 'Open the doors,' she proclaimed solemnly in stentorian tones. 'The digital clock is wrong.' It was one of the House of Commons better Gilbert and Sullivan moments.

Unlike so many of her more pompous colleagues, however, Madam Deputy Speaker has not allowed her new-found status to go to her head. For Betty still treasures what she perceives as the privilege of being a regular MP. She accepts the House of Commons with all its many failings but, like an over-indulgent aunt, continues to dote on it all the same. 'You see, love,' she explains, 'and I know to you it might seem odd and strange, but even after fifteen years here I still love this place. I still find it exciting. It's my place and I belong here.'

Yet for all her homely warmth and charm, Betty still remains the consummate politician. Although hotly tipped as a possible candidate for first woman Speaker, she resolutely refuses to be drawn on the subject. She is only too well aware that any ostentatious ambition for the office – a prize within the gift of fellow-backbench MPs – will only result in its being denied her. Besides, whatever happens post-Weatherill, this is one MP who is happy merely having her shot at one of the more fulfilling roles in the House, performing a job where she is growing daily more comfortable.

'What are we supposed to call you?' asked Labour's flummoxed Peter Pike, when she first took office back in July 1987.

Throughout a strangely silent House, the voice of Miss Betty Boothroyd reverberated clearly. 'Call me Madam!' came the resounding response. And no one, to my knowledge, has needed to ask the same question since.

Of course, Miss Boothroyd is only one out of 650 MPs. But her example is of universal application to the entire institution. For MPs are at their happiest when they have a well-defined role to fulfil, when they wield something at least akin to the power or influence which a career in politics is supposed to confer. Clearly, a specific job within the House is the best antidote to the hours of tedium spent forcibly immured there. Like attaining the heady status of prefect at school, existence at Westminster may be greatly improved by the prospect of making other people's lives vastly more miserable. Of course the job of presiding over the House or chairing a committee may hold its attractions for the more administratively punctilious or naturally domineering. But such tasks are still not everybody's idea of exercising genuine clout. Real influence, more Machiavellian inmates would feel, is best achieved through the tangled webs of intrigue that politicians habitually weave so well. For whatever his party, there will always be a certain category of MP who is at his best when 'fixing'. Life at Westminster could not function without its daily dose of deals, and for deals to be done, each side needs its squad of Arthur Daleys, of punters guaranteed to turn the odd débâcle into a party earner. Such middlemen are the very lubricants of life's wheels within wheels. And in the Houses of Parliament, they tend to end up as Whips, those indefatigable fixers who, according to Enoch Powell at least, are as necessary to the democratic process as sewers to civilization.

In the House of Commons, the government Whips are a fairly impenetrable brotherhood, a Mafia of faceless men who meet from time to time in Number 12 Downing Street around a long, highly polished table. Here, they drink white wine out of silver cups and, one can only assume, spend glorious sessions deep in conclave, immersed in that most delicious of parliamentary pastimes: gossip. For the Nigel Dempsters of Number 12, this is the basic stuff of their entire existence. Indeed, if for myriad transgressions in this life, I might be reincarnated as something so miserable as an MP in the next, it is right there in the Whips' office that I should like to do my penance. Far more than in the chamber, 'upstairs' or even in the bars, this is where the nub of parliamentary life is located. So much so, in fact, that one of these days Jackie Collins will probably write a book about it: *Westminster Whips* perhaps – the title certainly has a ring to it. And make no mistake about it: under the urbane and genteel SW1 patina, all the necessary blockbuster ingredients are there in plenty, busily seething away, ever ready to surface, yet always carefully controlled. There is not a single liaison, affair, relationship, passion, vested interest, fault, foible, failing or feeling that will slip unnoticed through the net of this curious *curia*. For, in essence, the Whips' business is to trawl. The most relentless investigative journalists have nothing on them. It is their job to know precisely where everybody is: When? For how long? And, preferably, with whom? It is their task to keep an ear to the ground for whispers, and scour the nooks and crannies for scandal. For Whips must become intimate with the parts of Members other MPs cannot reach. They must ascertain every individual's bottom-line and be prepared to hit below it. They must figure out his Achilles' heel and be ready, if the need arises, to shoot straight at it. They must report back to the PM and her ministers whenever the slightest signs of backbench revolt appear to be fomenting. And they must do whatever is necessary in the circumstances to nip such rebellions in the bud. They must sound out the rank and file and establish precisely what the party will and will not wear. In short, the Whips' remit is surpassingly simple. They must do whatever is necessary in order to 'fix it'.

Nowadays, however, a crushing hundred-odd seat majority has taken much of the excitement out of being a government Whip. For with that sort of margin to play with, where is the glowing sense of achievement in delivering the goods? Apart for the handful of Tory backbench revolts, this Parliament has produced few *frissons* of genuine contest. All in all, it has demonstrated the stomach-churning tension of a 100-metre sprint between Carl Lewis and Nigel Lawson. Of course, in order to get the government's business through relatively intact, concessions, threats and promises do still have to be made. Observers in the chamber may notice men nodding and winking at one another across the floor of the House. Suddenly, they will disappear around the back of Mr Speaker's chair like schoolboys behind the bicycle shed for a swift, illicit fag. One cheerfully imagines them, thus hidden from sight, frantically rolling up their trouser legs, baring their breasts and performing unspeakable Masonic rites. The truth of the matter, unfortunately, is somewhat less exotic. For these are merely the Whips indulging in their usual horse-trading practices, agreeing pacts on timetables, agendas, or the scheduling of debates. But for today's government Whips, how humdrum and uneventful third-term Thatcherland must now have become. How much more exhilarating those fraught years of a government hanging on by the skin of its teeth!

The years 1974–9: now that truly was the Golden Age of the Whip. For that was the period when a teetering Labour government was obliged to operate without an overall parliamentary majority, uncomfortable in the knowledge that at any moment it might suddenly be toppled. Those were the days when minority parties came into their own, as the Scots, Welsh and Irish wrung concessions from a government from whom every single vote was crucial. And this was the era when the government Deputy Chief Whip, Wakefield's Walter Harrison, ruled the House of Commons roost with a rod of iron.

'When you get to this place,' one old hand confided, 'you have to learn the ropes. Soon you realize that it was Walter Harrison who made those ropes.'

'I sometimes look at the state of the party today,' complained another of Labour's old-timers mournfully. 'I look at the shenanigans of the Ron Browns and his type. And I can't help thinking, none of this would be happening, we'd be in much better shape, if only we had someone like Walter around.'

Retired from active politics at the last election, Walter Harrison spent the happiest years of his career as Westminster's fixer *summa cum laude*. From 1976 onwards, he and Chief Whip Michael, now Lord, Cocks worked indefatigably in harness, an unassailable combination of velvet glove and iron fist. For if Harrison epitomized the tough, macho and ostentatiously aggressive image, Cocks, on the contrary, was all gentility and charm. 'But of the two of us,' Lord Cocks now happily confesses, 'I was really by far the nastier.' Over a decade later, it is difficult to believe that the suave, elder statesman Cocks was ever capable of putting the knife in. Still an avid cricketer, he exudes an air of good-natured sportsmanship and will cheerfully tell stories at his own expense.

'May I speak to Michael Cocks?' asked his Private Secretary on one occasion, urgently trying to locate the Chief Whip at a Lords and Commons cricket match.

'I'm afraid he's just gone out to bat,' came the response at the end of the phone.

'Oh, good,' replied the Secretary, by then inured to Cocks's legendary prowess at the crease. 'In that case, I can hang on.'

But the methods of clinging to power with a minority government in charge owe little to the principles of the glorious summer game. 'By fair means or foul' must be the basis of any Whip's operation. And Walter Harrison, more than any, had such an operation down to a fine art. Semi-affectionately nicknamed the 'Mushroom Man' for a legendary ability to keep his ranks 'in the dark and smother them with bullshit', Harrison struggled night and day to keep the terminal Labour case alive. He relished the daily battle for survival, projecting himself as a hard man, a blunt, abrasive type always ready to get physical. On a particular occasion, for instance, whilst ascending one of Westminster's countless stone staircases, he encountered a new TV political correspondent, jauntily wending his way down. Suddenly, the Harrison hand reached out, giving the unsuspecting chap a nasty tweak of the balls. The poor man's face turned ashen as, winded, he doubled up in pain. 'Aye,' said Walter, *en passant*, 'and that's for nothing. Just imagine what'll happen to you if ever you cross me!'

Of all the many weapons available to the current Chief Whip, Mr David Waddington, interference with *les bijoux de la famille* would no longer appear to be one of them. For in today's Tory Party, as everyone is well aware, the Whips may leave all the ball-breaking to the most effective member of the tribe. But in the Harrison heyday, politics was much more a matter of life and death . . . and often life and death taken quite literally.

On the floor of Annie's Bar one evening, lay the prostate body of a distinguished Scottish MP. Eyes closed, motionless, not a sound did he utter. Distraught compatriots held a mirror close to his nose, hoping for condensation, breath, any tell-tale sign of life. But alas, in their misery, the despairing Scots saw nothing. By the lost trousers of Donald, they moaned, what hope could there be? Their Honourable Member had shed his 78° proof mortal coil. He had popped his clogs. He had spiked his sporran. He had torn his tartan. He had, in a word, just snuffed it. All of a sudden, the life and soul of the party was dead – dead drunk. Morosely, Annie's regulars began to seek solace. They found comfort in the thought that he had gone to meet his maker, the greatest Glenfiddich distiller of them all, in a devoluted sky. Their spirits rallied for a while, but soon subsided as the clammy fingers of fear began to grip their Gaelic souls. In an atmosphere of some hysteria, Harrison was swiftly summoned. It was one of those nights, as indeed it was every night, when Walter knew the vote would be perilously close. Carefully, he eyed the cadaver: no flicker of intelligence; no sign of cerebral activity; a distinct lack of affect. Yes, it was definitely dead. Fortunately, the deceased was not a member of the Young Conservatives, so it was possible to tell. Well, concluded Walter, now that all hope was quite lost, he might as well apply his last-ditch resuscitation technique: the well-documented Harrison goolie-grasp.

'Ooooch,' gasped the corpse, responding immediately, the colour soon flooding straight back to its cheeks.

'He's alive,' surmised Walter briskly. 'Nod him through for the vote.'

Like Wellington's troops, it was difficult to know what effect the Deputy Chief Whip had on the Opposition but, by God, he certainly frightened his own lot! Every evening, about an hour before the 10p.m. vote, he would muster his foot soldiers for a final head count.

'Where is X?' asked Harrison in one particular tense situation.

Petrified, the assembled ranks remained sheepishly silent.

'Where is X?' he insisted, growing angrier by the minute.

'He's in Crete,' volunteered the form snitch, rightly fearing the worst.

'Aye,' exploded Walter, 'and when the bastard gets back, he'll be in bloody concrete.'

Despite his martinet tactics, however, there was never any trace of malice about Harrison. True, in the Whips' office, a hit-list could be seen hanging ostentatiously on the wall. But as soon as any of the culprits had been given his come-uppance, his name was duly deleted, he was invited for a drink and that was the end of it. Moreover, there were even a few characters – strangely enough, usually from the Conservative Party – who were entirely above reproach in Walter's book. For if, as a government Whip, he never missed a transgression, neither, as an individual, did he ever forget a kindness. Catapulted into a committee meeting on one occasion, Harrison was inadvertently about to vote against his own party line. Ever the gentleman, even to his political opponents, Francis Pym signalled by a shake of the head that he ought to reconsider. From that day forward, Pym was Harrison's best buddy and still, quite possibly, bears the scars of the relationship. For Walter's was the forefinger school of communication and Pym's sternum was supposed to sport a permanent, livid blue bruise, the legacy of many a confidential corridor chat with his overemphatic friend.

Nor was the mix-up in the committee room the Deputy Chief Whip's worst ever mistake. One evening he spotted Ted Heath in the chamber and quite obviously voting. Harrison was incensed at what he thought was the man's treacherous duplicity. He had Heath down as 'paired'. A recognized practice which makes an MP's life more tolerable, 'pairing' is a legitimate way of skiving off for the night. With approval from the Whips' office, and for certain specified evenings alone, a government MP and an Opposition MP may agree to cancel each other out by agreeing not to vote. It is a useful arrangement and, despite all their political differences, 'pairs' often develop into well-established, enduring and amicable partnerships. As Charles Irving, Conservative MP for Cheltenham readily admits: 'In a general election, as soon as you know your own seat is all right, the next thing you do is pray your "pair" is safe too.' (On a more mischievously salacious note, however, Great Grimsby's Labour MP, Austin Mitchell, has observed that many Honourable Members' interest in firm pairs has nothing to do with whipping.) But in today's House of Commons there is no longer any *official* pairing. The tradition still continues unofficially, of course, but for cosmetic reasons the Opposition cannot allow it to flourish openly. For even if every single Opposition MP were to be paired with a Conservative, the average vote would still be a 100–0 walk-over, not the sort of result to reinforce public confidence in British parliamentary control. In Harrison's neck-and-neck era, however, the practice was of necessity widespread. It was just another of those deals without which the ship of state would have foundered. So it came as something of a shock for Walter to see Ted Heath, a former Chief Whip himself, openly flouting the rules. Not a man to beat about the bush, Harrison crossed the floor of the chamber and accosted the ex-Prime Minister with some feeling. The forefinger went in as he launched into a vehement diatribe.

'You're paired,' exploded Walter, 'and you're not voting.'

'I am not paired,' responded Heath quietly. 'I have sent you a letter to that effect and I am voting.'

'There is no letter, you're down as paired and you're not voting.'

Oh no, he isn't. Oh yes, he is. Heath voted. Harrison went berserk. Heath would be outlawed, black-balled, put on a permanent hit-list. The press had a field day. And Ted remained aloof.

The very next day, whilst this headline news was doing the rounds, the inevitable happened. Tidying up in the Whips' office, what should they find but Ted's letter, somehow mislaid? Harrison was mortified. Having publicly flagellated Heath as man of no honour, and after all the furore his challenge had generated, what could he do but proffer the most abject apology? 'It's perfectly all right,' replied Heath graciously. 'It wasn't your fault, Walter, just a mistake made by the people who work for you.' No high horse, no recriminations: that was the end of the matter. Such magnanimity is a side of the much maligned Ted about which we hear very little. But it is hardly surprising that, to this day, Edward Heath has no more fervent admirer than Walter Harrison.

Not only may a government Whip exercise the influence of intrigue, but more important still, the power of patronage, a doubly potent force. The charming titles still conferred on many of the Whips are the legacy of a bygone age, of an era when messages had to be sent to the King's men in order to get them along to Parliament to support the monarch. Nevertheless, even today, such titles are not entirely redundant. As Deputy Chief Whip, and thus Treasurer to Her Majesty's Household, it was part of Harrison's job to help organize the Queen's garden parties. Snigger if you will. But we live in a society where people will still happily donate thousands of pounds to charity for the exquisite pleasure of being snubbed by His Royal Highness, the Duke of Edinburgh. So imagine the inestimable kudos involved in deciding who shall and who shall not go to the ball. Never, since Harrison's tenure of office, has Her Majesty had the pleasure of the company of so many of Wakefield's Labour councillors. But great and small alike were to bask in the privilege. The Parliament Square newsagent would also die a happy man, as police outriders escorted his old banger to Buckingham Palace, courtesy of Walter. It was also Harrison's duty to mingle with the crowds and select an interesting cross-section of the guests to introduce to the Queen. Her Majesty, he felt at one party, had had more than her fair share of City moneymen. It was high time she met a quota of the blue-collar boys.

'Good afternoon,' he said, accosting one cube of a man. Small, squat and stocky, the fellow was clearly every inch a comrade. 'Are you a member of a trade union?'

'Yes, I am,' replied the cube in a deep, guttural voice. 'I am the Third Secretary of Trade to the Soviet Union.'

But Walter's halcyon days of fixing and dealing could not go on indefinitely. It was only a matter of time before Callaghan's shoestring government was bound to snap. Indeed, it was no mean measure of the Cocks–Harrison success story that such a government had managed to stagger on for so long. Towards the end, however, the whole enterprise was beginning to look almost a trifle obscene. The sight of half a dozen ambulances ferrying dying or seriously ill MPs to the House was then not uncommon at Westminster. Since these MPs' physical presence on the premises was deemed to constitute their vote, they were often obliged to hang around well into the night. The Whips, conversant with every trick in the book, would even check up and ensure that the ailing MP was actually there on his stretcher, in a ghoulish, macabre practice referred to as 'the meat inspection'. Worse still, in the government Whips' office – not the most auspicious environment for sentiment, at the best of times – any news of an MP's death would invariably be met with the same two callous questions: 'Has he voted?' and 'What's his majority?' It was only, by that stage, a mere matter of time . . .

Finally, one evening in 1979, Walter Harrison saw the futility of his sisyphean task. For what was the point, night after night, of shoring up a government at the expense of basic human dignity? Over the phone, and despite rasping protestations, the government Deputy Chief Whip insisted that one dying Labour MP should stay at home comfortably in bed. That very night, in a motion of no-confidence, the Labour government fell by one single vote. It was the end of an era in more ways than one. But even today, with the benefits of ten years of Conservative-dominated hindsight, Harrison still knows that he made the right decision. 'The man died two weeks afterwards,' he recalls, 'and the government was bound to go, sooner or later. But, in the end, it occurred to me that nothing could be more important than a man's right to die in peace.'

There are few enough real characters in today's House of Commons, and it is without doubt a duller place since Walter Harrison's resignation in 1987. But at least, unlike so many of his parliamentary colleagues, Wakefield's erstwhile MP may look back with a feeling of relevance at his period of personal power, at his stint of wheeling and dealing, of fixing and broking in the corridors of Westminster. He may recall with some nostalgia that almost forgotten age, the days when the Labour Party looked like – and, indeed, actually was – an electable alternative. And he may derive some comfort from the knowledge that, while those years lasted, he, more than most, had his crack of the whip.

Of course, as in the case of Enoch Powell's sewers, Whips are operating most effectively when nobody is even aware of their existence. Sometimes, however, they may over-egg it, as did the delightful Lord Denham, government Chief Whip in the House of Lords, over their Lordships' anticipated poll tax rebellion. No mean detective novelist in his spare time, the unflagging sleuth, Denham, managed to track down quite a host of hitherto unearthed backwoods Tory peers. Obediently, they scrambled out of the stuccowork of their crumbling ancestral piles and turned up in their droves and Land Rovers to ensure an overwhelming government majority. As these unknown scions flocked through the division lobbies, a great flurry of excitement suddenly broke out. Surely, it could not possibly be true? But was that really the long-lost Lord Lucan voting with the 'Not Contents'?

The incident, unfortunately, did little to enhance their Lordships' popular claim of constituting a bulwark against the excesses of elected government. It discredited the Upper House in the eyes of the nation, and only further strengthened left-wing resolve either to abolish or radically reform this last bastion of undemocratic privilege, if ever the opportunity should arise. I, for one, was deeply disappointed. Naïvely, perhaps, I had not expected the Lords, of all folk, to be such servile forelock-tuggers, although their vehement – if ultimately unsuccessful – opposition to eye and dental health charges did achieve some minor form of rehabilitation. But it did seem odd that, for the issue of the community charge at least, strong-arm tactics fared better in the House of Lords than in the usually less independent Commons. For there, even the Whips' strategy of depicting a power-crazed, bogey-man, Michael Heseltine, as the prime mover behind the Mates amendment (a median solution designed to link the poll tax to a three-banded 'ability to pay' structure), did nothing to stop disgruntled government back-benchers from allying themselves to the cause. In the end, such scaremongering techniques did little but reinforce some of the younger Conservative MPs in their resolve to revolt – clearly not whipping of the Harrison school.

But if Whips are at their happiest and most influential in a state of anonymity, the same does not hold true for MPs generally. For what is the point of politicians in our putative democracy if not to convince the electorate of the legitimacy of their views? If the electorate is to hear and assess those views, then MPs must gain publicity and its inevitable concomitant, visibility. With the exception of the Prime Minister herself, the government had no better exponent of the art of PR than . . . well, is it really that difficult to hazard a guess?

In September 1988, an extraordinary poll conducted by MORI for *The Economist* revealed that, after Mrs Thatcher, the most instantly recognizable Conservative politician was not a cabinet minister, nor even a Minister of State, but none other than the then Junior Health Minister, Mrs Edwina Currie. Of the poll's respondents, 78 per cent recognized her photograph, whilst only 46 per cent could identify the Foreign Secretary, Sir Geoffrey Howe. Mr John Major, the low-profile Chief Secretary to the Treasury, fared particularly badly. He was spotted by only 2 per cent of the people polled, which just goes to show that a daunting intellect plus membership of the cabinet is certainly no guarantee of fame. Now, whilst nobody is seriously suggesting that there is any correlation between visibility and genuine power, Mrs Currie maintains that the yardstick for success as an MP, let alone as a minister, is that people know who you are. When she first ran for Parliament in the marginal constituency of Derbyshire South in 1983, she made sure that she was in all the local papers, 'usually a front-page story', most days of the electoral campaign. Her philosophy paid off handsomely, as she was returned to Westminster with a healthy Conservative majority of over 8,000.

Since then, of course, Mrs Currie's views and profile have been promulgated relentlessly. Within two years she was appointed PPS to Sir Keith Joseph during his stint as Education Secretary, and by 1986 had landed a ministerial position at the Department of Health and Social Security. Happiness, for the limited horizons of most aspiring MPs, is a job, any job, in government. But few ministers grasped how to exploit the situation more intuitively than Edwina. It was St Patrick's Day 1988 when I first went to interview her in the new DHSS, an impressively beautiful building, situated in Whitehall opposite the Cenotaph and the entrance to Downing Street. Punctiliously restored and renovated, it is just too bad that here, of all ministries, no one thought to include facilities for the handicapped. An old university friend chanced by as I sat waiting in the anteroom. A perfect product of the combined public-school and Oxbridge systems, he has always demonstrated that unshakeable conviction of 'knowing best' on an astounding variety of topics. Clearly, he has now found his natural *métier* as a career civil servant. Had he failed the exams, of course, he'd have had to make do and become an MP. 'What we want to achieve,' he proclaimed, scanning my newspaper and launching into an unsolicited explanation of some article on the Education Reform Bill, 'what we want to achieve with this legislation is perfectly simple. We simply want to engineer a new, rather nice sort of worker instead of our present, horribly odious ones.'

*We? Engineer? Nice workers? Horribly odious ones?* What sort of astonishingly obnoxious Whitehall philosophy could underpin this sort of jargon? I peered at him through the diffuse light of my incipient cataracts. Had he at last succumbed to a long-overdue sense of humour? No, he was absolutely serious. But protected from reality by the impenetrable labyrinths of Whitehall, would he ever really understand why we, the odious *hoi polloi*, just refuse to accept what other people insist is good for us? What is more, it occurred to me suddenly and with more immediate relevance, would the Junior Health Minister?

From her appointment in 1986 to her controversial departure in December 1988, no one could have failed to know Mrs Currie's views on issues as varied as exploding tomato ketchup bottles, exercise, cigarettes, alcohol, junk food, cervical cancer, woolly hats in cases of acute hypothermia and, her ultimate downfall, the dangers of salmonella poisoning from the nation's lightly boiled breakfast egg. For Edwina was the modern-day, popular newspapermen's Heaven-sent dream. Who wanted to rehearse dreary and arcane arguments for or against the European Monetary System, for instance, when copy could be filled so easily with animadversions on slobs, chip butties, excess booze, councillors collapsing after municipal booze-ups and fags? The minister's desk, during her tenure of office, was for ever laden with a promiscuous heap of newspapers, for she kept a weather-eye on the entire spectrum of the publicity market. Elsewhere, as might have been expected, sat a box of artificial sweeteners and a fruit bowl containing three green apples. On her office wall, neatly framed, hung a front-page tabloid newspaper story. 'Edwina's Guilty Secret' ran the banner headline. What on earth could it have meant? Not the stockings graciously accepted from a constituency hosiery factory? No, those had been duly noted in the Members' 'Register of Interests'. Not a major shareholding, surely, in British American Tobacco, Kentucky Fried Chicken or United Distillers? An unrequited passion, perhaps, for any one of Messrs Dennis Skinner, Ron Brown, Dave Nellist or Arthur Scargill? No, sadly, it was nothing so delicious. The truth of Edwina's guilty secret was . . . a family foray to a hamburger joint when everything else was shut!

Now, if some newspaper editors think that constitutes headline news, I'm afraid I do not. Neither, I'd like to think, in her heart of hearts, does Mrs Currie. But, able and intelligent woman that she is, she swiftly sussed the populist system and learned how to turn it to her own best advantage. 'And, of course,' she added disarmingly, 'being a woman in Parliament does help. There are so few of us and we are therefore that much more visible. It also means that when a woman says something, people notice her more. And, if she's a bit flamboyant, all the more so.'

Health Secretary Kenneth Clarke, Edwina's hierarchical boss at the DHSS, appeared to bear this theory out. Referring to himself on one occasion as 'the nominal head of Edwina Currie's department', he maintained that if either he or his Minister of State, David

Mellor, were to make the same speeches as their junior minister, the media would never pay them the same degree of attention. Nevertheless, despite all protestations to the contrary, the Currie phenomenon has always been person- rather than sex-specific. For in the same 'Name the Politicians' MORI poll, another lady MP, Angela Rumbold, Minister of State for Education, scored only 3 per cent on the recognition scale. Farther up the greasy, governmental pole than Mrs Currie ever was, either she has not sought or she has not managed to grab the headlines in quite the same way as her irrepressible colleague. Certainly, the two are very different types of Tory lady MP and there does not seem to be much love lost between them. One Currie grievance committed to the Members' Dining-room complaints book met with La Rumbold's very short shrift. She was fed up, wrote the former Health Minister, of being subjected to menus written in French, to descriptions of dishes and preparations which she, for one, could never understand. The grouse received a gloss, apparently in the Education Minister's own fair hand, implying rather deprecating conclusions about the level of certain MPs' general education. But unlike her unstoppable colleague, Mrs Rumbold is not to be found engaged in the business of controversy. Like most ministers, she is happier with her head beneath the parapet, anonymous to the masses if ever the solids should hit the fan. Besides, even if she were to develop into another incurable headline-grabber, her portfolio still fails to lend itself to the populist game in quite the same way. The thankless task of encouraging our illiterate and innumerate school-leavers to spend more time on their advanced calculus and Dickens could never acquire the same inflammatory potential as the great egg disaster.

'Edwina Currie,' claimed one distinguished Conservative back-bencher in early 1988, 'is the only phenomenon I can think of who could possibly lose us the next election. She is the Conservative Party's answer to Ken Livingstone. In fact, in terms of the publicity stunts the pair of them manage to pull off for their own personal benefit, the two have an awful lot in common.' Mrs Currie, however, is adept at defending herself against such allegations of self-promotion. It is all in a good cause, she claims. It is designed to make people aware. She genuinely does not care how much annoyance and upset she creates, so long as it encourages people to think about their health and to take proper care of themselves. 'Besides,' she adds, 'as Teddy Roosevelt used to say: "To be a successful politician you must say what the people are thinking, only you must say it louder and more often." '

There can be no possible doubt that Edwina has always taken the gold in saying things louder and more often than the majority of MPs. Most of the time she was even saying things that moderately informed people already knew to be true. For, nowadays, there are few of us still blissfully unaware of the attendant dangers of smoking, eating, drinking, having sex, breathing the lead-laden air, drinking the chemically polluted water, going for a walk through the now-thought-to-be-carcinogenic bracken in a shower of probably acid rain, and generally just getting out of bed in the morning. In Mrs Currie's book, many of the country's ills could be put down quite simply to 'the diseases of affluence'. She also believed, more realistically, that as a minister she had no actual power to do much about it. What she did wield, she would claim, was influence – the influence to ensure that 'If people don't do as you want, then you have the means of kicking up a fuss.' It was interesting to see this redoubtable politician's theories actually at work in practice.

My first opportunity came some weeks later, at the beginning of May. I had been asked by Judith Chalmers to speak at a charity luncheon in aid of the Women's National Cancer Control Campaign. The WNCCC had raised enough money to fund another of their much needed screening units, and Mrs Currie, whose remit included specific responsibility for women's health, was also invited along to address the 1,000-strong crowd. I suppose, in retrospect, we made a fairly balanced ticket: Edwina, the ideal woman to give everybody a lesson on how to behave; and me, the ideal woman to provide an object lesson in precisely how not to. Over a few pre-prandial, confidence-building measures, I soon discovered that all at the London Hilton venue was far from roses. We had hardly made a decent dent in the cheese straws before one leading fund-raiser told me how infuriated she still was. An all-male House of Commons committee had earlier refused to allow a WNCCC cancer-screening unit on to its Westminster premises, the suggested exercise designed to offer a free check-up to any woman interested. 'Of course,' she added with righteous anger, 'when we start talking about cervical cancer and breast cancer, everybody gets so terribly uptight and embarrassed. Brush it under the carpet! Women's problems! It's no wonder that women all over the country are still too "ashamed" to come forward. And then, by the time anything is detected, they have often left it far too late for really positive action to be taken. That's why the publicity a screening unit at the House of Commons might have generated would have helped our cause immeasurably. But for all Parliament's humbug about women's health and how concerned they are, the relevant authorities just turned our offer down.'

The House of Lords, in their infinite sagacity, had decided on the contrary to accept the offer. They should, by now, have embarrassed the more recalcitrant Commons into tolerating, if not welcoming, the gesture. Despite this particular undercurrent, however, and thanks to the almost boundless generosity of its patrons, the WNCCC luncheon went off very well. In fairness to the Junior Health Minister, one can only assume that, with her natural penchant for publicity, she personally had never been party to this scandalous, yet all too typical, male indifference.

She read out the usual prepared ministerial speech, a basic rehearsal of the Thatcherite belief in the responsibility vested in individuals, organizations and charities to stop the gaps, to darn the inevitable and increasing holes left by government. At the end of her speech, however, Mrs Currie did something quite extraordinary. It was difficult to know whether to be extremely impressed by her undoubted guts, or to squirm with embarrassment at her amazing *chutzpah*. She picked up an ashtray from the top table, and waved it meaningfully in the air. 'And next time,' she said, in her best schoolma'amish voice, 'I don't want to see any of these things around.' Seated just two places away from the minister, and on my immediate left, was Judith Chalmers's husband, Neil Durden-Smith. An impeccable gentleman, a superb cricketer and rugby player, he is the sort of chap who would never knowingly upset anyone. As if by some Pavlovian reflex, however, as soon as the ashtray warning had been delivered, he took out a cigarette and immediately lit up.

The incident, agreed, is insignificant in itself, but far more important in its general ramifications. For along with Neil Durden-

Smith, the rest of the country generally takes exception at being told how to behave. The adult population does not mind the idea of being objectively, calmly and scientifically informed. But what it tends to dislike is being hectored, lectured or downright patronized. Influence, unfortunately, is always a double-edged sword. Whilst it is perfectly possible, with sensitivity, understanding and persuasion, to bring the chip-butty brigade around to a healthier lifestyle, it is equally possible to influence them *negatively*, to make them *abreact*. Although much of Mrs Currie's message was incontrovertibly correct, her sharply didactic style merely alienated many of the victims she purported to save, by reinforcing them in their bad habits.

Besides, the premises of her arguments were often dangerously simplistic. Take, for instance, her references to obesity and all its related illnesses (coronary heart disease, high blood pressure, atherosclerosis, depression, lethargy, etc.). These may well have been, as Mrs Currie used to claim, 'the diseases of affluence'. If the Duchess of York, to cite one conspicuous example, decides periodically to eat herself into designer-dressed, aircraft-carrier shape, then few would disagree that that is a disease of affluence. But obesity, in addition to being the disease of plenty, is just as likely to be the disease of misery, poverty, unemployment and despair. Of course, the erstwhile minister's much castigated Northerners know they should be eating more fresh salads tossed in light vinaigrette, more fresh fish, more fresh fruit and a lot less fatty food. But as every *Reader's Digest* psychologist is well aware – indeed, as everyone who has ever been on a diet knows to their calorific cost – stodgy carbohydrate food is *cheap* food, it is comfort food, it is the food people go for whenever they feel unhappy. When individuals are under stress, when they are laid off from work, when they are told that they will have to wait a couple of years for their hip-replacement operation and in the meantime can make do in chronic discomfort, they do not tend to race off and make themselves a nice little beansprout salad by way of emotional compensation. Obesity in SW1 may indeed be the disease of affluence. But Mrs Currie should be wary of trying out her theories in places such as Salford.

At this stage, I suppose, it is only fair to declare an interest. If health policy attracts my attention more than any other domestic policy, it is because my entire family is, and always has been, 'medical'. My father died a young man, obsessively committed to the concept of the National Health Service and free medicine for all. To the day he died, after four coronaries and all the classic complaints of sheer overwork, he was proud of the fact that he had never once in his life seen a private patient. Instead, every one of his NHS patients was treated with all the highly personalized attention of today's private patients. In mid-Cheshire, even today, there are still three generations of his charges who will gladly bear me out. I often wish that Mrs Currie had been around with an apposite pearl of wisdom to advise him on his health. In such cases of acute stress, increasingly prevalent in the beleaguered medical profession, she might well have prescribed the therapeutic qualities of a nice hot cup of tea! Undeterred by such Thatcherite concepts as sweat-to-bread ratios, however, my three brothers – one gastroenterologist and two eye surgeons – have all followed my father into medicine. They, in their turn, have developed into equally fervent believers in the NHS, a system which, over recent years, has been allowed to deteriorate to the point of collapse. Even with the well-publicized but belated injections of cash, morale among staff has sunk disturbingly low. Nevertheless, an extraordinary intervention made by doyens of the medical establishment still took the government by surprise.

Royal Colleges are perceived as many things but not, traditionally, as hot-houses of radical left-wingers: of reds, so to speak, under the pay-beds. And so it came as something of a Hurricane Gilbert through these bastions of conservatism when the presidents of the Royal Colleges of Physicians, Surgeons and Gynaecologists banded together, and on 7 December 1987, issued the following joint statement to the government:

Each day we learn of new problems in the NHS – beds are shut, operating rooms are not available, emergency wards are closed, essential services are shut down in order to make financial savings. In spite of the efforts of doctors, nurses, and other hospital staff patient care is deteriorating. Acute hospital services have almost reached breaking point. Morale is depressingly low.

It is not only patient care that is suffering. Financial stringencies have hit academic aspects of medicine in particular, because of the additional burden of reduced University Grants Committee funding. Yet the future of medicine depends on the quality of our clinical teachers and research workers.

Face-saving initiatives such as the allocation of £30m. for waiting lists are not the answer. An immediate overall review of acute hospital services is mandatory. Additional and alternative funding must be found. We call on the government to do something now to save our health service, once the envy of the world.

The appeal was signed by the three Royal College presidents, Sir Raymond Hoffenberg, Sir Ian Todd, and Sir George Pinker, none of them gentlemen given to sudden bouts either of hysteria or hyperbole. Mrs Thatcher was not at all pleased by this unprecedented initiative. But home truths are often unwelcome and, if nothing else, they helped put the string of facile Currie gimmicks into their proper perspective. Woolly hats for cold pensioners, the suggestion that they consider mortgaging their houses to pay for earlier private operations, none of these ideas goes any way towards addressing the real issue: the fact that the NHS is still underfunded. Neither is the suggestion of 'opting out' of the NHS and moving into the burgeoning multiplicity of private health care plans as reasonable a government policy as is sometimes depicted.

The prime advantages of private health care, convenience and choice of doctor, have all been well rehearsed. And to be fair, the private solution is often just the ticket for swift *una tantum* operations. But which private health care plan is willing to concern itself with cases of chronic or mental illness? Which with terminally sick people? Which with AIDS patients? Which with the handicapped or geriatrics? Besides, there is no proof that increased privatization will actually improve the country's general health care. Certainly, it often increases a tendency to indulge in unnecessary and expensive procedures. And, secondly, a patient's free choice of doctor or consultant is only beneficial if it is *informed* choice, a decision based on something less spurious than a trendy Harley Street address.

The NHS must not be dismissed as merely another sacred Socialist cow. It is a system which, properly run and funded, could ensure the entire nation's health more efficiently and cost-effectively than any of the hybrid solutions currently on offer. If now, as is indubitably true, the NHS is suffering from the New Tory 'freedom of choice' syndrome (i.e. freedom of choice, but only for those who can afford to pay for it), a condition aggravated by bad attacks of advanced monetarist mania, then it is also true that it has suffered in the past at the hands of doctrinaire Socialism. Medicine, traditionally, does not tend to thrive when extreme political views hold sway. By now a healthy, adequately funded NHS should have become a *droit acquis* in this country, no longer a highly politicized football. Free, *readily available* health care should be considered as fundamental a part of the fabric of our society as free speech. It cannot be allowed to degenerate insidiously into a third-rate service just 'good enough' for the country's poor and underprivileged.

Despite an increasingly selfish society's 'I'm all right, Jack' attitude, I remain persuaded that the British are still, when shaken, a caring and compassionate people. Over the months, Labour's health spokesman, Robin Cook, has shown an unerring ability to tap that very rich sense of decency and fair play, to his party's incalculable advantage. If, for his part, Health Secretary Kenneth Clarke does not start convincing the electorate that the NHS is not only 'safe in our hands', but, indeed, 'safe *only* with us' (*dixit* Thatcher), then this issue could well remain one of the Conservative Party's biggest electoral liabilities. Clarke's task of heading up the government's much heralded health review will not be an easy one. Any National Health Service will always face the tensions of finite resources versus infinite demand in a consumerist society whose expectations are being raised continually. Constant advances in both techniques and research mean that more can be done for people now than ever before – at a price. I believe it is a price that many tax payers, including many Conservative tax payers, are prepared to pay. Failing that, the government may care to start considering alternative funding proposals such as this one, suggested by Professor David Anderson of Hope Hospital, University of Manchester Medical School: 'Since we are being attacked by AIDS rather than by the Russians, nuclear warheads, etc.,' argues Professor Anderson, 'and since we are spending £80m. per annum on AIDS care and research, then that money should come out of the defence budget, not the Health Service budget.' Simplistic?

Perhaps, though I happen to think its logic is particularly inspired. Besides, whatever its merits and demerits, it is still not half as simplistic as the suggestion we were used to hearing from that certain spokesperson at the DHSS.

It was only a matter of time, of course, before the Junior Health Minister would be hoisted by her own publicity petard. For one single moment, she forgot the most fundamental lesson of Conservative ministerial office and it cost her her job. Patronize pensioners and insult Northerners, by all means. No one gives two hoots. But upset the agricultural lobby and more than chicken feathers fly. Edwina's original assertion that 'most' of the country's egg production was infected by salmonella may well have been an overstatement. But what bitter irony! The country which ignored her advice on atherosclerosis and continued to eat its chips; disregarded her warnings on cirrhosis and continued to drink its booze; brushed aside her admonitions on cancer and continued to smoke its fags – this same country suddenly woke up to pay attention to her general alert on eggs. Edwina's much sought influence was finally brought to bear, with disastrous results. Overnight, egg sales dropped dramatically. Immediately, £500,000 of government money (i.e. as Mrs Thatcher tells us, 'our' money) was earmarked for an egg advertising campaign so wishy-washy, it merely reinforced consumers in all their worst fears. Public funds, never normally available under this government for folk who fall foul of the incontrovertible laws of supply and demand, were used to buy in unwanted produce, undiluted interventionism at its most blatant. Writs were issued against Mrs Currie for alleged malicious misinformation. Egg producers all over the country went bankrupt within weeks. Overall losses in the region of £200m. were being mooted. As 'the most expensive mouth' in the history of British politics, Mrs Currie clearly had to go. Both the farmers and the backbench shire Tories demanded their sacrificial victim, and she was duly given up to them. And yet, claimed independent clinical microbiologists, the scale of the problem was much closer to the Junior Health Minister's version than to the anodyne whitewash put about by the Ministry of Agriculture. This, surely, was the bitterest irony of all. The day Edwina got it right was the day she had to go.

Even before the great egg débâcle, Dr Owen, the man who arguably knows more about the NHS than anyone else in today's House of Commons, had dismissed Mrs Currie's behaviour as merely absurd. Her job was so insignificant, he maintained roundly during one episode of Sir Robin Day's *Question Time*, that she had to find compensation by playing the media game. Ironically, the good doctor's diagnosis of Edwina's complaint did not seem to carry even the vaguest trace of self-recognition. Nevertheless, despite Mrs Currie's many detractors, I still must admit to a soft spot for her. (The brothers have specifically requested to be dissociated from that remark.) For even if I did not always agree with the message or its style of delivery, I always enjoyed the messenger in person. Female politicians tend to share one shortcoming – a lack of a sense of humour, at least for public consumption. No doubt, this failing is precipitated by the earnest and understandable female desire to be 'taken seriously' in a predominantly male environment. But relaxed and in private, Mrs Currie still exhibits the Liverpudlian legacy of a fine Scouse sense of the ridiculous. She will happily recount tales from the Derbyshire 'tap-rooms' of her constituency, Lord George Brown's erstwhile neck of the woods. 'You remind me of George Brown when he was young,' one old-timer once told her. 'So I'm warning you. Don't *you* be getting yourself into trouble down there in London, what with all them bright lights, booze and flesh pots.'

Happily, Mrs Currie, with her box of artificial sweeteners, her three green apples and her ninety-hour working week, has yet to show much sign of thus going to the dogs. There is no doubt that she is a bright, capable woman, qualities which, combined with indefatigable stamina, have taken another lady right to the top. Edwina is not to be written off too easily. I am sure she will be back. Next time, perhaps, a less obsessive desire to convince, a trait which she recognizes herself, coupled with more compassion and sensitivity may help her hang on to her post. Whatever her failings, however, at least Mrs Currie was one minister who stimulated public debate, one of the few with the nerve to air unpopular views and the guts to cop the flak for them. Populist or mere publicity seeker, Mrs Currie was healthier for open government than the current anonymous slew of clones. It must have cost Mrs Thatcher dear to let her ideological soul-mate go. In the end, however, the envy of the backbench boys ensured 'that damn woman's' fall from grace.

The fact of being a woman in politics must often make life doubly difficult. To succeed, women must learn to outdo their male counterparts in every aspect, including the thickness of their skin. For if it is true, on the one hand, that membership of a minority increases visibility, then it is equally true that it often engenders antagonism and prejudice. In the embryonic stages of political life, women often find that selection committees are hopelessly biased against them, scrutinizing them on topics such as childcare and stamina, on domestic questions to which men are rarely subjected. On the other hand, according to Betty Boothroyd, unmarried women are equally victimized. 'What would you know about raising a family on a budget and making ends meet?' they are regularly asked. 'You're not even married!' Women are stymied either way.

Yet once the selection hurdle is overcome, research shows that the electorate votes not on a gender, but on a party basis. More damning still, incidentally, in terms of any individual MP's personal significance, is the conclusion that personality and assiduity in the constituency still only account for a maximum of 1,500 votes. As most early Labour renegades to the SDP discovered to their cost, people vote overwhelmingly for the colour of the rosette and not for the individual behind it. All of which goes to prove that a female candidate *per se* can in no way be considered a vote-loser. And yet, even in a country where *over* 50 per cent of the electorate are women, the overwhelming majority of candidates and MPs are still male, white, married, middle-aged and middle class. The House of Commons is thus representative only of a very narrow swathe of the British people – a club for the boys, and the Caucasian boys at that.

With forty-one female MPs out of 650 (i.e. 6 per cent of the Commons), Britain almost takes the wooden spoon in Europe's emancipation league. Only France comes out worse. In Scandinavian countries, for instance, 30 per cent of the parliamentary representatives are women; in Denmark, 29 per cent; in the Netherlands, 19 per cent; in the European Parliament, 17 per cent; in West Germany, 15 per cent; and even in Italy, 12 per cent –

twice our disgraceful figure. True, a pressure organization, the '300 Group', has now been established – its mission, to encourage more women into Parliament and into public office generally. But progress on this front is slow, directly proportional to the force of resistance. Anyone who believes that attitudes to blacks and women are really improving at Westminster, should first ask Tottenham's black MP, Bernie Grant, and then me about some of the consummately obnoxious *gauleiters* who police the various galleries in the House of Commons chamber. Ridiculous minions, got up in the glad-rags of a bygone age, like all ignorant people they wear their prejudices like a chain of office. Why does it sometimes seem that half my life has been spent fighting with people such as these for access to places where I am perfectly entitled and accredited to go? Cerberus-like gatemen at cricket grounds, morons guarding press enclaves, I have had more than my fill of all of them by now.

Enough! Such people, being simple, are only the rawest manifestations of much broader, often less obvious, yet generally far more insidious discrimination. Britain, despite the virtual red herring of its woman Prime Minister, still has a long way to go in changing its social attitudes towards the female sex. Take, for example, the most ubiquitous and yet most difficult discrimination of all to nail, the inherent sexism of our very language. It is a problem with which all women, but particularly high-profile women are obliged to contend. It is interesting to study how perfectly neuter words acquire positive or negative overtones depending on whether they are attributed to a woman or a man. Take the adjective 'aggressive', for instance. For a man to be aggressive is a very positive characteristic. Such a quality will help him head up Kleinwort-Moneybags; open the bowling for England; sell British television sets to the Japanese; win a war and drag a nation out of the doldrums and forward into unprecedented economic prosperity. But an aggressive *woman*? That somehow runs counter to everything society expects from the so-called weaker sex. Aggression is somehow not quite 'nice' in a lady. Neither are an ability to kick a man when he's down, a ghoulish pleasure in turning the knife, a perverse delight in the downfall of a friend – all the characteristics which make a successful politician and a fairly disgusting human being – perceived as remotely desirable in a woman. Insistence on such token verbal gestures as 'chairperson' or 'chair' instead of 'chairman' will change nothing whilst attributes such as 'resolution' in a man are decried as 'obstinacy' in a woman; 'conviction' in a man is depicted as 'narrow-mindedness' in a woman; 'paternalism' in a man, dismissed as 'condescension' in a woman; 'self-confidence' in a man denigrated as 'smugness' in a woman; 'natural authority' in a man, reviled as 'bossiness' in a woman; and 'articulate' in a man, reduced to 'can't keep her bloody mouth shut' in a woman.

All women who have the temerity to let their aspirations rise to anything above the level of the kitchen sink are liable to suffer from the insidious language trick, the greatest and most inimical obstacle to female emancipation, with the possible exception of the Polish Pope. But women politicians, particularly the outstanding ones, are more likely to come in for the treatment than most. There is a tendency to disparage them, to dismiss them as faintly comical creatures. I for one am getting extremely tired of the constant pooh-poohing references to Mrs Thatcher 'hitting things with her handbag'. Funny at first, they are now beginning to pall. Why? For the simple reason that far too often they are perpetrated by folk who are as covertly anti the fact of the Prime Minister's sex as they are ostensibly anti her policies. But, of course, anti-Thatcherism is just that much more trendy, right-on and generally acceptable than the ugly face of downright sexism. I am prepared to concede that many of Mesdames Thatcher and Currie's most vehement critics genuinely do believe that they are both obstinate, condescending and bossy characters. Fair enough. But let us not *unwittingly* fall into the language trap. It is always worth considering that, whatever mental images we hold of either the Prime Minister or her former Health Minister, they have all been shaped by a language which has never been over-generous to successful and assertive women, and especially not to those operating in the traditionally male-dominated arena of British politics.

Of course, it may well be that the sex which specializes in common sense has seen something its male counterparts often refuse to accept: the fact that, for the vast majority of MPs, the Westminster game is simply not worth the candle. More realistic MPs have long since forsaken any high-blown political aspirations to 'statesmanship' (a 'statesman', as Ken Livingstone once pointed out, being 'merely a politician who has died'). Instead, more useful MPs have concentrated their efforts on the social welfare aspect of the job, a particularly important task in the poorer and, therefore, usually Labour-held regions of the country. For no longer do MPs tend to represent the interests of a particular class, especially now class distinctions have become increasingly blurred. More often they will represent the concerns of a locality, or more specifically, of their own constituency.

Perhaps Middlesbrough's Labour MP, Stuart Bell, is the most outstanding example of this development in recent times. In his efforts to ensure that justice should prevail in the Cleveland child-abuse case, he was even prepared to resign his job as Northern Ireland spokesman and to incur the displeasure of many of his parliamentary Labour colleagues. Using parliamentary privilege to 'name' the over-zealous child-abuse 'experts' involved, Stuart was the first to blow the lid off the Cleveland scandal, that appalling witch-hunt which wrecked and continues to wreck hundreds of innocent lives. But such indefatigable efforts on behalf of his wronged constituents did not go down too well with everyone. Left-wingers, for instance, would hear no wrong of the social workers implicated. For social workers, those Calpurnias of the left, are always and always will be completely above reproach. The rabid feminist and loonier lesbian factions then moved in, soused in the belief that all men are repressed molestors in any event. Officially if not privately, the medical and social services professions also closed ranks against Bell, refusing to contemplate any possibility of malpractice by their colleagues. But despite such hostility, and thanks both to a concerted media campaign and a groundswell of popular outrage, the matter became the subject of a full judicial enquiry. And, as a direct consequence, the Queen's Speech of autumn 1988 outlined new legislation to prevent the recurrence of such blatant iniquity in the future. True, the crusade has cost Bell dear in terms of party promotional prospects. It is a small price to pay. For this, at least, is one individual who did what all new MPs *think* they can do and only a handful ever manage. This is an MP who actually succeeded in changing the legislative system for the better.

There can be no doubt, at least not listening to them, that many MPs do devote a lot of time to constituency duties. Indeed, whether he wants to or not, many a moderate Labour MP is obliged to work hard on his reputation as a 'good constituency MP'. He knows that when the 'hard left' attempt their probable putsch, this may be the only trump card available to play. But if they are honest, MPs from all parties must recognize that their role is now little more than that of glorified welfare officers, less capable even than local county or district councillors in solving the majority of problems raised. Indeed, a Citizens' Advice Bureau could do the same job far better, and not for merely one, but for five days of the week. 'I have to be honest with you,' confided one, extremely hard-working Labour MP. 'It's true, I *am* rushed off my feet in the constituency. But the fact of the matter is, a competent secretary with an address book of names and contact numbers could do the job just as well as any Member of Parliament!'

But if people, rather sentimentally, continue to believe their local MP has clout, then the myth becomes reality and the magic codicil will still carry weight with them. As large fish in small constituency pools, MPs must often find their insignificance back at Westminster rather difficult to cope with. For once inside the portals of St Stephen's Gate, it is only the confidence of their constituents which affords them any genuine *raison d'être*. The problem with so many MPs is that they forget it so easily. Others, on the other hand, remember it all too well . . .

The *Piper Alpha* disaster of July 1988 shall remain for ever seared across the nation's collective memory. By the afternoon following the explosion, the death-toll had already risen to over 150, as politicians of all parties in the Commons expressed their commiseration with the families of the deceased. Of course, it would only be a matter of minutes before the day of mourning would degenerate into the usual party-political dog-fight. The Energy Secretary would state that he and his department were completely blameless. And the Opposition would counter, naturally, that *Piper Alpha* was just another instance of worker safety being sacrificed to the heartless capitalist profit motive. But all that was to come after the grieving, the parliamentary *hors d'oeuvres*. For a few halcyon moments, the House of Commons would be seen to be united in its cross-party sorrow. The Prime Minister, clearly shaken, spoke with a discernible crack in her voice. Kinnock, too, a more naturally emotional man, was visibly moved. But the House of Commons show must go on, and after a few brief statements, Prime Minister's Question Time continued as planned. South-west Norfolk's Tory MP, Mrs Gillian Shephard, was to be called fourth on the list. 'Would the Prime Minister,' chirruped Mrs Shephard, with an inalienable sense of the appropriate on this day of national tragedy, 'would the Prime Minister care to congratulate the people of Thetford who have recently succeeded in reducing unemployment from 10 per cent to 6 per cent?'

For once, the Opposition was too stunned to react, though some may have wondered whether, when the nuclear balloon goes up, Mrs Shephard would again be there in the House of Commons, querying whether or not the 56B bus to Norwich would still be running on schedule?

Not for the first time that session, I decided I'd had enough of politicians and their interminable, inconsequential point-scoring. Leaving them all behind, I sauntered down the road to that place in Westminster where, unlike the House of Commons, Someone Really Important Lives. I felt a sudden and long-forgotten need to go and say a prayer. It was not, I need hardly tell you, for the good burghers of Thetford.

But if, in charity to Mrs Shephard, hers were merely a momentary lapse into the trivial and the trifling, there is, on the contrary, a group of MPs who have raised the art of trifling triviality to a media form. Indeed, they have made it the very stuff of much of their parliamentary existence. For there was never an issue so important, never a question so crucial, never an argument so water-tight that a few well-chosen remarks from certain members of this fraternity could not reduce to the risible. These are the omni-present, omni-available for comment, omni-preconceived idea on everything, omni-experts. They must not, under any circumstances be confused with *genuine* authorities, with people such as Labour's Nigel Spearing who knows more about European legislation than the rest of the Commons put together; or Conservative Michael Mates, just the man when you need to know anything about defence. No, the omni-experts are a different species altogether, backbench trumpet-blowers, MPs who believe that ubiquity in the press somehow compensates for a life of insignificance in the House. Up in the Press Gallery, they call these men 'Rent-a-Quotes'.

The Rent-a-Quotes, however, are a far from homogeneous group. Take Mr Terry Dicks, for instance, MP for Hayes and Harlington since 1983. Now, whilst no one in their right mind would ever dream of calling Mr Dicks in any way prejudiced, neither would anyone expect him to be first on the dance-floor when the reggae band started up. Dicks began making something of a name for himself as housing chairman for Hillingdon, a Tory-controlled council which refused to house a number of homeless immigrants, although not, so he argued vehemently at the time, merely those of the Asian variety. Since then he has worked hard at enlightening the masses with his comments on everything from rapists (ought to be castrated) to Sky Shops (a rip-off); from soccer hooligans (ought to be branded with dye on their foreheads) to the Master of the Queen's Music (ought to be sacked for calling the Prime Minister a 'philistine'); from 'do-gooders' (they can go to Hell) to the Notting Hill Carnival ('The police do not want this ludicrously named carnival ever to occur again, nor do the people of London, and the Home Secretary should ban it forthwith').

Somehow, from his personal Mount Parthenon in Hayes and Harlington, Mr Dicks appears to have gleaned some cosmic insight into what the people of London – indeed, of the entire country – seem to need and want. Not for men like Dicks the idea of leaving it to Notting Hill residents to decide for themselves whether or not they want their *ludicrously*(?) named Notting Hill Carnival. Not for the Dicks of life the concept of the public being allowed to 'waste' their money on charity fun days organized by 'the do-gooders and bleeding hearts in this country ... experts in hoodwinking the public into paying up money for unnecessary causes'. Why, if Ethiopians are starving, opines Mr Dicks, then let their own government sort it out. 'As long as they have got idiots like the British public giving them money, why should they worry about feeding their own people?'

Inevitably, homosexuals, too, come in for the Dicks treatment. Gay civil servants, he once argued, should not be allowed access to sensitive security information. Let's face it: as Mr Dicks and just about everybody knows, no heterosexual has ever been found guilty of leaked documents, security breaches, treachery or treason! Even today the Dicks diatribe continues. Foreign aid to countries such as Zambia and Zimbabwe should be cut off, averred Dicks on another occasion, manfully defending the Prime Minister against Commonwealth leaders' attacks on her anti-sanction stance. 'These black Hitlers should stop biting the hand that feeds them . . .' Let us thank our lucky stars, at least, that Dicks is unlikely to end up as Foreign Secretary.

The most telling Dicksism, however, created understandable furore in the national press. It was his widely reported claim that West Indians are 'bone idle, lazy and good for nothing'. On the basis of that allegation, one wonders, why are there so very few of them in today's House of Commons?

But if much of what Dicks has to say generally tends to shock, the utterances of his party colleague and almost namesake, Geoffrey Dickens, are usually received with little short of hilarity. It is difficult nowadays for most people to take this generously endowed figure too seriously. A large man, surprisingly light on his feet at the odd *thé dansant* or in the occasional Bananarama promotional video, he is perceived by many as a somewhat comic figure. Indeed, the last time I came across anything even vaguely analogous to Geoffrey Dickens was during the America's Cup in Fremantle. It was the Bond Corporation blimp and, in contrast to Mr Dickens, responsible for the most perceptive of all commentary.

Launched by a wily journalist into the stratosphere of media publicity, Dickens was originally encouraged to expose ex-diplomat paedophile, Sir Peter Hayman, under the protection of parliamentary privilege. Whether or not he was completely aware of what he was talking about has since been a matter of some conjecture. Certainly, his resounding denunciation of 'phaedopilia' (*sic*) had everybody bar certified dyslexics quite foxed to begin with. Overnight, however, Dickens was to become the Commons resident sexual-deviation expert, the Marjorie Proops of the Tory Party, but with none of the answers. This new-found authority was only further enhanced by revelations about his own double-dose of hanky-panky en route back to his abandoned wife, Norma. To be brutally honest, a cursory assessment of Mr Dickens, hardly the Imran Khan of the backbenches, does not suggest the traditional heart-throb genre. In terms of size and appeal, he is more the sort of mammal designed for Green Peace-style care and affection. But life and ladies of Littleborough and Saddlesworth are full of surprises. Only the spectre of AIDS, implied this reformed Casanova, has succeeded in denting his romantic ardour. 'I don't want to drag up the past,' confessed the man who felt obliged to call a press conference in order to broadcast his adultery, 'but I will say that AIDS has put a very different perspective on the morality of sexual relationships.'

Spurred on by the heady heights of fame, Mr Dickens was moved to play the 'naming' game again, this time alleging rape of an eight-year-old girl by an Essex doctor. He also threatened to expose vicars supposedly guilty of sexual offences. But weary by now of Dickens' headline-grabbing shenanigans, not to mention his interference in the affairs of other MPs' constituencies, some queried whether his actions were not becoming a regular *abuse*, rather than a justifiable *use* of parliamentary privilege. After all, the subjects of these allegations enjoyed no right of reply and, contrary to every tenet of British justice, were being found guilty by a combination of banner headlines and arcane parliamentary rules. It is all too easy for any MP to resort to the protective cloak of privilege, comfortable in the knowledge that the normal laws of libel do not apply. Great privilege implies great responsibility. Honourable Members happy to use the one must understand the other. I have often wondered to what extent Geoffrey Dickens really did.

The Dickensian volcano, thank goodness, seems rather quiescent of late. Of course, he has been suggesting, amongst other things, that there were three Moors murderers, not two, and – somewhat less likely – that a wave of witchcraft is now sweeping the country. But apart from that, Mr Dickens has been on a different form of self-promotion. For any artists in need of a nifty mover for their next pop promo, the MP for Littleborough and Saddlesworth could certainly fill a gap.

And yet not all members of the 'Rent-a-Quote' clan are of a piece. In fairness, Selly Oak's Tory MP, Anthony Beaumont-Dark, must be put in a different league to the Dicks and the Dickenses. An affable and not untalented man, Beaumont-Dark might have realized early on that the best way of increasing his erstwhile slim majority was to fight for all the popular causes and to let his constituents know it. To his credit, Beaumont-Dark was one of the few backbench Tories capable of withstanding the biblical Tebbit wrath at his opposition to the poll tax. Neither has he been afraid to tell the Prime Minister to 'get off her economic high horse and stop playing macho politics with the pound' – brave words indeed from any Conservative nowadays. And finally, as a fervent supporter of the NHS, Beaumont-Dark proposed massive cash injections for the service, even before opinion polls dictated that the government ought to make them.

But inexorably, sooner or later, the odd hint of eccentricity is bound to pop out. Cheekily populist calls for Anglo–American raids on Libya and demands that drunken drivers be made to sweep the streets may always be dismissed. But in this country, *bons mots* at the expense of the royal family certainly never will. Beaumont-Dark's jovial, throwaway remark allegedly made to the Duke of Edinburgh – 'You may know more about adultery than I do' – did not go down at all well. And his suggestion that the Queen's displeasure with the Prime Minister was leaked by Prince Charles himself has probably cost him his 'twenty-five years' good-behaviour' knighthood. By all means, call the Texans 'yellow bellies' for worrying about the security implications of Mark Thatcher as a neighbour. Insist that the father who sold his daughters as child brides should be deported from this country. Remonstrate with Sikhs for carrying swords around in Birmingham. Seek clarification on whether Mr Heath is or is not 'a nut case'. But never, in an entire career of successful rent-a-quoting, never, ever become embroiled in controversy over the nation's royal family.

You may, of course, if you are Labour's George Foulkes, be moved to aver that Lady Di should be married in a pair of Falmer's jeans, or that Prince Charles should test drive a truck. Absurd though such suggestions may be, offensive they are not. Indeed, when this particular Rent-a-Quote, once described by a Tory as being a 'fiscal illiterate', declares his intention of going off to the Channel Islands to expose tax-dodgers, amused eyebrows are merely raised. When the same man introduces a time-consuming bill to curb the evils of Space Invaders, his *gravitas* is called vaguely into question. When, as an outspoken critic of the Falklands war, he visits the Falkland Islanders, he is hardly afforded a conquering hero's welcome. But it is when he claims to have uncovered a link between political success and the stars that people start to wonder. Such statements suggest a thought-process the odd Exocet short of the full *Belgrano*.

But all grist to his oppositional mill, Mr Foulkes is surpassingly good at stirring up government embarrassment: Could Mr Norman Tebbit please explain the precise nature of his relationship with one Abdul Shamji, an Asian businessman whose empire collapsed with debts of some £40m. at the time of the Johnson Matthey banking scandal? Could the House please be told why a certain Miss Sara Keays knew details of the Falklands crisis denied to MPs? Could we have our fears allayed over allegations that the Prime Minister's son, Mark, was acting on behalf of a British company attempting to win a £300m. Middle East contract at the same time that the Prime Minister herself was trying to secure the deal for Britain? Yes, if ever there is a breath of scandal alleged, George Foulkes is sure to fan it.

Ealing North's Tory MP, Harry Greenway, if not a card-carrying member of the Rent-a-Quote ranks, is certainly happy to provide the press with instant quotes and seems able to live with the resulting publicity. A former deputy-headmaster, his pro-caning, anti-gay stance is well known to all those obliged to spend hours listening to him. The usual bees-in-the-bonnet are all there. *Growing Up*, a sex manual endorsed by the Royal Society of Medicine, is 'merely licensing pornography'. Some doctors shell out contraceptive pills 'like jelly babies', even to very young girls. Children are asleep in schools because of late-night videos. Fine old English puddings should be reintroduced in the House of Commons. And, most mind-boggling of all, 'I believe Jesus called us to be Conservatives not Socialists.' One can only imagine the gist of statutory religious education in Mr Greenway's ideal comprehensive! Yes, even today Harry Greenway is every inch the former deputy-headmaster, *circa* 1890.

For all that, this man is no fool in his choice of publicity stunts. What a wheeze! Conduct the *Miss World* contestants on a visit around the Commons. Go one better. Get involved with sportsmen. MPs just love sportsmen. For unlike politicians, sportsmen are athletic, high-profile and glamorous. People have actually *heard* of them. So, organize a cocktail party of Ian Botham after his John o'

Groats to Land's End marathon. Support John Conteh in his efforts to win back his boxing licence. And, if all else fails, call for a two-year British tennis ban on John McEnroe for calling the umpire a 'moron'. McEnroe, more canny that people think, soon had the measure of our British Rent-a-Quote MPs. 'He wants a lot of publicity,' concluded the tennis star with admirable insight. 'It's obvious.' And who am I to argue with the conclusions of Mr John McEnroe?

If the Rent-a-Quote phenomenon were not itself sufficient proof that far too many MPs have no sensible job to occupy their time at Westminster, then the statistic that 70 per cent of them are engaged in paid employment outside the House of Commons most assuredly is. Some of these extra-mural activities – such as writing newspaper articles to attain a wider audience – are perfectly legitimate. Others, far more liable to suspicion, go some way to answering that fundamental question: Why do MPs bother? Since the prospects of genuine political power are negligible, the reasons for many MPs' tenacity in hanging on in there do seem distressingly shoddy. Of course, so many MPs are such abject nonentities, they realize that the loss of the magic codicil would mean total oblivion.

Far more disturbing, when we question MPs' motives, is the accumulation of consultancies and directorships which some MPs manage to acquire, those 'jobs for the boys' rarely granted on grounds of sheer ability or expertise, but rather for the mere fact of being an MP. This somewhat insidious practice certainly deserves to be monitored more carefully, especially since some Honourable Members are known to hawk themselves around quite shamelessly. A friend of ours, a man who runs the country's most successful agro-industrial group, is perfectly sick of the weekly barrage of letters he receives from MPs, all explaining what tremendously useful contributions they would make to his board of directors. The friend in question, who, like Reggie Perrin's CJ, 'did not get where he is today' by carrying dead weight, will have none of them. 'It's not my practice to spend shareholders' money on people who are useless,' he claims. 'We believe in paying people top whack for the job they do, so long as they are good and do it properly. I know MPs keep groaning that their salaries are low. In point of fact, I pay my chicken eviscerators more – with profits! But I'd rather a decent chicken eviscerator on the books than a Member of Parliament any day!'

But not even those MPs coining the boodle by sitting quietly on company letter-headings are the most serious concern. Most insidious of all are those who have ceased to be active representatives of anything other than a range of vested interests. There is nothing new about the syndrome. It is just that the arcane ways of Parliament ensure that discussion on it is consistently stifled. Even as far back as 1965, James Callaghan, then Labour Chancellor, was moved to comment about the behaviour of certain Tory MPs: 'I do not think of them as the Member for X, Y, or Z,' he said. 'I look at them and say "investment trusts", "capital speculation" or "that is the fellow who is the stock exchange man who makes a profit on gilt edge." I have almost forgotten their constituencies, but I shall never forget their interests. I wonder sometimes who they represent, the constituency or their friends' particular interests?'

Callaghan's comments were considered a breach of parliamentary privilege at the time, and he was asked to apologize. It just goes to show what an incredibly useful little tradition this business of parliamentary privilege is! Whilst any ordinary citizen may be accused of the most heinous of crimes with complete impunity, an MP's blatant corruption must be allowed to continue unremarked. Of course, all MPs are encouraged to state their interests in the Members' Register designed for the purpose. But there is no compulsion to do so, nor to do so exhaustively. Conflicts of interest arise far too often. In committee discussions on the Finance Bill, for instance, that piece of legislation which deals with fiscal fine-tuning, some Labour MPs were shocked at the amendments tabled by certain Tory colleagues. They were clearly not being moved out of any interest for their constituents. It is high time the Commons put its own House in order, if only to ensure that those MPs of impeccable standards do not find themselves similarly besmirched by suspicions of impropriety. It is outrageous, for instance, that the irreproachable Sir Marcus Fox, a senior Tory with responsibility for appointing MPs to Commons committees, should find his position as director of a private firm of consultants being called into question. We are fortunate that, with a man of such principle, the possibility of his firm's having clients interested in legislation covered by certain committees could never possibly influence his decisions. But there are far too many MPs around who do not share

Sir Marcus's sterling qualities. It is those MPs whose activities should be scrutinized more thoroughly.

And so it is that the days are spent in that Ambridge of SW1: disgruntled Labour MPs, afraid to leave, clocking up a decent pension; disillusioned Tory MPs, hanging around, waiting for the knighthood; busy MPs, ever so slightly *louche*, looking after the old-boy network's interests; bored MPs, with nothing better to do, trying to grab the headlines; and some, it must be admitted, some MPs simply trying to get on with the job of being effective parliamentarians.

'My choice early in life,' President Truman used to say, 'was either to be a piano-player in a whorehouse or a politician. And to tell the truth, there's hardly any difference.' Who, observing Westminster's inmates, could quibble with Harry S. Truman? And who would deny that the best job in any 'whorehouse' is that of the madam who calls the tunes?

# 5 / Rule Margarita!

*"LUNCH IS FOR WIMPS!"*

If by some remarkable fluke, an extraterrestrial being should suddenly find himself transported into the House of Commons, it would not take him long to ascertain precisely who was boss. Seated ramrod-straight on the government bench, Margaret Hilda Thatcher stands out among her crumpled cabinet colleagues like an item of *haute couture* on a C&A sales rack. During Prime Minister's Question Time when the going gets rough, a more observant alien might even notice the Ken Lane pearl earrings, as they peep out from beneath her bouffant blonde coiffure in the manner of miniature missiles trained menacingly on her assailants. Whatever the situation, she always gives the impression of enjoying the fray, of relishing the fight, of being able to give just as good as she gets, of constituting, in short, the Mike Tyson of the frontbench. As with Mr Bill Frindall of Radio 3's cricket commentary team, she is constantly being bombarded with requests for the most spurious of statistics. As with Mr Bill Frindall of Radio 3's cricket commentary team, she is surpassingly good at providing them. And as with Mr Bill Frindall of Radio 3's cricket commentary team, nobody is the least bit interested in listening to them when they finally arrive. Yet still she continues in that relentless, 'I've started, so I'll finish' *Mastermind* mode. In the chamber she rarely appears anything other than unruffled and unperturbed, cocooned from oppositional opprobrium by that buffer zone of Brylcreem boys we sometimes call the cabinet. Indeed, as that undulating, occasionally hesitant oil-slick ebbs and flows between the frontbench and the government's Dispatch Box, cricket fans are often wont to reminisce about the Golden Age of Denis Compton in the act of negotiating a run.

And so it is that almost alone among the many and less memorable luminaries who inhabit the House of Commons, it is still this sexagenarian siren who never ceases to intrigue us. Women in general do not relish overt antagonism, yet Mrs Thatcher somehow seems to mainline on it. There can be no possible doubt about it. She has always been a handsome figure, though much smaller in the flesh than her TV image would suggest. And yet, she has somehow contrived to look better now than ever she did a decade ago when first she took office – a Westminster version of Dorian Gray, perhaps, but with none of the nonsense. Currently embarked upon this, her third and most radical term at the helm, the question which continues to invite most political speculation is when – if, indeed, ever – the lady is intending to go. And perfectly idle speculation it is at that, for Mrs Thatcher is showing not the slightest sign of letting up, nor of the usual mid-term blues. We may never discount, of course, the chance encounter with the proverbial bus although, as former Foreign Secretary, Lord Carrington, once averred, even if such a misfortune were to befall the PM, 'The bus wouldn't dare.' No, despite growing murmurings of dissent from various quarters, there is every indication to suggest that Mrs T. will still be leading the country well into the 1990s.

But with her place in the pantheon of history already assured, it is difficult to imagine why anyone, bar a certified basket case, would want to hang on so tenaciously in the first place, why anyone in her right mind would even think in terms of going 'on and on . . .' What, with the constant threat of terrorist attacks, the interminable red boxes of bumf to assimilate, the daily barrage of criticism from every direction – and all on a couple of hours' sleep a night – it is a job only a mutated humanoid like a politician could conceivably relish. Now in her sixties, Mrs Thatcher is at an age when most women would simply long to rest the old varicose veins in the 'Dunhustlin'-Dulwich-equivalent-townhouse of their choice, or to sit swinging gently in a hammock, sipping improbable green drinks on the beach at Ocho Rios. She, and industialist husband, Denis, are a wealthy couple. She is not short of the odd spondoolick, and so she cannot, like the rest of us, be doing it for the money. Indeed, to her credit, she has never even taken the full Prime Ministerial salary, making do instead with a lesser cabinet minister's stipend. No, the major motivation, as with most leading politicians other than those of the more dubious third-world variety, must be something else. Perhaps the secret of the Prime Minister's tireless determination is best encapsulated by another formidable lady, Mrs Barbara Castle, in her diary entry of 1975. It was the day after Margaret Thatcher had been formally declared leader of the Conservative Party, much to the surprise of many people, particularly to that of the Conservative Party itself. 'She has never been prettier,' wrote that indefatigable, red-headed rabble-rouser, 'she is in love with power, with success, and with herself.'

Nice one, Barbara! Build them up to knock them down, the usual politician's ploy. And yet, the lady herself once tipped as the first Labour woman Prime Minister should know what she is talking about. Most political leaders do tend to fall in love with the power they wield, and with all its meretricious trappings. This is presumably why all but the most gracious are incapable of relinquishing the reins with any degree of decorum when they must. Witness Ted Heath, Mrs Thatcher's immediate predecessor as leader of the Conservative Party. Today, almost fifteen years after his momentous defeat, he still sits lugubriously under the gangway, in the seat first earmarked for Sir Winston Churchill himself. Reserved once upon a time for eminent statesmen only, the bench is now packed with Maggie's many cabinet casualties, those growing ranks of sad men who were called and found wanting. But Ted, despite indications of increasing bitterness, still stands head and shoulders above the rest. For it was Heath, after all, who virtually single-handed took the United Kingdom into Europe, though to our eternal credit, no one really holds it against him today.

Now in his post-PM era, he seems content to spend his parliamentary days ruminating in the chamber, seething semi-silently like the bubbling mud of New Zealand's most famous tourist attraction, Rotorua, and always, like the boiling gushers of that place, dangerously liable to erupt with some scalding outpouring at any moment. Not a gracious loser, really. He appears to detest Mrs Thatcher with the sort of passion that men traditionally reserve for the mother-in-law. More often than not, he stares straight ahead, as if unwilling to favour the lady with even the most cursory of glances. Sometimes, however, he does seem to turn a wistful eye to those few former friends and colleagues whom Mrs T. has not yet relegated to the trash heap of history, to Douglas Hurd, Geoffrey Howe or Kenneth Baker.

And yet Heath is not quite of the classically tragic tradition. He does not, for instance, bear the hallmarks of a character riddled with anorexic angst. Indeed, nowadays, with his increasingly generous girth, he would be far better cast as a Falstaff than as a Lear. I can never look at him, however, without thinking of that most sympathetic of Shakespearean tragic heroes, of Antony as all his feckless friends deserted him, and of that ruined Roman's final comment on the pendulum of political pragmatism:

> The hearts
> That spaniel'd me at heels, to whom I gave
> Their wishes, do discandy, melt their sweets
> On blossoming Caesar.

Poor old Ted, indeed. It cannot be much consolation for him to contemplate that it was his own detached and supercilious manner which finally alienated backbench support and gave Mrs Thatcher her shot at the leadership in the first place. Perhaps the finest irony is that it was due to him in large part that she was even considered for the job at all. For already Heath, a middle-class, grammar-school boy, and a bachelor to boot, had broken the traditional Conservative Party leader mould. He was certainly never the archetypal 'huntin', shootin' and fishin'' type of Tory.

'He had two things against me,' one discontented cabinet colleague was later to remark. 'I was a gentleman. And I did take a first at Oxford.' Cruel words, yet even Ted's second-class academic credentials failed to endear him to the Tory grandees, to folk whose brains had long since been addled by years of judicious inbreeding.

Like Mrs T. after him, although less wholeheartedly, he first appeared to have little time for their patronizing, paternalistic ideas, advocating instead the 'own two feet' philosophy combined with a fleeting flirtation with Mistress Monetarism. Indeed, it was in more ways than one that Heath was the precursor of Thatcherism, the man who, after his fashion, played St John the Baptist to the Blessed Margaret's Messiah. In the end, however, Heath foundered, overcome by a bad attack of decency and conscience. Confronted by a potentially disastrous miners' strike in 1974, he went to the country and, albeit by a narrow margin, lost. It was then that Ted felt obliged to test the water and tentatively proffered his head on the Tory Party chopping-block . . .

Now, there are many things the Conservative Party does not like, but most of all it does not like losers. And Ted had lost. What is more, he was now judged to be unsound. He had lost his bottle when unemployment figures soared, and committed an unforgivable U-turn in reintroducing a statutory incomes policy. Even so, the Conservative Party is known to forgive men almost anything if they happen to be personally popular. Witness the rise and fall and rise again of Mr Cecil Parkinson. But Cecil has learned to operate on high-octane smarm whilst, in the charisma league, Ted has always been a resolute non-starter. 'I can remember the only time I ever saw him in the Smoking Room,' one disenchanted backbencher recalls. 'He had just popped in to give someone the most frightful earful. He didn't seem to realize that people needed to be thanked and encouraged from time to time, not consistently sat upon.'

And so, not for the first time in her political career, Mrs Thatcher was in luck. Encouraged by disgruntled backbenchers, mainly from the lower and middle ranks, and also from the right wing, she stood against Heath in the first round. Tory malcontents wanted a more resolute character in charge, yet quite why they rallied to Maggie's banner is rather curious. There was nothing in her then relatively undistinguished track record which could have so readily impressed them. For it was only much later on, when Pandora had well and truly emptied her Aquascutum box, that the characteristics so beloved of hangers and floggers were to become fully apparent. As the token woman Education Secretary, she had never been a particularly outstanding or outspoken member of the cabinet.

Indeed, as Heath himself recalls with relish, she might even have been classified as one of those high-spending ministers of whom she so disapproves today. But she looked sound, and she sounded straight. Besides, as the old adage runs, people do not win elections. Other people lose them. The grandees' natural choice, William Whitelaw, loyal lieutenant to the last, refused to stand against Heath in the initial skirmish, though – with the benefit of historical hindsight – he would probably have won if he had. Potential pretenders, such as Keith Joseph and Edward du Cann, realizing that their own chances were slim, decided to stay out of the contest altogether. And so, in the best *I, Claudius* tradition, whilst the obvious antagonists cancelled one another out, the dark horse came up on the outside lane and beat the rest of the field by lengths.

'Being a woman in politics can be useful,' says Mrs Edwina Currie. 'Amongst other things, it means that people tend to underestimate you. And that can be the most tremendous advantage.' Certainly, at that early stage most people failed to grasp the significance of the Thatcher phenomenon. Even veteran politician Rab Butler, a man who should have known better, was heard to wonder out loud about 'this Thatcher woman', and whether or not it was necessary to take her 'seriously'. But the fervently Roman Catholic Norman St John Stevas was far more enthralled. To him, the image of the Blessed Virgin Mary seemed oddly appropriate. It was not an election, he was heard to enthuse, it was an Assumption. But no one, not even the ecstatic Norman, could possibly have divined the full significance of this most remarkable of apotheoses. Neither could the more sceptical top brass, whose sporting instincts were merely 'to give the filly a run', have guessed that Margaret Thatcher would stay the course so well.

The rest, of course, is history. In 1979 a country weary of constant strike disruptions and sickened by a 'winter of discontent' returned a Conservative government to power with a forty-three-seat majority. Already, Margaret Thatcher had started breaking British political records: the first woman to lead a party; the first woman Prime Minister; and, incidentally, the first Prime Minister with a science degree. Even at that early stage, her remit and her message were perfectly clear: to curb union power; to cut taxes; to master inflation; to control the excesses of the welfare state and to maintain a strong line on defence. And even then critics and colleagues alike were finding it hard to cope with the novelty of a woman in charge. It was a hard grounding, but with the help of a heavily sexist Parliamentary Labour Party, the lady soon became inured to her fair share of verbal abuse.

And yet despite the hurdles, despite the endemic Tory snobbery towards the grocer's-girl-done-good, despite the opposition, the male chauvinism and the vested interests which have all conspired against her, Mrs Thatcher has not only survived, but has positively flourished to attain a virtually impregnable position. In the House of Commons, thanks to the idiosyncrasies of our first-past-the-post electoral system, she now enjoys a majority of over 100 seats, unfettered power on the basis of 43 per cent of electoral votes cast. In the House of Lords, thanks to the inbuilt Tory majority of a goodly bunch of hereditary backwoods peers, she is rarely in real danger of not having her way. In the country as a whole, despite deep pockets of resentment, particularly in the inner-city areas, she is constantly being accorded those meaningless 'Woman of the Year' awards.

Abroad, her standing is even higher than at home. In the USA, one revealing survey suggested that the Americans would far rather have her for President than any of their own lacklustre lot. During his period in office, President Reagan made every effort to single her out as the European head of government with whom he was most inclined to do business. In the USSR, her apparently warm, personal understanding with Mr Gorbachev has combined with the original 'Iron Lady' image to produce the profile of a western leader of some considerable stature. In Brussels, proligate continental farm ministers cannot see her coming without clasping their agro-wallets tightly to them and running for cover. And in Spain she is lauded as the only 'macho' in the cabinet: 'The best man in the Tory Party,' as Harold Wilson rightly quipped. At the beginning of 1988, Mrs Thatcher exceeded Asquith's record as longest continuously serving Prime Minister this century. One cannot help wondering what records she has set her sights on now . . .

For many people of my age, Mrs Thatcher is the only Prime Minister we can really remember, the only one who has truly stamped her hallmark on our generation. I suppose, with an effort, that I do recall Ted Heath and the miners' strike of 1974, but by that time I was immured from the vicissitudes of British politics by a whacking great Euro-salary at the Commission in Brussels. My more pinkish friends, who, like me, had just graduated, would write me vituperative screeds, incensed at Ted's putting them all on a three-day week. They failed to see why they should be doing an extra day's work for anyone, let alone a Tory government. And then there was dear old Jim Callaghan and his 'winter of discontent', a man who, even be-gartered as he is today, still has all the appeal of a fern plant, but less of the colour. Not to mention Harold Wilson, the pipe, the Gannex mack and the 'lavender-coloured note-paper'. No, there is no doubting the rich and meaningful heritage the average politician leaves behind him. But, putting all that aside, mine is a generation whose post-schooling (forgive me, those of you outside the South-east: I was about to say 'working') days have been spent almost entirely under the influence of one woman.

For the past ten years Mrs Thatcher has used her increasing authority to reshape this country and its citizens along the lines of her own homespun philosophy. It is the philosophy of the Lincolnshire Nonconformist society whence she hails, the self-help philosophy of her grocer father, Alderman Alfred Roberts, Mayor of Grantham and the greatest influence in her life. For Mrs Thatcher's is the simple creed of good housekeeping; Sunday chapel; an honest day's work; thrift; the nest-egg set aside for the rainy day (preferably in some nice, Department of Trade and Industry-registered outfit, Barlow Clowes, for instance); law and order; support for the police; self-reliance; self-respect; and the very definite existence in life of distinct strains of good and evil. Political commentators may well accuse Mrs T. of being a bit short on the old political theory. But even if her personal *Credo* does read rather like a litany of well-worn clichés, the 'Grantham theory' seems no worse than many others. At least it sounds a good deal clearer than most. Besides, Mrs Thatcher has never been afraid of voicing the odd platitude. As Mr Julian Critchley, the MP who has made a cottage industry out of Maggie-bashing, maintains: 'She is a woman of common beliefs and uncommon abilities . . . a radical populist.'

It is, in other words, the power of her convictions – not merely those convictions themselves – which sets her aside from her colleagues. It is that extraordinary ordinariness which makes her so extraordinary, and which explains the directness of her appeal to so many ordinary people throughout the country. But as ever onward and upward she pursues her own Socialist-free utopia, her relentless zeal and growing self-righteousness are beginning to worry even her strongest allies. For whilst no one could ever doubt the morality of the good alderman's basic beliefs, we now live in an era where such values have become increasingly confused with a selfish, pushy, grasping and ruthless society, the 'unacceptable face' of a nation which Mr Roberts and his kind could not possibly have condoned. For Mrs Thatcher has presided over a country which grows daily more divided between the 'haves' and 'have-nots', between the 'loadsamonies' and the 'lumpen proletariat'. We are a people gradually reverting to the upstairs/downstairs dichotomy of bygone Victorian days. Perhaps, if he were still around today, that most famous Mayor of Grantham might even consider counselling his daughter a degree of caution.

There seems little hope, however, of stopping the Thatcher juggernaut now. For the Prime Minister has had a vision. Oh, yes, brothers and sisters, she most assuredly has had a vision. She has been to the top of the mountain, looked over, and found the Lambeth Council lookalikes, the louts and the layabouts on the other side not at all to her taste. So come Hell or high water, she is jolly well going to root them all out before she calls it a day. She will not rest, or so she has assured us, until every last vestige of Socialism and 1960s permissiveness has been eradicated from our midst. This, dearly beloved, is the gospel according to Maggie. And this is the message that will be ringing in our ears until our teeth rattle – at least those of us who can afford preventive dentistry charges. We have in Mrs Thatcher a Prime Minister who knows the Way, has found the Truth and, at an economic rate, will provide the Light. After tentative beginnings, the New Conservative Crusade is now on with a vengeance. Faint of heart need not apply.

At times it seems incredible that, for all her radical and unpopular third-term legislation and despite the well-publicized backbench revolts, Mrs Thatcher is still indisputably in charge. Her ability to ride any storm, to survive and prosper in adverse conditions, has confounded even her most ardent critics. With the exception of Mrs Nancy Reagan, no acting head of state could possibly have foreseen the extent of the Prime Minister's personal triumph. Only Nancy, in her wisdom, might have been vouchsafed the slightest clue. For it was Nancy who, during her sojourn at the White House, would consult an astrologer on what was about to happen in the future. For the wife of a man rarely conscious of what was happening in the present, I always thought the exercise peculiarly redundant. Besides, although I am always happy to see what Mr Patric Walker and his stars have in store for me (for an overextravagant, hyperactive Leo this usually involves impending financial gloom and doom, combined with a distressing shortfall of tall, dark, handsome strangers), I am otherwise loath to spend time on forecasts of any sort, especially not political. It's just as well. For, so far, the career of Margaret Thatcher has defied even the most professional pundits. Had they thought to consult their pet astrologers way back in 1975, they might all have fared much better. For then they might have realized that the lady falls under the astrological sign of Libra, and Libran women are well known as strong and resolute characters, eminently capable of knowing exactly what they want and how to get it. Perhaps, if it is not too late already, someone really should co-opt Mr Walker on to the political staff.

Yet, even back in the hot-bed of university politics, where peer groups tend swiftly to identify their own future high flyers, no one fully grasped the true measure of Miss Margaret Roberts. Part of the post-war Oxford generation, she did succeed in becoming the third woman president of the Oxford University Conservative Association. Nevertheless, whilst people spoke of Shirley Catlin (later, Williams) as a potential first woman Prime Minister, no one really considered the hard-working Somerville undergraduate in the same light. Later, whilst a research chemist at J. Lyons and Company, she would proselytize in vain on the works bus, creating wry amusement among employees more interested in creating the perfect Neaoplitan ice cream than a free-market economy. But then, after the usual round of selection committees and unwinnable seats, she was finally elected for Finchley in 1959 and moved swiftly and efficiently up the greasy pole, stopping merely to say in 1969 that it was not yet time for a woman Prime Minister. A working wife, she was vocal in her awareness of all the attendant problems, though once, in an unusual admission of non-omnipotence, was moved to admit that 'When the children were young, I always had an English nanny.'

Clearly, though in no way to denigrate the Prime Minister's own personal achievements, the presence of a wealthy and sympathetic husband in the background does not hinder a thrusting young woman's political career. Indeed, it is precisely because the majority of mothers cannot afford a nanny – even at scandalous 'Philippino' rates – that there are so disgracefully few of them in the House of Commons. And a saner and more leavened and sensible place it would be if there were! Never the less, despite such material advantages, none of them has ever been allowed to affect the Prime Minister's own image of herself as a self-made woman, of someone who came up the hard way. The success story often seems to set too little store by the contribution made by that most supportive of political spouses. For Denis Thatcher, far from the buffoon so joyously depicted in *Private Eye*'s fictional 'Dear Bill' letters, has always been the female politician's perfect ''im indoors'.

Lady Luck has played a useful hand too. When we think of the Prime Minister's virtually unchallenged position today, it is staggering to look back to 1981, a far from happy time for the Tory Party in power. It was a time when Mrs Thatcher's tough monetarist policies were beginning to bite. Unemployment was soaring at around the 3 million mark – bitterly ironic, considering that the successful 'Labour Isn't Working' campaign was based on unemployment figures of around a mere 1 million! Inflation, the arch-enemy, was running at about 20 per cent. Street violence was rife in Toxteth and Brixton. And alarming ratings showed Mrs Thatcher to be 'the most unpopular British Prime Minister' since polling began. Despite a degree of dislocation between the inflexible 'Iron Lady' image and some very definite policy fine-tuning, colleagues were beginning to feel that the intransigent 'not for turning' rhetoric was developing into a major electoral liability. Throughout the country, Conservative MPs braced themselves for a long stint back in Opposition, or for those of them unlikely to be re-elected, back in work. So what an unexpected stroke of luck it was for all of them when, in April 1982, General Galtieri's Argentinians invaded the Falkland Islands.

The Falkland Islands! Who on earth had ever even heard of them at that stage, except as some far-flung, distant lands where men were men and sheep were scared? And who on earth even particularly wanted them anyway? Certainly not the British government, who had just decided that the Falklanders did not even merit the full great and glorious British passport. And certainly not the boys at the Foreign Office, whose unofficial policy has always been studiously to disregard the sort of spots they would rather not be posted. No, as with tediously faithful wives, nobody is ever interested in places like the Falkland Islands until somebody else decides to steal them. Then men wage war. Or at least, in this case, Mrs Thatcher waged war. For as John Nott, then Defence Secretary, openly admitted: 'Men would have done a deal . . . She had to win.'

And win she did, to the overwhelming acclaim of a country gone mad on a fix of somewhat spurious chauvinism. For, overnight, this sick-man nation was in the game again. Overnight, Maggie had put the 'Great' back into 'Britain'. Suddenly, a people relegated for years to the second division of the international league was back in there pitching with the big boys. Britannia was thrilled to be ruling the waves again: the glittering liberator of downtrodden nations; saviour of the oppressed and defender of the helpless. There were, of course, a few minor niggles, minutiae which would continue to bother such tenaciously pedantic MPs as Mr Tam Dalyell (Labour, Linlithgow), details such as the direction in which enemy boats may or may not have been sailing when British forces decided to sink them. And there were also the inevitable casualties of war, the young men maimed and destroyed on both sides and, so some claim, covered up and forgotten. Besides, few of the people and virtually none of the press were going to allow such inconvenient considerations to spoil this ritual gorging on glory, this splurge of new-found patriotism. The country was high on its own hyperbole. And nobody embodied the exuberant feeling more, nobody represented the decisive and optimistic profile better than Margaret Thatcher, the victorious Boadicea of Finchley. The 'Iron Lady' image which had fast been developing into a Tory Party problem was suddenly ideal. Where others had vacillated, the heroine of the Falklands had always stood firm. As the nation rejoiced, it toasted a Prime Minister who now, more than ever, looked precisely the part.

The tough, domineering and resolute leader, how assiduously over the years the Prime Minister has courted that style! Even in the early days, with a cabinet fractured by Heathites and 'wets', by people who disagreed with her Friedman monetarist fanaticism and told her so openly, she seemed to project an almost despotic image, the image of a woman in total control, of a starchy headmistress occasionally obliged to round up her sillier and more recalcitrant 'blue bunnies'. 'I don't mind how much my ministers talk,' she claimed in 1980, 'as long as they do as I say.' The rhetoric, however, as is usual with politicians, has always been somewhat at odds with the reality. If press 'leaks' on cabinet proceedings are anything to go by, Mrs Thatcher actually appears to have been overruled by her colleagues on various issues, on matters such as MPs' pay; teachers' salaries; Rhodesia; Vietnamese boat refugees; expenditure cuts and the sale of Land Rover. But nevertheless, like Heath before her, she has always managed to convey the impression of a leader surrounded by a bunch of yes-men, 'a brilliant tyrant surrounded by mediocrities,' as Harold Macmillan suggested to a contradiction-in-terms Conservative Philosophy Group. It is an image which the public has grown to expect and which television satire has been happy to exploit. One particular *Spitting Image* sketch sums things up completely: the scene, one of those unsubsidized cabinet dinners where one fondly imagines the PM handing everyone individual, itemized bills, and the Chancellor of the Exchequer collecting VAT at the door.

'And what about the vegetables?' asks a waiter, somewhat timorously.

'Oh, they'll have the same as me,' replies the Churchillian-cigar-toting Prime Minister without a moment's hesitation.

But the well-honed image is changing to accommodate slightly different times. Now, apparently, the Prime Minister would wish to be portrayed as a more 'caring, sharing sort of person', something akin to that other remarkable housewife and superstar, Dame Edna Everidge, perhaps, but without the *appliqué* koala bears up the front of the frocks. And a new image, as Mrs Thatcher has long understood, is far too important an aspect of politics to be left to mere chance.

We live in an age which is dominated by the media in general, and by the small screen in particular. In the land where television rules, one visual image is worth a hundred thousand words. In the days of Winston Churchill, Harold Macmillan and Alec Douglas-Home, leaders could remain mysteriously distant and remote, more awe-inspiring. For in politics, as in every other area of existence, familiarity may certainly breed contempt. Nevertheless, in a country where, according to the MORI statistics quoted earlier, one in four people does not even read a newspaper, the small screen has developed into the most powerful, if not the most reliably analytical, medium of communication. As every aspiring politician knows, if he is going to percolate through to the brain-bleached masses, he must be good on the box. He must be able to exude that indefinable amalgam of fortitude and charm; charisma and conviction; softness and strength – or is that the ad for toilet tissue? Anyway, since television is an immediate medium, time is of the essence. Every politician's message must be clear, simple, and repetitious: the 'tell them, tell them again, and then tell the stupid blighters that you've told them' school or rhetoric. Even more important, the image conveyed must be simultaneously attractive, impressive and resolute. With her relatively straightforward, uncomplicated vision of life, Mrs Thatcher has always had a clear, simple story. Moreover, she is perfectly happy to repeat it until the EEC's 'adult bovine animals' come home. After so many years in the limelight, the Prime Minister now has the TV performance down to a fine art. Naturally didactic, she has always been happy to preach the glad tidings of New Toryism. And as for the image – that is one sphere at least where she has never been afraid to seek advice.

Politicians nowadays must all be individually 'packaged'. Out for Mrs Thatcher and the 'gals' goes the hackneyed image of the prototype Conservative lady: sensible shoes; large hats looking like David Hockney swimming-pools turned inside out; cashmere twin-sets; dowdy tweeds; the lot compounded by that inevitable accessory, the double string of cultured pearls. Nowadays, Tory lady MPs constitute a far more heterogeneous bunch. Of course, there is still the odd Lady Bracknell ringer around, ladies such as Dame Jill Knight. A generous, handsome woman, always well turned out, the fabric of Dame Jill's frocks would more than furnish the spinnaker of the average twelve-metre yacht. This excellent lady also displays a certain penchant for fur collars of interesting pedigree, a foible which has been known to provoke concern in more left-wing circles. A keen supporter of the controversial Alton (anti-abortion) Bill, the great Dame was highly embarrassed when Labour's Ann Clwyd wondered vaguely why anyone so very supportive of life should waltz around wearing something so very reminiscent of a dead cat. But for all her radical right-wing persona, Dame Jill still manages to convey an air of amiable niceness about her, the ineffable whiff of the strict yet over-indulgent maiden aunt. The same can hardly be said for her distinctly more daunting colleague, Dame Elaine Kellett-Bowman. Squeezed into tight, short, sleeveless, cotton numbers – even in positively sub-zero temperatures – Dame Elaine eptomizes the 'all-weather' Tory look. She is also a fully paid-up member of the bulging-handbag brigade, that crack force of Conservative ladies capable of flattening the most menacing of miscreants with a swift smack across the head with a well-stuffed Enny. What on earth they keep in there is anybody's guess: life-size inflatable dolls of Mr Norman Tebbit; cardboard cut-out replicas of Selsdon Man; hand-tooled, gold-embossed copies of the last three Conservative Party manifestos – who would ever dare get close enough to find out?

The newer breed of Tory MPette is different again. There are the earnest, angular types like Mrs Virginia Bottomley, a lady who looks for all the world like the school hockey captain, only twice as likely to crack you on the ankles if you happen to cross her. Or the health- and weight-conscious joggers such as Mrs Edwina Currie, the ex-Junior Health Minister who, despite her avowed fondness for Janet Reger lingerie, no longer has the time for labour-intensive silk. (One of my naughtier journalistic friends has even dubbed her the 'polyester princess'.) But for all the richly coloured backcloth of the Tory ladies' tapestry, there is not a single one of them who could hold a designer candle to, say, the French European Affairs Minister, Socialist Edith Cresson; or the French ex-President of the European Parliament, Liberal Simone (never seen without a Chanel) Veil; not to mention the most dazzling politicians of all, the Italian lady Communists, 100 per cent pure Marx with Armani accessories.

Traditionally, however, and despite the enviable style of our European cousins, the grander type of British woman has always been vaguely ashamed of looking glamorous, of seeming as if she had gone to any sort of trouble. Mrs Thatcher's efforts in this department have met with admiration from some, but with the utmost contempt from others. For there is a certain form of inverted snobbery which tends to thrive among the self-acclaimed female intelligentsia, the distorted Cartesian logic of 'An absolute scruff I always look, an undoubted intellectual I therefore am.' Even in these post-feminist days, there is a fair proportion of learned ladies who still feel that the mere fact of smoking Gauloises *sans filtre*, and looking as if they had been dragged through a hedge backwards, is enough to qualify them for a Nobel Prize. In her battle for the 'image', Mrs Thatcher and her style have always found their most damning detractors among those not-sufficiently-blue, blue stockings. 'Margaret Thatcher ... has one great advantage,' confided that prodigious lady of letters, the late Dame Rebecca West, to Jilly Cooper on one occasion. 'She is a daughter of the people and always looks trim, as the daughters of the people desire to be. Shirley Williams, because she's a member of the upper-middle class, can achieve the kitchen-sink-revolutionary-look that one cannot get unless one has been to a really good school.' Dame Rebecca was far from alone in her mischievous dismissal of the grocer's daughter's style. Baroness Warnock, philosopher and Mistress of Girton College, Cambridge, is even more vitriolic about the Prime Minister's 'odious suburban gentility', the well-groomed clothes and hair 'packaged together in a way that's not exactly vulgar, just low'. Of course, such comments disclose as much about the perpetrators as about their victim. But clearly, the Prime Minister's scant regard for ivory-tower tenants is more than reciprocated.

And yet do we really want our Prime Minister – especially a female Prime Minister – looking like Shirley Williams just emerged from a de Havilland wind tunnel? Do we really want Mrs T. rocking around Red Square in a Michael Foot designer donkey-jacket? Of course not. We want our head of government to look smart, and Mrs Thatcher does look smart, or at least as smart as anyone condemned to wear British-designed outfits can manage to look. Like the Princess of Wales, the Prime Minister conspicuously flies the Union Jack couture flag abroad, and the domestic rag trade is grateful for it. But still, even with such restrictions of choice, getting *le tout ensemble* together is no easy matter. In the early years, Mrs Thatcher used to rely heavily on the advice of Lady Guinevere Tilney, a stable-mate from their years together at the National Women's Commission who was swiftly elevated to Lady of the Bedchamber. Lady Tilney had very definite ideas on most things, and even government ministers were known to worry about the extent of her influence. For with all people in power, access is everything, and for many years Mrs and Lady T. were extremely intimate. Initially they saw eye to eye on everything, from legislation on equal rights for women (against) to hanging and birching (for). Like many Tory ladies, both shared an irresistible urge to declaim about morality. At Tory gatherings in Liverpool, for instance, where her husband, John, was sometime MP, Lady Tilney was often heard to pontificate about 'slimy foulness' and 'seedy excursions into irresponsible sexual behaviour'. Inevitably, it was only a matter of time before the two Tory doyennes fell out. Perhaps, in the end, Mrs Thatcher grew weary of her cabinet favourites being thus flagellated in public.

Nevertheless, despite Lady Tilney's departure from the scene, Mrs Thatcher has never been short of 'image' advisers. In Mrs Thatcher's current kitchen cabinet, it is the PR man rather than the political theorist who wins hands down as favoured son. It is, without doubt, an index of the superficiality of our society. But images win elections and winning is the name of the game. Take Mr John Major, for instance, the brilliant Chief Secretary to the Treasury. He could be in with a chance of succeeding Mrs T., so the gossip goes, but only if he changes those appalling specs! He may well have the mind of an IBM number-cruncher, but that owlish sort of profile will not deliver the votes. Mrs Thatcher, though certainly no slouch on the cerebral front, has always been more intuitive than intellectual. She has known instinctively what the electorate wants. On the advice of ex-TV producer Gordon Reece, she simultaneously dropped the hats and the voice. Dennis Skinner, naturally, was the first to notice the lower register, focusing the entire Commons attention on the new 'Janet Brown Mark II' delivery.

The image-creators lightened, softened and heightened her hair. Lessons in make-up were organized at the Joan Price Face Place. A touch of cosmetic dentistry was suggested. Gradually, the Prime Minister dispensed with those fussy pussy-cat bows, fawn acrylic versions of which are still much in evidence at Women's Institute gatherings everywhere. Mrs Thatcher's favourite outfitters, Aquascutum, have since been commissioned to provide suits 'designed to stun', as if the Prime Minister's trenchant attitudes were not sufficient in themselves to achieve the result. But fashion designer Marianne Abraham's new, uncluttered necklines and shoulder-pads have certainly succeeded in producing an overall well-tailored look which combines power dressing with overt feminity in a way which appears to impress the President Mitterrands of life. Whilst the disdainful President Valérie Giscard d'Estaing never cared for her 'either as a woman or as a man', François feels the PM has 'the eyes of Caligula and the mouth of Marilyn Monroe'. Myself, I prefer the Bolsover approach, but one can hardly blame a woman for revelling in the attention of an admiring bunch of susceptible men. It was by all accounts Michael Heseltine's immunity to such feminine charms which helped contribute to his downfall. He was never really 'one of us', whilst more enthusiastic courtiers, men such as Cecil Parkinson and Jeffrey Archer, clearly were. But for all that, it is not as a fashion-plate that Mrs Thatcher most wants to be remembered. She knows that there are plenty of very important clothes knocking around with absolutely no one inside them. She must do. After all, she has met Mrs Nancy Reagan. No, good grooming is only implicit in, and very much secondary to, the image the Prime Minister most seeks to achieve: that of a woman completely in control. And here again, nothing in the package has been left to mere chance.

When Saatchi and Saatchi were brought in by the Conservative Party for the 1979 election, the concept of political advertising was not entirely new. But did those boys manage to revolutionize the business! Superimposed on posters of a dole queue, their 'Labour Isn't Working' slogan won plaudits from Central Office and the everlasting friendship of a grateful new Prime Minister for their smart, young executive, Tim Bell. It was the same Bell who was behind the post-Falklands 1983 election success also, with a campaign based almost entirely on the Prime Minister's gutsy, patriotic image. And it was Bell who, four years later and by that time no longer with Saatchi, still continued to advise the Prime

Minister privately during the 1987 election as a member of the unofficial inner sanctum nicknamed the 'Exiles'. Again, he felt sure that the campaign, like Labour's extremely snappy counterpart, should focus heavily on the personality of the party leader. Indeed, after a rather worrying and wishy-washy beginning, it eventually did, with well-known results. Since them, whilst Saatchi and Saatchi and the Conservative Party account have gone their separate ways, the favoured 'Tinkerbell' remains a regular visitor to Number 10 and always – dyed-in-the-wool public relations man that he is – with a bunch of flowers in tow. If the Prime Minister, as so many political commentators maintain, is rapidly developing into a personality cult, it is indisputably Tim Bell who must take much of the credit . . . or, as his critics would have it, a lion's share of the blame.

But politics is not about personalities, we hear the Westminsterocracy cry. It is about issues. Let them say it until they are blue in the face. We, the mere electorate, have always known different. To prove it, all you have to do is imagine a Sir Geoffrey Howe rendition of Churchill's 'We'll fight them on the beaches' speech. Hardly electrifying. Hardly the sort of thing to rouse the spirits of a nation. Of course not. Individual personality has always been the most important factor in convincing, cajoling and consoling the masses and, in our TV-dominated age, more so than ever. For all their talk of issues, even politicians have come to recognize this fact. Not that the personality phenomenon need necessarily be a bad thing in politics, so long as it is used as a means to an end, not merely for self-promotion.

The politically anonymous, however hard-working or worthy, have never been vote-catchers. Nowadays, particularly, a well-projected and forceful personality is the most effective vehicle for any policy or, indeed, for any party. Despite their ever-increasing sniping about the 'empress' and her 'new clothes', most post-1979 Tory MPs recognize that their majorities and their seats are due to the strength of the Prime Minister's personal image, to that and to the implacable clarity of her Messianic message.

Mrs Thatcher has always been portrayed as a 'conviction' politician, as a woman who has no time to argue the toss with folk who fail to share her vision and her methods of implementing it. One of the most outstanding hallmarks of her period in office has been the end of what the old-school political commentators call, rather sentimentally, the 'consensus'. Myself, I cannot really remember those halcyon days, but it was a time, so they tell us, when post-war Parliaments would sit happily basking in the sunshine, all sharing similar beliefs in matters as fundamental as the welfare state and a mixed economy. They were days when Labour and Conservative politicians would disagree vehemently across the floor of the House, only afterwards to slap one another gamely on the back, and share a few pints of Federation brew in the Members' Bar. Ah, no. Nostalgia certainly ain't what it used to be. But, whatever the real truth of these rose-coloured reminiscences, there seem fewer signs of such cross-party fraternization nowadays. Gradually, but certainly by the mid-1970s, the two major parties had begun to polarize, an ever-yawning gap opened as testimony to the growing influence of extremist tendencies in both. In the current political climate, the chances of any form of 'Thatchnock-ism' inheriting the 'Butskellism' mantle as a constructive *modus vivendi* are about as likely as Sir Cyril Smith's sudden conversion to the Cambridge Diet.

Today, British politics seem quite genuinely confrontational, not only between the various political parties, but equally within them. As far as possible, however, the Prime Minister has managed to ditch the majority of eleventh-columnists from her own top table. Waverers and 'wets' (a Tim Bell-inspired expression, by all accounts), were soon axed from her early cabinets, sliced off one by one with 'salami' tactics, and replaced by men who owed their elevation (and therefore their loyalty) entirely to her: men like Norman Tebbit, Cecil Parkinson, Leon Brittan, and Nigel Lawson – self-made men more in her own image and likeness. Indeed, of the first cabinet formed by the Prime Minister in 1979, only three ministers have survived the test of time: Geoffrey Howe, George Younger and Peter Walker (this last, perhaps, to obviate the danger of a potentially subversive agent roaming free on the government's backbenches). But the list of casualties, and the reasons for their resignation or dismissal, makes instructive reading, embracing as it does some of the Conservative Party's brightest and many of its best: Humphrey Atkins; John Biffen (too sardonically dry whilst politically too damp); Leon Brittan (leaked *billets doux* during the Westland affair, now off to Brussels); Mark Carlisle; Lord Carrington (an unintentional Falklands 'casualty'); Lord Cockfield (sent to the European Commission as a non-believer and prematurely recalled for 'going native'); Nicholas Edwards; Sir Ian Gilmour (too amusing by half, and too wet by plenty); Lord Gowrie (trouble making ends meet on a cabinet minister's pittance); Lord Hailsham (retired); Michael Heseltine (resigned over Westland, a spectacular *reculer pour mieux sauter* move if ever there was one); David Howell; Patrick Jenkin; Michael Jopling (retired); Sir Keith Joseph (retired to the Upper House with a bad attack of soul-searching); Angus Maude (retired); John Nott (resigned over the Falklands, now doing very nicely, thank you, as chairman of Lazards); Cecil Parkinson (resigned over a well-publicized affair now apparently forgiven and forgotten by everyone bar a certain Miss Sara Keays); Jim Prior (too kind); Francis Pym (too nice, especially to Europeans, not an attribute to be encouraged in British Foreign Secretaries); Lord Soames (off to Europe); Norman St John Stevas (too iconoclastic about all except Roman Catholic icons); Norman Tebbit (left to look after his wife – who was badly injured in the IRA Brighton bombing – but also miffed as party chairman for being side-stepped in the 1987 campaign); Lord Whitelaw (retired for reasons of health); and Lady Young (retired).

All in all, that makes about two dozen cabinet ministers obliged, for one reason or another since 1979, to hang up the red box, forgo the black limo and dispense with the little luxury of a bag-carrying PPS splashing soda in the Scotch. Not that the Prime Minister has had it all entirely her own way. Efforts to appoint the ambitious Lord Young, a man who has the PM's impeccably clean ear, to the position of party chairman were successfully thwarted. And ideas of bringing best-selling novelist Jeffrey Archer – the favoured, crowd-pulling ex-deputy chairman – back into government by appointing him to the Lords as Sports Minister were also quashed. The only man alive capable of attracting more attention than Mr Colin Moynihan, the current incumbent, Jeffrey would have been a dynamic if controversial choice. Of course, Mr Moynihan, a hyperactive rowing blue who keeps fit by running rings around his less enthusiastic civil servants, is growing into and, if he continues upsetting sporting bodies, possibly out of the job. A small but perfectly formed person of charm-bracelet proportions, he has always been an absolute demon at synchronized publicity stunts. But Jeffrey, who rallies 500 non-believers where Sir Geoffrey Howe only manages forty to any wet, windy November evening meeting in Newcastle, might have proved, in footballing parlance, just 'magic'. 'Actually, though, I'm not that interested in the idea of red boxes any more,' claimed the millionaire novelist, gazing out from his South Bank penthouse flat to Westminster's Gothic 'dream in stone'. 'Now, all I'm really interested in is people.' Perhaps the Tory Party's Number 1 fiction scribe might try a word in the ear of the Nimbys' Number 1 pet-hate, Mr Nicholas Ridley . . .

But despite achieving more or less the sort of mix she wants around her, the Prime Minister does not appear to take her cabinet chaps as seriously as some of them would like. Under her leadership, according to Sir John Nott, the full cabinet has gradually been relegated to the role of mere rubber-stamper. Another disgruntled ex-minister, Henley's double-breasted Croesus, Michael Heseltine, stoutly maintains that his resignation was not only over the fate of a helicopter company. It was also his protest over the way the entire government was being run by a Prime Minister who appeared on occasion to exceed her constitutional role by manipulating cabinet agendas and minutes. Nott is also critical of Mrs Thatcher's method of arriving at a decision by 'strong' discussion, a practice which the more gentlemanly type of Conservative minister apparently finds difficult to stomach. Not to mention the fact that she often mistakes the usual courtesies a man extends to a woman as a sign of mere weakness. Certainly, the traditional Tory gent must find this authoritarian lady very wearisome to deal with. If cabinet divorce statistics are anything to go by, most ministers obliged to deal with an awkward woman have simply axed her and moved swiftly on to a more malleable mate: the sweet, silent, secretary-type, perhaps. But Mrs Thatcher confounds them all. As the woman in charge, they cannot dispose of her. Neither can they, as they might an argumentative fellow-man, even tell her to belt up. In an organization like the Conservative Party, the fact of the Prime Minister's femininity simply floors them all. Ironically, in the Labour Party, the would-be more sexually egalitarian faction, she would doubtless be given a much rougher ride. But with the Tories, a group still very much nurtured and natured by public-school matrons and surrogate-mother nannies, Mrs Thatcher's now-no-nonsense-and-do-as-I-say approach has reduced them to a state of stuttering, inky-fingered schoolboyishness.

The odd thing is, of course, that far from being confrontational, most women have traditionally thought of themselves as society's natural conciliators, the ubiquitous Bostik in the fissures of family life. And for her part, Mrs Thatcher is for ever reminding us that she, too, is a mother and a housewife. Indeed, the term 'housewife', which ex-French Prime Minister, Jacques Chirac, once applied in tones of deprecating frustration, is one label of which she seems quite inordinately proud. After all, as she lectured government heads on that occasion, if the European Community were to manage its finances as sensibly as the average housewife, it would not constantly be obliged to lurch from crisis to crisis. And besides, she went on to claim at a Conservative Women's Conference in early 1988, it took a woman and a housewife to 'balance the books'. But despite all such appeals to the Tupperware vote, Mrs Thatcher is hardly one of the downtrodden sorority. She is certainly no women's libber: on one occasion she wondered what women's lib had ever done for her, stating the undeniable fact that 'some of us were making it' before women's lib was even invented. Perhaps, in some strange way, Mrs Thatcher belongs to a much later generation than her own – to the post-feminist sisterhood of females better educated, harder working and far more capable than the majority of men they find around them. It is a league of ladies no longer saying 'Yessir' to anybody, for now they themselves are boss; a clique whose natural affinities are not with other women specifically, but rather with other high-flyers. Statistics in this country show that, as the more confident and qualified ''er indoors' grows tired of domestic compromise and conciliation, there are more women than ever instigating divorce proceedings. Perhaps it is not only in politics that the time-honoured concept of 'consensus' has gradually collapsed.

But if you are a 'conviction' politician; if you are sure you are right; if, like Luke Skywalker, the adolescent hero of *Star Wars*, you 'trust to your instincts', then there is absolutely no point in struggling to compromise, in discussing things, in wasting time, as the Prime Minister herself puts it, 'having internal arguments'. The benefits of such an 'accept it or go' approach to government colleagues are perfectly clear. With the back-up band operating more or less in harmony, at least the party theme tune will always sound the same. But the obverse of such a coin is far less appealing. Unchecked, such attitudes may swiftly lend themselves to total intolerance of any individuals, categories, classes, ideas and, indeed, entire nations who are not 'one of us'. It is a blinkered philosophy which sees only black and white, and which rarely stops to concern itself with the infinite nuances of grey in which the greatest parts of life are sketched. It is an approach, nevertheless, which does have one distinct advantage over almost every other style of government. Without recourse to the compassionate spoonful of sugar, it will force people to swallow the nastiest radical medicine.

Nevertheless, that unhappy patient, the British underclass, has refused to take his treatment lying down. The gradual dismemberment of the welfare state has been a far from painless process. In the House of Commons, particularly, the final death-throes have been violent and convulsive. I watched Mrs Thatcher's coolly clinical performance at Prime Minister's Question Time in the angry April of 1988, as she endeavoured to explain social security 'reforms' (read, 'cuts') to an extremely ugly House. Coming, as they did, a mere month after a budget reducing the highest rate of taxation from 60p to 40p in the pound, the proposals enabled the Opposition to have a field day in moral indignation. Now, the 'Palace of Varieties', despite the promise of its name, stages disappointingly few variations on the original theme. Only a few weeks later, almost exactly the same scene was to recur as the joys of the 'community charge' (read, 'poll tax') were joyfully adduced for a sceptical House in the plummy tones of Mr Nicholas Ridley. One of the dwindling batch of Old Etonians now left in the cabinet, and always slightly stymied by the apparent presence of at least a dozen golf balls in his mouth, Mr Ridley was to enjoy an equally rough ride. In fairness, however, he could hardly have expected otherwise. The 'tribunes of the plebs' are hardly liable to swallow explanations of a tax quite unrelated to any ability to pay from a man who appears to dismiss the 'less well orff' (*sic*) as a mere matter of nasal nuance.

Opinions about Nasty Nick are divided even among his own backbenchers. Some hate him, others merely loathe him. Even his rather good impression of a supercilious turnip does little to endear him. Indeed, such is his popularity within the Tory Party that sometime rumours of his moving over to the Exchequer apparently met with threats of defection to the Labour benches. But for all that, underneath the tough exterior beats a heart of solid rock. A gifted dabbler in watercolours, Mr Ridley hit on an ingenious plan for people whose life savings amounted to over £6,000 (later, under pressure, increased to £8,000), and who were thus to lose their housing benefit. Why, wondered the in-house aesthete of the Department of the Environment, did such folk not simply breeze along to Sotheby's and blow the lot on a nice little painting, just the sort of investment the good Alderman Roberts might have considered for the entire family fortune? It was a solution which, even by Nick's own inimitable other-worldly standards, seemed to indicate all the political acumen of the Marie-Antoinette cake solution. Later that year, his attention was redirected to whingeing green-belt Tories, to those MPs in favour of enterprise and development anywhere but 'not in my back yard'. So high is Ridley's mind that revelations of *his* objections to planning applications near his own Cotswolds home could hardly be dismissed as mere hypocrisy. Many of us accepted the more charitable explanation: that, despite a deeply cherished belief in his own intellectual superiority, Mr Ridley's behaviour, on occasion, seems a few bangers short of a barbie!

But anyway, back in the House of Commons, early that April, members of the Opposition had been doing their confrontational homework well. There was not a single one of them who had not managed to come up with some poor unfortunate 'victim' of the 'evils of Thatcherism' with which to taunt the 'hard-hearted Prime Minister'. Every one of them had been out combing the land for examples of housebound-handicapped-housewives, horribly beleaguered by hoards of unspeakable ailments, and even greater hoards of unspeakable offspring, all of whom had had their benefits halved overnight and were soon to expire completely at the imminent introduction of the pernicious poll tax.

Moral indignation is a cheap commodity. That is why the Tory Party has stacks of it. It is also completely non-elitist, which is why the Labour Party has even more. But moral indignation sits easier on some political shoulders than on others. It must often be difficult, for instance, for earnest Labour MPs to pontificate about the breadline in Barnsley, with the pungent post-prandial aroma of Havanas and Remy Martin emanating from certain members of their own frontbench. And yet when the genuine article does pipe up, that dying breed of working-class hero so cherished by the Parliamentary Labour Party, then even the most hardened of cynics is obliged to pay attention. 'Answer the question,' heckled Dave Nellist, left-wing Labour MP for Coventry South-east. 'Answer the question,' he continued to roar for the full fifteen minutes of Prime Minister's Question Time. The poor man rumbled and shook quite alarmingly, like a hirsute Vesuvius intent on engulfing us all with his own molten-red brand of care and concern.

Now I for one am implacably suspicious of folk who believe they have a monopoly on compassion. The 'bleeding heart on sleeve' approach is such an easy one and, for all the hot air, does not necessarily make a man more genuinely humane than his fellow. Indeed, the very next day the same Mr Nellist was expelled from the Commons for merciless cruelty to a pathetic-looking invalid purporting to be the Social Services Secretary, Mr John Moore. But all the same, I did feel a degree of sympathy for Nellist's impotent frustration, if not for his counterproductive behaviour. In his late thirties, Mr Nellist is still the quintessential angry young man and I admire his relentless perseverance. In fact, there was a time when I knew plenty of the same genre back in the Cambridge days of the early 1970s. Lean, bearded and ascetic, they all wanted to take over the running of the Junior Common Room, legalize cannabis and paste Che Guevara posters all over the bar. The latter, incidentally, used to blend in quite nicely with the double-strength Capstan smoke smears on the wall, and the Greene King Ale stains on the broadloom. From time to time, these tireless class warriors from Weybridge would demonstrate by picketing Noam Chomsky lectures on the more esoteric aspects of structuralism. For such disruptions in our higher education, we are all, of course, extremely grateful. But then the silly blighters would spoil it all by plotting to immolate dear old Rab Butler, Master of Trinity, together with his lodge. Well, I was all in favour of rejecting capitalism as much as the next comrade. I had the guitar, the Joan Baez LPs, and was one of the few who actually knew the second verse of 'We Shall Overcome' in descant. However, upsetting Noam Chomsky on a miserable Monday afternoon was one thing. Being struck off Rab's Sunday morning sherry party list was quite another. Even universal anarchy has its limits! But as is the manner of things, and as rabid revolutionaries generally do, these chaps have all gradually simmered down, and are now extremely happy working in the City, coining the boodle, flashing around in BMWs and communicating with one another courtesy of the Cellnet system of the Car Phone Group. One ex-Trinity Trot, so the story goes, is now so loaded that when his son asked him for a cowboy outfit last Christmas, he just went straight out and bought him MI5!

Mr Nellist, on the contrary, is not a man to be diverted from his rightful purpose. He is no revisionist, being a Socialist of the ideologically and chemically pure variety. He refuses to become a homogenized Westminster man, joining in the clubby atmosphere of the House and doing the embassy cocktail party rounds. Instead, he tries to insulate himself from such endemic Commons 'corruption' by accepting only the average Coventry skilled worker's wage, about £130 per week. The rest of his parliamentary salary he donates to the Labour Party, the Militant-dominated wing of the Labour Party, the Young Socialists, and a fairly eclectic selection of strike funds. You may not like Mr Nellist's politics, but there is no doubting the man's sincerity. Yet as this rather overexcited chap stood barracking Mrs Thatcher on that occasion, his face contorted with something very close to hatred. It was interesting to watch the PM ploughing on regardless, genuinely oblivious to attack, undaunted by hostility, a crusader borne up by the fortitude of her own conviction and unquestioning sense of righteousness. For now the free-market message of economic prosperity is no longer enough. Mrs Thatcher has started to set her sights on less tangible goals. Now into its third term of office, the New Conservative mission has decided to pitch camp somewhere up there, somewhere in the rarefied atmosphere of the high moral ground.

High moral ground fever! The country seems to be ever more strangulated in its insidious grip. For all the Prime Minister's promises of less government, not more, there seems to be a growing swell of censorious folk busily telling us what to do, what to think, what to watch and how to behave. More and more, Britain is beginning to feel like modern-day Singapore since the advent of its 'benevolent' dictator, Mr Lee Kuan Yew. That, too, is a country where commercial freedom is almost total, but personal, individual freedoms are quietly curtailed by people who think they know best. A British Prime Minister, more so even than the President of the United States, is in a uniquely powerful position to promulgate her own views, to influence the thinking and direction of a nation, to make it up to match her own complexion. If she cares to wage a moral crusade, then there are a thousand ways of rallying the troops and tacitly teaching them the strategy.

The Prime Minister has an entire arsenal full of patronage at her disposal, an armoury of favours far more effective than any emaciated, post-Falklands fleet. At a political level, it is the Prime Minister who holds all cabinet posts within her gift. She, and she alone, is the woman who can make or break you. On the merest whim she can change your parliamentary days from the tedium of backbench obscurity to the limo-cushioned luxury of frontbench oblivion. The same goes for the 'payroll vote', that five-score *Rag, Tag and Bobtail* legion of junior ministers, Whips and Parliamentary Private Secretaries all of whom owe their unswerving allegiance to 'She Who Must Be Obeyed'. In the House of Lords also, the twenty-six Church of England bishops who are entitled to vote have all been the subject of Prime Ministerial *placet*. Not that these turbulent priests have been as prostrate as Mrs Thatcher might have wished them on occasion. But, nevertheless, a good half of their number have still been personally 'rubber-stamped' by her.

Perhaps the indicator which most reveals the colours of a British Prime Minister's would-be landscape is that quaintly archaic system, the Honours List, that ritual awarding of privilege where a Prime Minister exercises quite inordinate influence. Twice annually, at New Year and on the Queen's Birthday, people scan *The Times* to see whose contributions to the fabric of society have been recognized and to what extent. The first thing that strikes us, of course, is the superabundance of people of whom no one has even heard, career civil servants who have sagaciously kept their heads beneath the parapets of Whitehall and faithfully got on with the job, whatever it

## Rule Margarita! 139

was. But these are mainly *ex officio* honours: they go with the rations and are therefore no true gauge of prevailing political winds. Then there are the captains of industry, men like P&O's Sir Jeffrey Sterling, chaps whose companies' generous contributions to the well-being of the nation have been meaningfully channelled into Conservative Party coffers. Let us only hope that the families of the Zeebrugge disaster are treated with similar largesse! Then we get the personalities from the world of sport, entertainment, the arts, and so on. These are without doubt the most interesting honours of all. For as names we recognize, they may, at least, give rise to comparison and complaint. Why, we all ask, should the glorious David Gower end up with nothing, when the disgraced Mike Gatting gets an OBE? ('Order of the Big Eaters', according to sceptical English cricketers at the time, reassessed as 'Opportunist Barmaid Escort' some twelve months later.) Then come the knighthoods for the years of dreary backbench drudgery, compensation prizes for the runners-up of Westminster life who never made it to the Lords. The Labour Party leader, though quite prepared to make his own nominations for the coronet-and-ermine mob, is less eager to participate in the elitist knighthood game. Other Opposition leaders, on the contrary, are only too delighted to come up with their own list of suitable Sirs. In his SDP leadership swan song, for instance, Mr David Steel suggested the Rabelaisian Cyril Smith ('for services to Rochdale bedsprings', as one distinguished lobby correspondent somewhat enigmatically suggested).

Not that suitability seems to have much to do with who gets what nowadays. Even a few Tory eyebrows were raised when Mr Nicholas Fairbairn was singled out for the treatment. The party popinjay, Mr Fairbairn is the sort of man to tell you to the nearest £1,000 what he paid for his new suit, tailor-made by the 'in trade' family of Mr Speaker Weatherill. Done up like a Liberty's display window where the dresser has had a brain storm, Mr Fairbairn once announced that he was adopting frockcoats in order to avoid a 'shiny bottom'. He knows more than most of us, perhaps, what the sight of a shiny bottom does to the average bored backbencher. And later, in an Edwardian morning suit, he went on to attack Labour's 'scruffs brigade'. In short, Mr Fairbairn is a chap who has to be loud in order to be heard over the clothes he wears. But let us not concentrate entirely on this excellent fellow's good points. His recreations in *Who's Who* are listed as 'serving queens' and 'entertaining knights', a thinly veiled reference, one assumes, to his self-proclaimed genius as wit and Romeo *extraordinaire*. Once a lady of his acquaintance tried to hang herself from a lamp post outside his London flat. Who will ever really know the motives behind the scandal? No doubt she had fallen hapless victim to a surfeit of his wit.

Such mavericks are few and far between, however, and hardly representative of the Prime Minister's personal thinking. Far more indicative was the elevation of Chief Rabbi, Sir Immanuel Jakobovits, to the House of Lords in the New Year of 1988. Rabbi to Lord Young, the Chief Rabbi's clear moral leadership and emphasis on self-help, family life, and the ennobling effects of hard work were clearly consonant with Mrs Thatcher's own philosophy. Like the Prime Minister herself, Lord Jacobovits is not afraid to propound his own message, be it never so unpopular. No namby-pamby prelate, he takes a very hard line on the sin of adultery though, as certain members of the cabinet will be relieved to hear, has not yet called for the restoration of stoning. Indeed, when compared to the majority of Mr John Selwyn Gummer's pinko Protestant priests, Lord Jakobovits is one of the old school, an upholder of Victorian values, unchallenged as the representative of Judaism in Britain. Quite rightly, the Church of England's moral monopoly of the House of Lords is gradually being broken. There is now a Methodist peer, Lord Soper, and a Presbyterian, Lord Macleod of Fuinary, Moderator of the General Assembly of the Church of Scotland. But surely, if we are going to have it at all, then it is time that this extra pulpit was extended to embrace an even broader cross-section of races and religions. Leading British Roman Catholics are now pressing to revive the idea of a Catholic bishop or cardinal in the House of Lords, though the obvious contender – Cardinal Basil Hume, Archbishop of Westminster and sometime Abbot of Ampleforth – would not be able to find the time. And even if he could, his resistance to a gung-ho Thanksgiving Service after the Falklands, a jingoistic jamboree where Mrs Thatcher wanted to read the lesson, has hardly endeared him to the PM. No, Benedictine

Basil, a free-thinker more comfortable in a House of God than Lords, could certainly never be relied upon to act as 'one of us'.

Love or loathe her, there can be no doubt that Margaret Thatcher, that remarkable woman, has made her mark on our society. Since 1979, Britain's economy and world standing have both improved dramatically. But only history will tell how profound and indelible the Thatcher mark really is. For even the Prime Minister herself appears to have doubts about the permanence of her revolutionary changes. Certainly, her desire personally to carry the Thatcher banner into a fourth election indicates a definite want of confidence in the radical philosophy she has espoused. For if, after over a decade, the very narrow precepts of Thatcherism have failed to make irreversible progress, then perhaps they were not so incontrovertibly, so intrinsically, right after all. But in this stated desire to 'go on and on', the Prime Minister is courting three very real dangers. First, with wholesale privatization, her policies now seem based more on notions of dogma than on any of 'common sense'. Second, her memory is becoming increasingly, even disturbingly, selective. For if the Grantham grocer's girl is an object lesson in 'standing on your own two feet', then so is she an archetypal representative product of Britain's welfare state. And yet it is this very state, ironically, which the Thatcher government has worked so hard to undermine. As Nobel Prize winner and Mrs Thatcher's tutor at Oxford, Professor Dorothy Hodgkin, was moved to imply, it ill behoves those who have climbed the welfare ladder selfishly to pull it up once they themselves have completed their ascent. Indeed, in considering the government's plans to replace part of student grants by loans, the professor urged the Prime Minister to remember her own good fortune as an undergraduate. 'She was not so outstanding as to achieve a scholarship to Somerville,' Professor Hodgkin revealed. 'She was in a second category of very talented students from poorer backgrounds.'

Yes, in later life politicians do develop quite astonishingly selective memories! But the third and greatest danger is even more pernicious. It is not a problem for the Prime Minister alone, but for the prospects of the entire Conservative Party. For however dominant he or she may be, every leader must recognize that the day will come when it's time to bow out gracefully. The question is, will

Margaret Thatcher recognize that day even when it dawns? The prospects are beginning to seem increasingly doubtful. And yet, looking around both at the Opposition and the alternatives on offer within her own party, it is really not that difficult to understand why . . .

# 6 | *The brothers at Blackpool*

"OK, THE MOTION IS CARRIED — 457 TO 388. IT'LL BE COFFEE SERVED DURING TEA-BREAK!"

There is doubtless some sound anthropological reason why, every autumn, the party faithful feel the need to decant into those third-rate hostelries which so pock-mark the promenades of Britain's once-glamorous seaside resorts. Perhaps this annual pilgrimage is necessary to revivify and reinforce their more obnoxious political prejudices. Certainly, a week in Blackpool with the Labour Party did much to convince me that my natural home must lie with Mr Enoch Powell and his clique of right-wing Monday Club bigots. Just as a week in Brighton with the Tories helped persuade me that my real affiliations resided rather with Comrades Benn, Heffer, Livingstone, Skinner, Abbott and their 'hard left' Campaign Group philosophy. Yes, party conferences have strange effects on normal, disinterested observers. For party conferences are at once the emetic and enema of the British political system, the colonic purgation of the entire body politic. They are, in theory if not always in practice, the yearly opportunity for the rank and file to spew it all out, to get it off the collective chest, the cathartic experience to cleanse and restore the true believers, to set them up for yet another year's proselytizing in a largely indifferent wilderness.

Of course, party conferences differ wildly in form and in content. The first of the 1988 season, that of the SDP, might well have been convened with room to spare in a telephone kiosk in Torquay. The Rump of Three, or Gang of One, tried hopelessly to mend fences with their erstwhile bedfellows in the SLD. But Paddy Ashdown, flushed with a combination of TV-staged jogging exertions and recent leadership success, declared solemnly that he was 'not in the business of throwing lifelines to people', an interesting insight into the psyche of the average Special Boat Service marine commando. Nevertheless, like those profligate NHS General Practitioners of whom Mr Kenneth Clarke so openly despairs, the good Dr Owen continued to dispense prescriptions for the nation's every ill. Sadly, however, most of his erstwhile patients are no longer impressed by the placebos he has to offer. What a tragedy it has been for the health of current British politics, the fact that the physician has never quite managed to treat his own debilitating complaint: a terminal inability, as Roy Jenkins diagnosed it, to work with anybody but himself. And what a bitter, final epitaph it will make for Dr David Owen. For the man who succeeded in splitting two political parties will surely go down in history as a major, if unwitting, architect of Mrs Thatcher's unprecedented electoral success.

The SLD conference in Blackpool was an equally cosmic affair. Certainly, the SLD were not going to change the habits of a political lifetime by allowing policy discussions to interfere with the myopia of myriad minutiae. The high point of the conference, it soon emerged, was to be a decision on the party's 'name'. Casting aside the 'Liberal' legacy of Asquith, Lloyd George and Gladstone, the new name, it was agreed, would be quite simply 'Democrats' – in terms of subterfuge, about as convincing as the recasting of 'Windscale' as 'Sellafield'. Lonely and discarded, the 'Liberal' label was soon to find a friend, however, in none other than the person of Screaming Lord Sutch. For it is his party, in future, which will proudly carry on the tradition, transmogrified for ever as the Monster Raving Loony *Liberal* Party.

But the new Democrat baby had barely been christened before the assembled bad fairies began to fall out. All those who had so excoriated Dr Owen for his refusal to accept the democratic decision on merger were now, in their turn, refusing to accept the democratic decision on 'Democrat'. A compromise, happily, was eventually reached. They could all call themselves more or less anything they wanted, since by now the polls were indicating that everyone had forgotten who on earth they ever were to start with. Heartened by such public apathy, issues such as defence, which had so ostentatiously divided the old Alliance, were swiftly swept under the carpet. Instead, Paddy Ashdown unfolded his two-point plan for power, a simple strategy which involved beating first Mr Kinnock and then Mrs Thatcher. He might have done better, as Kenneth Baker later commented, to tell it to the marines. For Ashdown's only realistic hope of ever beating either of them is in single unarmed combat or courtesy of the Queensberry Rules. 'There is,' claimed Mr Ashdown, 'a gaping vacuum at the centre of British politics.' It is comforting that, even at this early stage of his career, Paddy has managed to reach such a comprehensive assessment of himself.

Yet the real fireworks, as ever, were to be reserved for the Labour Party Conference, that annual ritual of group *hara-kiri* merrily trailed by months of internecine back-stabbing and self-inflicted foot-shooting. This was to be my first ever party conference and the train trip up to Blackpool proved an unexpected eye-opener. Seated opposite in our London-Euston-to-Glasgow-Central-change-at-Preston-for-Blackpool-without-so-much-as-a-dining-car-for-the-Intercity-first-class compartment was a large man of relentless conversation and improbable diction. For the best part of four hours, he regaled all within earshot of his growing mastery over the party machine, of how, spotting a loophole in the rules, he had secured promotion from deputy-chair of the sub-group of the liaison committee of the working party to joint-chair of the sub-committee of the working group of the liaison party. He was clearly a man with a high boredom threshold, the sort of bloke who would still be there at constituency party or union meetings, arguing over the first sentence of the second indent of sub-paragraph three whilst all sensible folk had long since cleared off home to have a pint and watch 'Match of the Day'. He was, in short, traditional left-wing activist material, constitutionally incapable of seeing the wood for the trees, of ever perceiving the broader picture. He was just the sort of stuff of which Militant Tendency had originally been made, the very personification of the mindless, unswerving and unyielding commitment which is both the strength and the weakness of the palaeolithic wing of the Labour Party today.

With its celebrated illuminations, the town of Blackpool looked extraordinarily attractive, albeit in the dark. As with the Labour Party itself, it is surprising what a few bright sparks can do to camouflage a heap of otherwise out-moded, out-dated and antiquated dross. Don't get me wrong, at least not about Blackpool. I, too, become most aggravated with snotty Southerners who think that everything north of Watford is nothing more than black pudding, slagheap and chimney-stack land. Blackpool really does sport some excellent hotels. It was just a matter of extreme misfortune that I was not in one of them. Earlier on in the season, impresario Andrew Lloyd Webber and his wife, Sarah Brightman, had been invited to switch on the lights, and indeed Lloyd Webber's smash-hit musical *Cats* was playing to packed houses somewhere in the Winter Gardens. It was elsewhere, however, in the Empress Ballroom of that same venue, that all the genuinely dangerous claws were soon to be bared.

The long-heralded 'leadership battle' was swiftly laid to rest as the electoral college of trade union representatives (casting 40 per cent of the leadership vote), Constituency Labour Parties (30 per cent) and Parliamentary Labour Party (30 per cent) went overwhelmingly for the old Kinnock/Hattersley 'dream-ticket'. Clearly, the new-look Labour Party now has very wet dreams. But with an impressive eight-to-one victory over veteran left-wing challenger, Tony Benn, the thoroughly modern Kinnock proved once again what a canny in-fighter he is. 'The right-wing press like to depict Kinnock as an incompetent idiot,' complained one disgruntled Benn supporter, 'but the fact is, they haven't got a clue. He now has more of a strangle-hold over the party than any Labour leader I can remember. Talk about democracy! Wait and see if he doesn't use this to consolidate his own position even further. He'll make sure that the rule on 5 per cent of Labour MPs having the right to call a leadership election is amended as soon as possible. That'll ensure a smooth run for him, at least until after the next general election. I've never known such a fixer.'

Of course, Neil Kinnock's position as leader had never really been under serious threat. He has, until recently, enjoyed the status of darling of the constituencies, favourite of the parliamentary party and, on this issue at least, beneficiary of overwhelming union support, including that of his own union, the mammoth Transport and General Workers' Union. Benn's challenge had always been a non-starter, merely orchestrated, according to Mr Benn at least, as an opportunity to air 'the issues' – in other words, the growing tensions between traditionalist Labour Party policy and modernist/revisionist Labour Party policy. And yet it might have been a very different kettle of block votes had Kinnock been challenged by any one of Messrs Brown, Cook, Gould or Smith, all potential pretenders whom Kinnock had taken pains to get on-side in the early stages of his own campaign. Naturally, the Kinnockites had dismissed the battle as an unwelcome distraction from their real Oppositional task, that of taking on the Tories. But in the putative people's party, a party whose National Executive Committee is elected every year, many of the rank and file still fail to see why the same should not also apply to the leader and his deputy. For egalitarians, by definition, resent the very concept of leadership. Moreover, they pride their purity over any possibility of power. Even if it means forfeiting any hope of seeing 'their own man' at Number 10, they continue to insist that their own internal procedures must be paralysingly, counterproductively democratic. With the stunning exception, that is, of the profoundly dubious system of union block votes . . .

But if Kinnock's victory was virtually assured from the outset, the same could not be said for his deputy, Roy Hattersley. Whilst one challenger, the old left-wing warhorse, Eric Heffer, was never really in with a chance, the prospects of the other contender, John Prescott, seemed increasingly rosy as the campaign progressed. Prescott's hard, straightforward, if never perfectly polished style struck an appealing contrast to essayist Hattersley's seeming sybaritic, sibilant and spluttering softness. Certainly, Roy's well-trumpeted reputation as a *bon viveur* and raconteur laid him wide open to criticism from the Wonderloaf-and-dripping brigade. 'Roy Hattersley's idea of campaigning,' sneered one Prescott supporter, 'is to send back the sweet trolley.'

John Prescott, on the other hand, despite his many physical

similarities to a roadie in a heavy-metal rock group, had gained very positive exposure over the year, particularly during the *Herald of Free Enterprise* disaster, the seamen's dispute, and the *Piper Alpha* tragedy. Sponsored by the National Union of Seamen, he had earlier served his time as a steward aboard passenger liners. On one occasion, he had even served Anthony Eden at table, much to the merriment of the public-school element on the Tory backbenches. 'Hey, Giovanni,' they would shout across the House of Commons chamber, 'another gin and tonic!'

If nothing else, however, Prescott emerged as an honest, hard-working rough diamond, whilst Hattersley's qualifications as an aspiring polymath were exploited to portray him as a less-than-fully-committed political dilettante. At the same time, though hardly yet the ideal *tabula rasa* of which political admen's dreams are made, Prescott's antagonism to the usual PR tricks seems to have been tempered over the years. In his early days, he was one of the few Labour MPs who refused coaching in television and public-speaking techniques, and it showed. He would come across as inarticulate, unclear and hence far less effective than he might otherwise have been. I clearly remember his period as leader of the British Labour Group to the European Assembly, the European Parliament before direct elections. His was always the 'quintuple negatives combined with any old preposition will do' school of argument. The fact that the foreign interpreters found him totally incomprehensible was bad enough. But the admission that we, the English interpreters, were equally in the dark was considered serious indeed. Interpreters from other booths would often request a *cabine blanche*, a suggestion that we might interpret Prescott's English into Queen's English for the benefit of our struggling colleagues. Only then, they argued, would they have the slightest hope of translating it into the other Community languages for the rest of the Assembly. All that, however, is now well over a decade ago. On current performance, Mr Prescott has obviously come a very long way since then.

Not far enough, however, to oust Mr Hattersley, who saw off the challenge quite convincingly with a three-to-one majority. Hattersley, of course, was fortunate to have basked in the warmth of his leader's wholehearted support, and delegates were left in no doubt that Kinnock would have found it well-nigh impossible to work in tandem with Prescott. A vote against Roy, it was implied quite openly from the outset, would be seen as the most damaging snub to Neil. And snubbing Neil, as the nation soon discovered, was to be left to someone else, to the General Secretary of the Transport and General Workers' Union and the Tories' favourite bogey-man, Mr Ron Todd.

The Labour Party has always simultaneously suffered and benefited from its traditional association with the trade union movement. Whilst it continues to benefit financially from the arrangement, it suffers increasingly in the eyes of an electorate well versed in the adage of people who pay fiddlers insisting on calling tunes. The British people still remember the shambolic state of a strike-riven country in 1979, with uncollected rubbish piled high in the streets, their dead left unburied, and appalling little shop stewards on hospital picket lines dictating, on the basis of a CSE in Elastoplast, who should and who should not be admitted into Intensive Care. It is hardly surprising, therefore, that even today the majority of voters continue to baulk at the prospect of a Labour Prime Minister, strings pulled courtesy of a handful of powerful union barons. True, when the Labour leader is in tune with the unions, this relationship may remain happily camouflaged. But when, as often happens, a major disagreement on policy breaks out, it is then that the block votes really hit the fan. As the new-look Labour leadership is beginning to realize, the more visible its links with the unions, the more damaging it is for the party's electoral prospects. For the resultant fall-out of such squabbles is inevitably to Conservative advantage, to the party which, as it never ceases to remind us, was the first to put these union wallahs in their proper place.

Poor Neil Kinnock! There he is with his 'pollsters and admen', his bright Walworth Road backroom boys with their 'sharp suits and cordless phones', trying to drag his party screaming into the 1990s, to make it an *electable* party, trying to convince it that, without power, it can do nothing but dispense impotent sentiments of compassion and solidarity to the 'victims' of apartheid, Thatcherism, etc. Yet try as he may, such laudable efforts are being constantly stymied from every side. And somehow the luckless Kinnock always manages to come off worst. On the one hand, the die-hard traditionalists of the party – the folk who cannot open their mouths without reflecting on the glories of 1945 or their hero, Keir Hardie – all believe that the new-look Labour leader means what he says. They are convinced that he genuinely does intend to modernize the party and, in the process, dump such electoral embarrassments as unilateral nuclear disarmament, wholesale renationalization and, not to put too fine a point on it, *their* ideas of Socialism. Such folk are positively horrified at Kinnock's acceptance of – indeed, conversion to – the concept of free markets. They are poleaxed by his assertion that the Labour Party must prove its ability to run a capitalist society better than the Tories! Mind you, with thousands of pounds of losses accruing in the Labour Party's own marketing section, the comrades need not lose too much sleep worrying about that! Nevertheless, such an eleventh-hour conversion to capitalism, be it never so bland, does not go down well with those who feel that they, and they alone, hold the touchstone of Socialism. The Todds and the Scargills are not likely to sit quietly on the sidelines, idly watching their deeply cherished beliefs and dogmas being swept aside in the interests of mere electoral expediency. Todd's controversial Tribune rally speech, restating his and 'his' union's traditional commitment to unilateralism, was only to have been expected in the circumstances. But coming as it did, a few hours after Neil Kinnock's own triumphant leadership speech, and hardly a day after Todd himself had thrown 'his' union's weight behind the substance of the party's half-finished policy review, it was a positive body blow, and a body blow from which Kinnock will struggle hard to recover before the next general election. For as if the foot-dragging of his own party's die-hards were not sufficient problem, Neil Kinnock is again confronted with a far greater one to deal with. The name of Kinnock's major hurdle now is, quite simply, credibility.

Perhaps, as is his wont, the irrepressible NUM leader, Arthur Scargill managed to put his finger on it first. Nowadays, argued Scargill, the leader of the Labour Party has become virtually indistinguishable in his stated beliefs from the leaders of the SLD and SDP. If Kinnock gets his own way on policy review, the Labour Party, especially with its new-found Euro-fanaticism, will have developed the very policies the Gang of Four once felt obliged to leave the fold in order to pursue. And this is precisely what the hard left so bitterly rejects: a near-as-dammit David Owen-genre Labour Party being gradually thrust upon them. But need Messrs Benn, Heffer, Skinner, Livingstone *et al.* really be so concerned? There is, after all, an obverse to Mr Kinnock's bright, new, trendy Labour Party coinage which should militate in their favour. For the trouble with the average elector is that he is not such a wide-eyed trusting soul as Mr Arthur Scargill. He does not find it easy to believe that a lifelong CND supporter – and, indeed, a man whose wife and mentor is also a lifelong CND supporter – can change his spots overnight. Neither is he overimpressed by Damascan conversions to free markets and economic efficiency. It is just unfortunate for Neil Kinnock's credibility that life is full of cynics. When the nice Mr Gould, one of Kinnock's most right-on, right-hand men, mentions 'social ownership', those of little faith hear warning bells pealing something close to 'nationalization'. And when Mr Kinnock supports a motion calling for 'unilateral, bilateral and multilateral disarmament', those same people all cry 'fudge'. It is to the Labour leader's overwhelming disadvantage that his policies now seem increasingly concocted to mean all things to all men, nothing but designer policies, designed to get the beleaguered Neil into power at any ideological price. And the infamous 'policy review'? It is scheduled to be concluded in time for discussion at the 1989 conference. The question is, will it turn out to be little more than the Turin Shroud of British politics: convincingly presented and eminently capable of fooling the masses, but rumbled, in the end, as just another brilliant con? Or will it, on the contrary, be a clever Trojan Horse, attractive, acceptable, perhaps even electable, but still hiding in its flanks that most unwelcome host of inmates, the vandals of winter 1978–9, the British trade unions.

It is difficult to know what Tory ministers' gag-writers would have done without Ron Todd to liven up their own far drearier conference proceedings. 'All on your Todd.' 'Not on your Todd.' 'We always thought it was Glenys running the Labour Party until we discovered it was Ron Todd.' Gosh, the jokes were almost as funny as Mrs Thatcher's poll-indicated conversion to a new Marvellian shade of Green. But seriously, if there had never been a real Ron Todd, the Tory admen would have been obliged to dream him up. For he has all the hallmarks of a fellow conceived to strike fear and loathing into all true Tory breasts. The General Secretary of Britain's largest trade union, the Transport and General Workers' Union, wielder of a massive 1.25m. block vote at party conferences (despite the fact that 30–40 per cent of his members do not even vote Labour): yes, Ron has plenty of negative public relations potential. And yet the facts of the man are rather less sensational. For Ron Todd is an anachronism in today's Labour Party simply because he is straight, honest and perhaps a trifle naïve. It is some cause for concern that, across the entire political spectrum, such folk went out of fashion along with flared trousers. An enthusiastic amateur palaeontologist, Todd is still painfully rooted in the past. He is proud of his dinosaur credentials, pointing out that the dinosaurs ruled the world for over 200 million years. Unfortunately, as Denis Healey was moved to aver, and as Ron has so far failed to grasp, it was a sudden change in atmosphere which finally killed the poor beasts off.

Nevertheless, as long as Labour purports to be the natural representative of the organized working class, there is no chance of killing off union influence over party policy. Neither would such a move be entirely desirable. For the unions, after all, provide the party with its most direct conduit to the blue-collar masses, to the realities of which the 'sharp suits and the cordless phones' and the trendy, left-wing Chianti-swilling ideologues have little direct experience. But when 92 per cent of votes at conference are cast by the unions, and when those votes come in indivisible blocks from memberships which have often not been balloted for their views, then clearly conference decisions owe little to democracy. In many ways, Ron Todd did Neil Kinnock a favour in bringing the block vote scandal so clearly to the fore. In voting against Kinnock's fudged and mudged disarmament motion, Todd focused everyone's attention on the enormous influence of his 1.25m. block vote. Like some outrageous feudal overlord, the union leader spoke quite unselfconsciously of 'my' vote and 'my' union, and proceeded to exploit both to maintain 'his' and his predecessor's, Frank Cousins's, personal views on unilateralism. Kinnock found himself in a particularly uncomfortable predicament. The same block vote which now so embarrassed him had earlier been used to return him as leader and to support his on-going policy review. Even at his worst moments Kinnock is astute enough to realize that you cannot have it both ways. Yet just when he least needed the aggravation, the union block vote shenanigans have once more become a major political, constitutional and electoral liability. It is time to grasp the nettle. Fortunately for Kinnock, many of the more enlightened union leaders, the John Edmonds and the Gavin Lairds of life, have also understood the stakes. They realize that if the Labour Party is to accede to power in the foreseeable future, it must clean up its own internal act, and fast. If Neil Kinnock manages to put policy-making more into the hands of Labour's rank and file, if he succeeds in implementing a truly democratic system of one-member-one-vote more widely throughout the movement, then he will have achieved no less radical a change in his party than his arch-rival, Mrs Thatcher, has wrought in hers. The question which confounds us all is, 'Is Neil Kinnock up to it?'

Of course, if Kinnock were to succeed, such a move would further undermine the already decimated influence of British unions today. Certainly, despite the majestic card-vote posturing at conference, their self-esteem must currently stand at an all-time low. And yet, only the fading prospect of a Labour victory – perhaps even a victory purchased at the price of union dominance within the party – can restore their slightest hope of renewed significance in national life. They have taken a severe pounding from the Conservative government since 1979, with a drastic loss in legal immunities, not to mention a drop in membership combined with the humiliation of impotence in the face of mass unemployment. Their power is on the wane on all fronts, further exacerbated in late 1988 by the highly publicized schism between the TUC and the forward-looking electricians' union, the EETPU. The nation has been brought to believe that the unions deserve their fate. For this, we have been told, is what happens to organizations who refuse to move with the times, who allow themselves to be overwhelmed by the dinosaur brigade. And yet, even dinosaurs at their most terminally daft never got around to stabbing themselves in the back. To its detriment, sadly, the TUC has never shown any such inhibitions. Its rejection of the government's Employment Training Scheme, in autumn 1988, gave Employment Secretary Fowler an ideal opportunity to weep profuse crocodile tears and immediately set about planning the abolition of the tripartite Training Commission. Well-orchestrated leaks from Whitehall followed. And since the unions were such a curmudgeonly crowd, why not, while the government was at it, remove TUC representatives from the National Economic Development Council, the Equal Opportunities Commission, the Health and Safety Executive and a bunch of other less important quangos besides? Neil Kinnock had warned the TUC of the possible consequences of its decision. And Ron Rodd had duly told him to keep his nose out of TUC matters. A Labour leader who cannot express a political opinion at a TUC conference, and a trade union baron who sits at a party conference and dictates general policy – this is a partnership which has yet to give the impression of a winning combination. Perhaps the mindless yokels chanting at the Conservative Party Conference really have got it right. With that sort of power-split in the major Opposition party, Mrs Thatcher can surely bank on another 'Ten More Years' at least.

Poor Kinnock indeed. Too powerful in the party to resign, too incompetent in the Commons to dominate, and too weak in the country to win, he will just keep rolling along until his next, now almost inevitable election defeat. Nevertheless, despite his growing and, in many quarters, resented dominance over the party today, he still knows that no Labour leader can ever afford to adopt Thatcher-genre smugness. For as if the unions and their leaders were not sufficient millstones around his neck, Neil Kinnock is also kept uncomfortably aware of the 'hard left' electoral liability within the parliamentary party itself. 'Oh, no,' the Walworth Road boys are supposed to have groaned when, in 1987, the unstoppable 'Red' Ken Livingstone was returned for Brent East. 'Another Tory gain!'

And yet, we are constantly advised, such Socialist skeletons in the cupboard represent an ever-dwindling constituency within the Labour movement. Even before the failure of their leadership challenge, the Benns and Heffers were already being neatly – indeed, complacently – written off as 'yesterday's men'. Such blanket dismissals, however, are always very dangerous and perhaps, in this case, even a trifle premature. For there is no shortage of precedents for small and unfashionable cells, characterized by indefatigability and extremism, propagating against all expectations to achieve pre-eminence. Who, for instance, would ever have imagined that the embryonic New Right philosophy being adumbrated by a certain Keith Joseph in the early 1960s would so dominate the political scene of the entire 1980s? The day may still come when, at the other end of the political spectrum, this nation's growing group of have-nots decides that it has had quite enough not-having, when a large and angry underclass begins to see red – and extremely red – again.

It was such thoughts as these that wafted through my mind as I sat watching an ironically relevant performance of *Les Misérables* one evening. That same day, in late October 1988, the government had decided to freeze child welfare benefit for the second year running, effectively allowing it to wither on an already ill-tended vine. Oddly enough, the concept of 'universality', so totally acceptable in arguments in favour of the poll tax, was suddenly quite outrageous when applied to this, the most popular of all benefits. Nigel Lawson, claimed Gordon Brown, Labour's Shadow Chief Secretary to the Treasury, must now count as the first Chancellor in history to have spent £6b. on tax cuts and, in the resultant reductions in public spending and social services, actually succeeded in making the majority of families worse off. With concomitant interest rate and wage increases, not to mention record balance of payments and trade deficits, the image of golden boy Lawson, the senior architect of Thatcher's 1987 success, was starting to look just a wee bit tarnished. For his own, and for the Thatcher government's sake, things would have to start improving very soon. Otherwise, the Chancellor could be finding himself, as Dan Quayle watchers used to put it, 'in real deep yoghurt'.

Certainly, by the end of 1988, the burgeoning British economy was beginning to feel some pressure. But such a flourishing economy, the main theme of the Thatcher success story, has never, according to her detractors, been anything other than an illusion based on North Sea Oil and privatization receipts plus a whisked-up topping of related consumer-boom froth. Home-owners hit by higher mortgages, businessmen made uncompetitive overseas through higher interest rates at home, many such 'typical' Tories began to feel concerned for the first time in years. For all that, Mrs Thatcher and the lads still have until 1992 to try and get things sorted out. And even if they fail, the Conservatives will always have one massive advantage to exploit over their adversaries. Personality-sated though the electorate may be after thirteen years, and indeed, the prospect of a further five years of Mrs Margaret Thatcher, will they be sufficiently bored to gamble on the major alternative?

'The Labour Party,' argued Tony Benn, 'is only electable when the left is strong and represented . . . It is at its most popular when it is at its most Socialist. Witness the setting up of the NHS'. In making his point, Benn, for all his alleged 'yesterday' status, is still the most lucid of Labour MPs. There is little doubt that the revamped Labour Party, currently exuding its new SLD-cum-SDP flavour of the month, is leaving many voters utterly confused. In a party which now seems beset by trimmers, a party which has somehow managed to navigate itself at least half-way across the political spectrum, it is refreshing to witness the stubborn intransigence of a few unrepentant class warriors. There is, however, just one insurmountable problem for these, the thinning ranks of the left's ideologically pure. They must, in order to remain unsullied, stay exactly where they are, in that hopelessly neutered limbo of eternal opposition.

At any Labour Party Conference, fringe meetings abound. Issues as diverse as 'The House of Lords – Who Needs It?' to 'Tabloid Porn' are all given, if not an easy ride, then at least a good airing. The 'hard left' Campaign Group, now operating in virtually self-imposed exile within the Labour Party, hosted many such fringe debates, at least one convened specifically to discuss the problems now facing the left after the great leadership débâcle. It was to be held in the Spanish Hall of the Winter Gardens, a strangely mock-baroque/pseudo-Tudor/loco-rococo venue for such arch-spurners of life's many fripperies and frills. Indeed, it was that very Spanish Hall which was later to be set alight by the virtuoso performance of the notorious el Todd, the greatest matador of them all, and the man who took no time in laying Señor Kinnochio's bull to rest.

I suppose the most impressive characteristic of the participants – many of them women in boilersuits busily bonding babies – is that they genuinely do not care. Oh, these *tricoteuses* of the revolution care about their rather blinkered vision of utopia all right, but not about much else that might crop up along the way there. Concessions to such bourgeois considerations as common civility and normal, relaxed social intercourse are definitely out. To their undying credit, such people cannot be accused of compromise, nor of making their concept of society in any way a meretriciously attractive one. But what sort of society is it that they have on offer, whose grassroots support is surly, antagonistic and motivated by nothing, it would seem, but the politics of hate?

'Waged or unwaged?' demanded the daunting, deadpan woman guarding the plastic spondoolick bucket at the entrance. What a good old capitalist wheeze the organizers had rumbled – the idea of charging everyone, especially the media, for the privilege of coming in. Already the Benn/Heffer supporters had been vocal in their criticisms of the dreaded right-wing press. Neither Tony nor Eric, they argued, had been given proper coverage during the leadership campaign. Mind you, with television cameramen being asked to cough up anything from £50 to £250 to film their Blackpool fringe meetings, such a dearth of interest in the duo was at least partially self-inflicted.

'Waged or unwaged?' repeated our Campaign Groupie impatiently, the inevitable John-Lennon-dig-me-I'm-a-revolutionary spectacles bouncing petulantly on her nose.

Call me reactionary. Call me old-fashioned. But the self-proclaimed custodians of some ill-defined humanity will always fail to convince me so long as they insist on being churlish to the individual human beings they meet. By this stage, the waged–unwaged issue had developed into a clear matter of *feminismo*. I was determined not to answer this woman until she spoke to me, rather than the bottom of her plastic bucket, direct.

'Waged or unwaged?' she heaved emphatically, finally looking up. 'Ugh!' she gasped, taking in the *Mail on Sunday* press accreditation and the Ungaro ensemble disapprovingly. 'Clearly waged. That'll be a pound.'

'Socialism', as Peter Brooke, the Conservative Party Chairman was later to declaim at his gang's jamboree, 'thrives on failure.' Certainly, such 'hard left' nuclei as the Campaign Group appear to flourish by encouraging Nature's underdogs to wallow in the bitterness of their state. 'In politics there is only one absolute,' argued Ms Diane Abbott, Hackney North's black woman MP, at that meeting. 'Power!' It was unfortunate, however, that the overall impression generated on that particular occasion was nothing but the general hopelessness of their quest for success. For the will to win, after all, is essentially an anti-egalitarian pursuit, the very reason why, presumably, they do everything not to embrace it. Indeed, anyone who appears to have gained any advantages at all is *persona* very much *non grata* within their curmudgeonly ranks. It is ironic, but even the figure of the erstwhile Lord Stansgate in their midst fails to remind them of their relatively recent history, where the leader of the most spectacular revolution of all was an out-and-out aristocrat. But no. In this forum, even Robespierre would have been classified as 'waged' and doubtless given the same 'Ugh' class-envy treatment.

Of course, nowadays, the Campaign Group has no monopoly over the ugliness of intolerance. Neither Thatcher nor, increasingly, Kinnock has any time for dissenters within their ranks. With their highly personalized styles of leadership, disagreement with the leader is cleverly cast as outright treachery against the party as a whole. Labour's John Prescott soon paid the price for the 'impudence' of his deputy-leadership challenge, as the high-profile energy portfolio was swiftly removed from his control. On the Conservative side, rebels against the controversial eye and dental charges – an *ad hoc* policy decision never even mentioned in the party manifesto – were horrified at the bully-boy tactics employed by their leader against them. A conscience vote against the charges would be viewed as a vote against the empress herself with all its ugly implications, as Dame Jill Knight and Michael Mates both found to their cost. For not only, on that occasion, were the rebels assured that their own personal career prospects would be effectively strangled, usually sufficient threat in itself to sway the more pusillanimous backbenchers. But even worse, according to Macclesfield's Nicholas Winterton, potential dissenters were also warned that their constituency problems would no longer find a sympathetic ear if they continued their rebellion. It seems ironic that Winterton, a man once sickened by Edward Heath's identically abusive tactics, should have been one of those whose efforts brought the current despot in.

But of all factions, it is arguably those on the 'hard left' who are most damaged by this sort of intolerance, by an overriding bitterness and envy. For wherein lies the attraction of their brand of care and compassion when those qualities fail so obviously to embrace so many? In their company, anyone unfortunate enough not to be a 'minority', to be either unemployed, underprivileged, black, gay, or a one-parent family, is made to feel quite ridiculously uncomfortable. In such a hostile environment, I had only one thing going for me. At least I am a fully paid-up member of that unique 'minority' which constitutes 52 per cent of the British population. How few parties anywhere, including those on the 'hard left', have done much to deserve the support of our massive membership! For whether a country be north or south, east or west; whether a religion be Catholic or Protestant, Hindu, Muslim or Jewish; whether a prevailing ideology be right wing or left wing, Socialist or capitalist; whether a country be rich or poor, developed or third world, the only immutable constant in the political equation is that our 'minority' always manages to come off worst. For we, in fact, are *women*. Of course, at Labour conferences nowadays, there is constant lip-service paid to the bravery of our female forbears, to the glorious suffragettes. And yet, at the time, the same movement was viewed with the greatest suspicion, particularly by those on the left. Indeed, many were quite openly and vehemently opposed to its aims. For the women's fight would only result, or so opponents argued, in returning *right-wing* women to Parliament.

Back at the Campaign Group, however, any embarrassment over inconsistency is reserved for MPs alone. Out among the comrades, Labour MPs feel obliged to writhe in self-abasement for the disgrace of having risen above the rest, for the very fact of having been elected, for having acquired that modicum of kudos which the letters 'MP' are supposed to confer and, not least, for benefiting now from the perks of their Westminster upper tax-bracket job. 'It's a cushy number,' apologized Dennis Skinner MP by way of exordium to his speech. 'It's a bobby's job. Well paid. Provided you vote for the leadership, you're considered sound. You might even end up getting a desk!'

Hard working and as straight as a die, Skinner is one of the few MPs on entirely safe ground. Absolutely nothing to be ashamed of there. Unrestrained by any niggles of conscience, he proceeded to denounce the hypocrites amongst his own parliamentary colleagues, those quislings who had sold their Socialism short and now belonged to nothing, in his opinion, but the 'careerist tendency'. Whatever their claims, thundered Skinner, such MPs were not 'real hard left', they were not doing the job for which they were elected. Why, as soon as they arrived at the Palace of Varieties, their first move was to sortie unashamedly with the despised opposition, to find themselves a 'pair', and to set about organizing a nice easy life for themselves with evenings off. What they ought to be doing, argued the Beast of Bolsover, currently the most astute parliamentary operator in the entire House, was to be hanging around like he did till all hours of the night, ever in the hope of organizing the odd, surprise ambush on an unsuspecting government.

I must admit that I was rather surprised to see Ms Diane Abbott applauding so vigorously. Usually one of the more sartorially chic in Westminster, she appeared for some reason to have dressed down for this occasion. Generally speaking, I have a lot of time for Diane Abbott. Her thoughtful maiden speech on immigration, her reputation as an excellent constituency MP, and her quiet, constructive approach to policing and race relations indicate a degree of soundness belied by her more demagogic public posturing. But in her enthusiastic response to Mr Skinner's rousing rhetoric, she seemed to have forgotten one small detail, the fact that she herself belongs to one of Dennis's contemptible 'pairs'. Even worse. The other half of the pair is one of the Tories' more affluent and glamorous backbenchers, none other than the great nephew of Lord Beaverbrook himself, Mr Jonathan Aitken. What, one cannot help but wonder, would Mr Skinner make of that?

'Don't mourn,' the overwhelmingly defeated Eric Heffer had earlier advised the audience. 'Organize. The left has been down before, but it has always come back.' But even Eric's claims of unbounded stamina were beginning to sound a trifle hollow. There was an odd air of aggressive despair about it all, like an England pre-Test Match team talk after the fifteenth consecutive defeat. Bright and chirpy as usual, Ken Livingstone ignored the shouts of 'traitor' from the floor. What the Labour Party needed, he had argued, was a leader in the mould of Harry Perkins in *A Very British Coup*. I tended to agree with him, however, and contemplated the distinct improvement if such an idea could be extended to embrace the entire British government. Since all ministers ever do is read out scripts prepared by other people, why not go direct to central casting and hire a more professional lot to do the job? How much more palatable, for instance, if we could enjoy the mellifluous tones of John Hurt delivering notice of the next interest rate hike. Even social service cuts could be made to sound attractive if outlined by the inimitable and irresistible Mr Robert Powell. For the really funny stuff, like 'The Conservatives have always been the truly Green Party' sketch, perhaps the help of Messrs Rowan Atkinson and Stephen Fry might be enlisted. And to deal with all those appalling little foreigners in the European Community, Harry 'Stavros' Enfield could be relied upon to create almost as much hysteria as Mrs T. herself.

Those in the Campaign Group, however, perceive no need to change their own current protagonists. Already, they feel, they have acquired the necessary touch. Strolling along the Blackpool promenade one evening that week, Mr Livingstone was recognized by a group of pensioners on a day's outing from London. From the other side of the road, they all shouted and waved. 'Look,' exclaimed 'Red' Ken excitedly to his journalist companion. 'I'm even more popular than the illuminations!'

And yet, as Mr Benn had duly reminded us for the umpteenth time, politics is not about personalities. It is about issues and policies. It was all the more ironic, therefore, that the same Labour Party policy changes, which these radical dissidents dismissed, should be precisely those the Tory critics would winkle out for closer scrutiny. A vote of confidence, the left complained, had just been given to an overweeningly dominant and remote leadership, to a leadership which had stage-managed the conference in true Tory fashion and tried, in the process, to stifle real debate on foreign policy, defence policy and employment policy. Labour's traditional opposition to the European Community had also been reversed without so much as a by-your-leave. Concepts such as wholesale renationalization had been abandoned overnight. Neither, though such policy *lacunae* would exercise the Tory critics less, had any genuine thought been devoted to the sort of problems which the Labour Party, of all parties, ought to be addressing: issues such as black and women's rights. 'Half the young blacks in this country are unemployed,' claimed Ms Abbott, citing an alarming statistic which speaks volumes for the growing racial divide, that increasingly dangerous split which, if it continues untended, will one day make Toxteth seem like the teddy-bears' picnic.

Despite their dislocation from the mainstream, however, the concerns of the Campaign Group did much to pinpoint the current dilemma confronting the Labour Party. How much easier for the 'hard left' if life, as Eric Heffer seems to see it, really were so black and white: the bosses in charge of the means of production versus the down-trodden and exploited workers; the frockcoat-and-silk-topper battalions versus the cloth-cap-and-muffler brigade. But life in the late twentieth century is no longer comprised so simply of haves and have-nots, of people who have always had, and people who will always be have-nots. It also sports a growing class which has recently managed to acquire and is now justifiably petrified of losing it all again. And it is hardly surprising that this new blue-collar society is being weaned away from its traditional Labour Party roots. For this is precisely the category which, thanks to the acceptable face of Thatcherism, is now doing quite well, thank you. It has bought its own council house, acquired its full quota of British Telecom and British Gas shares, enjoys its two weeks' continental holiday per annum and holds, perhaps for the first time ever, its own real 'stake in society'. Such folk, once the mainstay of the Labour Party, are now more likely to belong to that ever-expanding band of radical Tebbitites. They are as alarmed as any true-blue Tory at dirty words like 'renationalization' or even 'social ownership'. Renationalization might have been perfectly fine in the past. But not now that they study their own share portfolios.

To his credit, Kinnock has understood the importance of winning this new type of voter back to the Labour Party. Together with the thrusting ranks of ambitious, young professionals, these categories constitute a new, more heterogeneous and electorally volatile middle class. It is, agreed Kinnock, in his spirited leadership speech, a very affluent middle class at that, but a class living constantly 'in *anxious* affluence'. These are the very people whose fears must be exploited to the full. For although they may be thriving now, warns Kinnock, will their beloved Tory government care for them when illness or unemployment come knocking at the door? The 'super-class', Kinnock realizes, will always be quintessentially Conservative. Just as the 'underclass', the 9 million people on supplementary benefit and the 9 million people on low pay – in short, the 18 million people living in dire poverty – will always be a safe Labour bet. But the king-makers of the future will be the swelling ranks of the anxiously affluent. It is their confidence that the new-look Labour Party is now out to gain.

Of today's party leaders, Neil Kinnock is without doubt the most accomplished orator. Of course, there is no one more competent than Mrs Thatcher in mastering a brief or assimilating the facts. And there is no one to touch her at statistics, the scientific way to bend the truth. But despite the engineered hysteria of Conservative Party Conference ovations, her oratorical style has all the passion, humour and spontaneity of the Talking Clock. Certainly, the Reagan-inspired autocue system which she and her cabinet use on such occasions has one major advantage. It is capable of producing a passable speaker out of the biggest dimwit, though even that is not completely Reagan-proof. When, for example, the erstwhile American President came to address the European Parliament in Strasbourg, his specially imported system failed. Unable to change the habits of a lifetime, Ronnie had, of course, turned up without a single idea actually consigned to his head. Denied his idiot board, and much to the embarrassment of everyone except himself, the President just stood there, grinning inanely, until the device could be fixed. Such breakdowns, mercifully for politicians like Reagan, are few and far between. But whilst the autocue system facilitates a word-perfect delivery, the performance often tends to be of the lacklustre, passive, newsreader type. Kinnock, on the contrary, is capable of generating real emotion. He works himself up into rousing crescendos, trails off compassionately into tales of human tragedy. Margaret Thatcher's society, he claimed in his most stirring oratorical flight, was a society with no number other than one; no time other than now; a 'Me and Now' society. Perhaps Mr Kinnock should have popped his head in at Brighton the following week. For there, the glorious Michael Heseltine, together with that motley crew of major ministers with minor speech defects, would all be at it – desperately trying to impress the faithful of their leadership credentials. Not only has Mrs Thatcher spawned a 'Me/Now' society. She has succeeded in filling her party full of frustrated 'Me/Next' heirs-apparent.

Unfortunately for Kinnock, his performances at the Dispatch Box are far less impressive than his speeches. In these snappy exchanges, where short, sharp jabs are of the essence, the same rehearsals of repetitions of reiterations, the very oratorical tricks which add *gravitas* to a thirty-minute speech, swiftly deteriorate into redundant verbiage and waffle. The Prime Minister's has always been the steam-roller as opposed to the rapier school of argument. But unfortunately for the Labour leader, he has always allowed his response to be guided by his worst, Welsh, macho, rugger tactics. He attacks the Prime Minister head on, trading fact for fact, statistic for statistic, the very front on which she is most impregnable. Indeed, such an approach invariably allows the Prime Minister to quash him with one of her only two jokes: (a) the Right Honourable Gentleman does not seem to be completely in charge of his facts; or (b) of course, the matter is far too complicated for the Right Honourable Gentleman ever to understand. More dated even than *Morecambe and Wise* repeats, these old chestnuts still never fail to produce an accommodating response from the tittering tiers of Tories. For such jibes are the very stuff of knock-about life in the Commons, important to keep the troops amused at the twice-weekly workers' playtime.

It is one of the Commons more intriguing phenomena. But however important a politician's television image today, it is still essential to be able to perform well on the floor of the House. High-flyer turned DC-10, John Moore, saw his reputation and prospects reduced to tatters after one miserable performance at the Dispatch Box in early 1988. And the morale of the Parliamentary Labour Party is similarly deflated by Kinnock's bi-weekly humiliations at the Prime Minister's merciless hands. How much sprightlier was the PLP step when Neil went off to the front-line states and left Roy Hattersley in charge. The old *Punch* essayist had Mrs Thatcher on the ropes a dozen times at least, cleverly exploiting her Achilles' heel, a vulnerability to mockery. 'The Prime Minister,' Hattersley was moved to assert on one occasion, mischievously filching a leaf from Mrs Thatcher's own book, 'does not seem to be completely in charge of her facts.' The Prime Minister, if no one else, was glad to see Neil Kinnock safely home.

But even if, against all odds, the Labour leader managed to turn the tables in the Commons, he would still have the Herculean task of regaining a majority in the country. Robin Cook, one of the brightest and the best, refuses to deceive himself with specious talk of Labour's next electoral victory. Along with the Austin Mitchells, the Jack Cunninghams and the Jeff Rookers – along, in other words, with the realist wing of the Labour Party – he too is beginning to realize that electoral reform is the only way of ending the Tories' disproportionate advantage in the House. In this, of course, they are all out of line with, or rather, streets ahead of mainstream Labour thinking. For neither the overwhelming majority of Labour nor, of course, the Conservatives have ever supported a change in the status quo. Both sides still prefer the outright majority which our first-past-the-post system generally tends to deliver. With the outstanding exception of Mr Arthur Scargill, even a majority of the left within the Labour movement are unwilling to contemplate any change in the current set-up. For their day, the believers in the 'pendulum of political change' theory continue to argue, is bound to come again. And when it does, they too, like Mrs Thatcher before them, will need a fail-safe parliamentary majority to push their radical package through.

But the pendulum, it would appear, has now finally snapped. The system which could once be relied upon to provide alternating yet strong government has now disappeared for ever. With at least 57 per cent of the voting population against her, Mrs Thatcher has nevertheless achieved a virtually unassailable position. And she is using – or, her critics would claim, *abusing* – the idiosyncrasies of our electoral system to consolidate that position even further. Her government (note, nowadays, how folk say 'Mrs Thatcher's government' and not 'Her Majesty's government'), claims the Prime Minister, has given us *less* government not *more*. But what it has given us in reality, is fewer alternative *loci* of power and a more centralized government than ever. Since 1979, nearly all the necessary checks and balances on elected government have been gradually undermined. The trade unions have been flattened. Tripartite fora have been axed. Local government has had its teeth pulled. Once-great municipal authorities are degenerating into mere management companies. Putatively independent organizations such as the BBC and the IBA have gradually seen their governing bodies filled with people who can be counted on to act as 'one of us'. Universities have been deliberately starved of cash. The mechanisms which guaranteed tolerance, restraint, dialogue and government by general consensus have nearly all gone. The very safeguards which meant that we, as a nation, never before felt the need for a Bill of Rights or a written constitution, all those guarantees of freedom and fairness have been stealthily whittled away. 'We have been turned into a society,' argued John Mortimer, he of *Rumpole of the Bailey* renown, 'where the freedom to make a million on the Stock Exchange has become more important than the freedom of speech.'

Unlike most barristers, perhaps Mortimer's mistake is that he tends to overestimate his fellow-man. Forget the million on the Stock Exchange. The people's price is nowhere near as high. Rather, we have been turned into a society where the freedom to ingest a daily diet of bonking and bimbos has become far more important than any desire for informed public debate. But Mortimer had been moved to speak out during an extraordinary week in late 1988, a week which had witnessed the Home Secretary's attempts to ban direct broadcasting of extremist groups in Northern Ireland. Such access to the media, Mrs Thatcher has long felt, provides the supporters of terrorists and assassins with the 'oxygen of publicity'. An overwhelming body of opinion, however, takes quite the opposite view. Whenever bus-loads of young soldiers are blown up by the IRA, whenever families of innocent by-standers are mistakenly mown down, whenever such obscenities occur is precisely the time to *demand*, never mind ban, an interview with a spokesman from Sinn Fein. For that is precisely the opportunity to expose the IRA ideology for what it truly is: a bankrupt philosophy based on nothing but malevolence and hate. On such occasions, apologists such as Gerry Adams do not bask in the oxygen of publicity. On the contrary, they are made to inhale the toxic fumes of the IRA's putrid policy of mindless violence and destruction. Why on earth does anyone suppose the IRA have not yet 'silenced' the Reverend Ian Paisley? For the simple reason that whenever that man opens his bigoted mouth, it is worth a hundred converts to their cause and another million dollars in the IRA coffers. Refusing free speech to legal political organizations such as Sinn Fein will not spike one IRA gun, nor prevent one IRA bomb. It will merely allow the supporters of the men of violence to escape live cross-examination with impunity. What a great advance in the war against terrorism! And what a sad indictment of the strength of our democracy, the fact that our government should now believe proscription rather than argument is the answer to all evil.

Almost simultaneously, the suspect's right to silence, traditionally an inalienable right under British Law, had also been withdrawn. And along with that, argued Mortimer eloquently, the presumption of innocence, that most crucial cornerstone of our entire legal system. Designed to convict more IRA terrorists, it was a policy decision, like most policy decisions nowadays, based exclusively on Mrs Thatcher's gut reactions. But in the process, a basic human right enjoyed by all for centuries has suddenly disappeared. You might as well say, for the sake of argument, that this country is just as full of rapists as it is of IRA terrorists. The logical conclusion, by analogy, would be to castrate the nation's entire male population! The summary withdrawal of time-honoured rights is now an increasingly alarming phenomenon. Where, I cannot help wondering, will it all end?

But our country is so besotted with Mammon that a few 'minor' losses of freedom simply go through on the nod. Whatever conciliatory platitudes our poor dummy of a Home Secretary is wound up to rehearse, it is a society becoming daily more secretive and anti-democratic. By the time the new Official Secrets Act becomes law, for instance, the information that 30,000 phones are currently being tapped in this country without Parliament's knowledge or approval could net its herald a good two years in the slammer. Serious investigative journalism, another necessary check on the excesses of government, will be progressively stifled. It is odd but, over the past year or so – certainly since I have been engaged on his book – I have started to notice an extraordinary change in my own attitudes. I have never been what anyone would call a congenital rebel. Indeed, I have always thought of myself as conservative with a small 'c', with a vague penchant for the Gilmour style of politics. I have fervently admired the fortitude of a Prime Minister who has tried to change an entire nation's attitudes and has managed to salvage its economy from the brink of disaster. Whatever her critics may say, such achievements should never be underestimated. Neither shall I forget the lessons of my interpreting days at Council of Ministers meetings in Brussels during the 1970s. They were times when the signal for everyone to repair to the bar for a swift tincture of the necessary was precisely whenever a British minister took the floor. Britain was simultaneously the sick man and the laughing-stock of Europe. Mrs Thatcher, to her undying credit, has succeeded in changing all that. But the less acceptable face of the Prime Minister's success is now making itself visible. Mrs Thatcher's avowed intention of continuing for a fourth term is a source of concern, even to some of her most ardent supporters. She cannot leave, or so she argues, until she has found a worthy successor, some bright light under the dismal Tory bushel for whom she is 'always on the look-out'. It is all quite alarming, really. For if, as the Prime Minister's statement seems to indicate, her cabinet colleagues are such a pile of hapless dross, then what on earth are such no-hopers doing in the cabinet at all? Such conclusions are hardly designed to imbue the country with confidence in the government of the day. Neither can they be particularly encouraging for the senior ministers of that government whom they so openly disparage. The college of second-class vegetables now has only one hope of revenge. Such hubris, they can only hope, must surely tempt the gods.

But with our winner-takes-all electoral system, the empress will almost certainly be allowed to carry on unchecked. Only a fairer representation of the population's wishes, argue proponents of electoral reform, can stop the Thatcher juggernaut now. How different the political picture would have looked, for instance, if a system of proportional representation had been in operation for the 1987 election. The Conservatives, with 43 per cent of the vote, would have had their current 375 seats in the House of Commons slashed to 279. Labour, with 31.5 per cent of the vote, would have suffered slightly with a 202-seat haul instead of 229. But the

Alliance, with 23 per cent of the vote, would have gained an amazing 149 seats instead of their miserable twenty-two. No overall Conservative majority there. And no justification for spurious Tory claims to 'an overwhelming mandate from the British people'. Strong government, as in circumstances such as those of 1979, may be precisely what a country needs. But without the necessary constraint of strong opposition, such a form of government can swiftly degenerate into something far less acceptable. More than ever, with the disappearance of our traditional curbs and restraints, we need an electoral system capable of reflecting the strength of that majority opposition adequately. Since the pendulum, sadly, can no longer be relied upon to swing, alternative methods for arresting the excesses of unrepresentative, one-party dominance must be sought. Perhaps it is even time for the much maligned system of proportional representation to be taken out of the cupboard, dusted down, and looked at afresh. For proportional representation need not necessarily result in fragmented governmental chaos *à la* Israeli. Countries such as Australia, Sweden, Austria and Spain have even managed majority government on the basis of the system. Elsewhere, proportional representation has at least allowed minorities (e.g. Greens or blacks) and even badly organized majorities (e.g. women) to choose more precisely the persons and the policies they wish to represent their views. At this stage, however, even the Labour leadership is too proud and too short-sighted to recognize the need for change. They may soon be forced to see the error of their ways. Thanks to population shifts, as Labour's Jeff Rooker has calculated, the Boundary Review Report to be delivered around 1993 will mean a *loss* for Labour of between twenty and thirty seats, and a commensurate seat gain for the Conservatives: in other words, a further forty-to-sixty seat differential between the two major parties. And all this without a single extra vote being cast for the Tories.

Already, among the realist left, there is talk of organizing a broad-based, anti-Thatcher coalition, though quite how this hotchpotch coalition would operate after victory is anybody's guess. Nevertheless, even if Messrs Kinnock and Hattersley refuse to see the writing on the wall, the realists see such a deal as the only possible way of breaking the Thatcherite monopoly. In Chile, it was just such a consensus among the opposition parties which succeeded in ousting the redoubtable General Pinochet. Luckily for Mrs Thatcher, however, such a triumph for compromise is currently inconceivable among the left of this country. But as the Prime Minister moves inexorably on, perhaps even into her fifth term of office (who knows?), this is one fundamental debate which is bound to gain momentum. For once, both Opposition and cabinet pretenders stand united in the question: How do we get her out?

# 7 | Brighton flock

♫ *HERE WE GO – HERE WE GO – HERE WE GO* ♫

Imagine, if you will, a frenzied crowd of people, some – the lager lout element – still coming round from the intemperances of a heavy session the previous night. All individual identity has suddenly been lost, subsumed into the corporate animal which has taken on a life of its own, behaves as no one part of the sum total would ever dream of behaving. Totemic Union Jacks are vigorously waved, symbols to confused intellects that the hyperbole of herd hysteria somehow equals patriotism. From the belly of the beast, the mindless chanting gradually gathers momentum, relentless, meaningless, yet comfortingly hypnotic and swells to its chorus.

'Ten more years,' they wail in catatonic unison. 'Ten more years.'

'Heysel?' you may well ask, or, just conceivably, 'Chelsea?'

No. The scene is Brighton, and the mob, the Conservative Party faithful. How proud the Prime Minister, like Millwall FC, must be, to know she has such unquestioning supporters so staunchly on her side!

But all in all, this final episode was a fitting climax to a week of almost Kafkaesque surreality. The unprecedented £1.5m. security operation had tried the patience of the good burghers of Brighton, yea, even unto breaking-point. After the IRA bombing of the Grand Hotel some four years beforehand, no preventive stone had this time been left unturned. For days preceding the conference, the town had been positively crawling with policemen, specially bussed in from the regions for the added advantage of accent. A clever ploy, designed to confuse the enemy, it ensured that none of them could give directions which anyone would ever really understand. In the bay, grey and threatening, sat a minesweeper brooding darkly on the horizon. Every moment of every day, we were made painfully aware, the government was operating under the most terrible of threats. Indeed, we were apprised, our entire nation was under attack from the very worst of all the foes of Thatcherism: a Socialist, a Frenchman and, more pernicious still a *genuine* intellectual. Yes, at least the minesweeper would stop the dreaded Jacques Delors, President of the European Commission, from making an unsolicited landing on our beaches. For already this Euro bogey-man had made his initial incursion into our green and pleasant land, rabble-rousing to resounding effect at the TUC conference earlier in the season. What with dangerous talk of Europe's 'social dimension', and treacherous assertions about workers' and guaranteed social rights, Delors was clearly the sort of trouble-maker all good Tories could do without. Invasions of continental thinking would make few inroads among the Little Englanders of Brighton.

Up above, the sound of a couple of helicopters droned interminably on, like an Edwina Currie health lecture, only slightly more instructive. For months beforehand, the media and constituency 'representatives' had been filling out their forms, gaining the necessary security clearance and eventually the cherished conference pass. A triangular security 'fortress' had duly been established, embracing the Grand and Metropole hotels together with the conference centre itself. Access to the fortress was a biblical pursuit, owing much to the concept of camels negotiating a passage through eyes of needles. Never, since the hey-day of the Wigmore Club, had so many been groped and massaged so thoroughly at such exorbitant unit cost. State-of-the-art technology was in evidence everywhere. One poor fellow even had his placatory box of chocolates ripped unmercifully apart. The silver foil on the raspberry and caramel whirls, it appeared, kept tripping the alarm. How distressing it was to witness the de luxe, super-gourmet, executive selection swiftly reduced to a promiscuous heap of Woolie's Pick 'n' Mix!

No, security at a party conference had never been so tight. Hotel residents were even ordered to advise reception of their every expected visitor. 'How many people will be staying in your room?' one check-in question ran, the answer to which more optimistic punters would carefully leave a blank. Yes, old habits still die hard at the Tory Party Conference. Not even the joint spectre of AIDS and terrorism could usher the New Morality in.

It was therefore all the more surprising when, on the second evening, an unexpected knock shook the very lintels of my door. Of course, I assumed immediately, it would have to be the chambermaid, her mission to place an unwanted After Eight mint tenderly on my pillow. I often wonder who was first responsible for this disgusting nocturnal practice. How often, all over the world, have I tumbled exhausted into bed, only to wake up the following morning with a melted wodge of dark chocolate smeared all down the Janet Reger!

But instead, the fellow towering there outside the door was a frightening sight indeed. With a swollen, broken nose and two big black eyes semi-hidden by shades, you'd have had to conclude that here was a refugee from the Mafia or – at the very least – a Kray twin. Or possibly an escapee from a late-night rendezvous with Mike Tyson in the Lanes. From behind the bluey-bruised features, however, this desperate-looking hoodlum began to look familiar. Why, it was none other than the Edmonds other half himself, face recently remodelled during a charity cricket match courtesy of Mr Graham Roope!

So much, then, for the £1.5m. security cordon. The dear boy, looking every inch a villain, had simply rocked into the hotel, slipping in unheeded through a door marked Exit.

'Which room is Mrs Edmonds in?' he had asked the ultra-accommodating receptionist.

'Room 409,' she had replied. 'Take the first lift on your left.'

How fitfully I slept that night under my artificial duck-down duvet, not entirely happy in the knowledge that my visitor might have been a hit-man from the Test and County Cricket Board. But as it was, the poor mangled Philippe-Henri was there to bring glad tidings of great joy. For it had been confirmed that very day that the first Edmonds minor was on the way. Immediately, I felt quite astonishingly relieved. It was not, after all, the bobbing waves of blue rinse that had been making me feel sick.

But the week, stage-managed to hallelujah perfection by evangelist Billy Graham's erstwhile *metteur en scène*, was to provide few such surprises. The conference platform itself, a symphony of blues, was heavily engulfed in rows of washed-out-looking creepers. But there were plenty of others too, apart from the cabinet. Some ministers even had their long-suffering wives up there on show, looks ranging from the desperately ambitious, doting dormouse (Elspeth Howe), to the happily horsey (most of the rest), with few gradations in between. Or all the speakers, however, only Mr Cecil Parkinson, he of the infinite smarm, saw fit to thank the missus. Perhaps the Energy Secretary, on reflection, has more to be grateful for than most.

Punctured into either side of the celestial backcloth, two eye-like apertures appeared to survey proceedings closely, their lenses designed to carry closed-circuit TV coverage of the star performers in the show. The overall effect, however, was more disturbing in its implications. 'Make no mistake,' that lidless gaze seemed tacitly to be warning. 'Big Sister is watching you.'

Elsewhere in the conference centre, the enterprise culture was busily plying its trade. Conservative Party Products by Blue Rosette were doing roaring business at Ye Compleately Redundante Gifte Shoppe. Now, I have yet to meet the person so desperate that an 'exclusive cuckoobird' Conservative Party egg-cosy at £1.75 is going to make his day. But such unhappy individuals clearly do exist. For the more affluent, however – those just sloshing around in cash since Nigel's top tax cuts – perhaps something a little more 'tasteful' might be more in order? A Wedgwood-lookalike bust of the Prime Minister herself, for instance, an indispensable addition to the lares and penates of any Finchley semi's mantelshelf. Besides, as the Blue Rosette director cajoles in one Conservative Central Office publication, everyone really should be lending their support to this value-for-money, fund-raising initiative.

'By so doing,' runs the message, 'you are helping the Conservative Party to develop it's [sic] work throughout the country.' Perhaps Mr Kenneth Baker's great educational reforms, so hot on reading, 'riting, 'rithmetic and times-tables off by heart, might also include a few tips on the neuter possessive pronoun for the benefit of his party's own HQ!

Like the Houses of Parliament themselves, the place was swarming with lobbyists for every conceivable issue. Some would be organizing cocktail parties. Other would be inviting MPs – a few genuine 'opinion-formers', but mostly just useful lobby-fodder – to expensive lunches and dinners. All would be expecting a certain return on their money, an ultimate quid pro quo. For when stripped of its PR blarney, the theory behind much professional lobbying is little, in effect, but mutual back-scratching. Some might even say corruption. For industries and interest groups who want either to see or to stop legislative changes will spend hundreds of thousands of pounds on these mushrooming consultancies to promulgate their views. Much of this, of course, is money completely wasted, insufficiently 'targeted' to achieve its end. For on most issues, other than those few moral questions on which a free vote is allowed, MPs' support or hostility is already pre-ordained. The relentless efficiency of the party Whip system sees to that. More astute lobbyists might do better to ignore MPs altogether, and to try instead to get the odd top civil servant on their side.

Nevertheless, the proliferation of PR and lobbying outfits is becoming an increasingly worrying phenomenon. Of course, no one is seriously suggesting that in our Parliament, a forum reserved exclusively for people of impeccable moral rectitude, anything untoward could possibly happen. For in this country, unlike in every other country under the sun, no one could ever imagine an MP's support being bought for a few dinners at the Savoy Grill Room, or a couple of all-expenses-paid trips abroad. Whilst in the United States, drug companies spend billions ensuring that their pharmaceutical products are viewed sympathetically by the relevant governmental authorities, we all know that nothing similar could ever happen here, could it? The same goes for the armaments industry, where multimillion-pound defence contracts are often at stake. Thank goodness no leading light in our Defence Select

Committee could ever be nobbled into espousing the cause of one manufacturer as opposed to another.

However, the sad day may well come when folk of more malleable disposition grace the benches of Westminster. It will be a time when, thanks to the vast resources behind these professional lobbying organizations, our entire legislative process will become effectively privatized, when the industries and pressure groups with most money will stand most chance of ensuring that their wishes prevail. Already, in this country, we are witnessing a similar degeneration in genuine policy debate. For why should any government bother trying to convince the population of the irrefutable logic of its arguments, when it can bamboozle them instead with a multimillion-pound publicity campaign? This Conservative government is now second only to the giant multinational Unilever in its public relations spending. The Education Department alone has increased its advertising budget by a massive 3,000 per cent over the last eight years! Surely, it is high time some neutral ombudsman monitored how much of this expenditure is devoted to objective public information, and how much to more or less subliminal party political propaganda. Lobbying activities, similarly, should come under much closer scrutiny in the future. For who knows when the odd MP or 600 might be led into irresistible temptation?

Of the more legitimate lobbyists, Mr Trevor Clay, General Secretary of the Royal College of Nursing, was ubiquitously in evidence. His college's no-strike record during the nurses' extended pay dispute of 1988 had earned the nurses increased affection and support from an already sympathetic public. But the new Health Secretary, Kenneth Clarke, refused stubbornly throughout the conference to give him a hearing, a decision which did much to undermine Mr Clarke's position in my previously well-disposed view. Yes, I have to admit it. I used to be quite a fan of Kenneth Clarke. But bitter and disillusioned by the aftermath of his divisive nurses' regrading exercise, he seems to have become less sympathetic – like Thomas Hobbes's definition of man's condition simply 'nasty, brutish and short'.

At the BUPA stand in the conference foyer, the indefatigable Edwina was passed as A1 fit. Less impressive, after four weeks on the conference razzle, a leading Sunday broadsheet correspondent was advised to write his copy as soon as possible and to consult a solicitor about his will. Elsewhere in the coffee queue, a large Tory lady was proclaiming that she too, along with the Prime Minister, had always been a Green. Indeed, she had escaped for the day from behind her St George's Hill privet-hedge and, if called upon, would inform the entire conference of the fact.

'We've always been "proper Greens" around there, you know,' she bellowed. 'And we're a growing band of believers.'

Did she think, I ventured the question, that with PR the Greens might even manage to win a few seats in the House of Commons?

'PR?' she mulled the idea over carefully for a minute. 'Yes,' she conceded finally. 'So long as Saatchi and Saatchi are employed as the firm.'

Could all Tory ladies, I wondered, looking at her, be as thick as their ankles?

Outside the entrance of the Grand Hotel, another Tory doyenne was being interviewed for television. Was she, the interviewer asked, 'an active citizen'? This was the new conference buzz concept dreamt up, allegedly, by Home Minister John Patten over a cosy cup of tea with the PM. A Reaganite idea, embracing successful Home Watch schemes in the USA, it had originally been dismissed by the British government as excessively patronizing. Since then, it has developed into the leitmotif of third-term Thatcherism as the practice of excessive patronizing has become the Prime Minister's special style. Yes, replied the lady emphatically, she most certainly was an active citizen. Why, every time she looked out of the window and saw the Pony Club trotting home unchaperoned, she would ring up the local police station and tell them to send an escort round immediately. Golly gosh! How stressful and fraught life must be for the active citizens of deepest Thelwell country.

The conference hall itself was chock-a-block with active citizens, all actively intolerant of anyone who dared mutter the slightest word of disagreement. Unfortunately, this prerogative, reserved for Mr Edward Heath alone, was unexpectedly usurped by Labour councillor, Mrs Patricia Hawkes, the Worshipful Mayor of Brighton, in her official welcoming address. The poor lady could hardly have been described as over the top in her comments. She exhorted the conference to enjoy the opulent façades of Brighton. At the same time, she suggested, representatives might care to consider the struggling pensioners and bedsit-land folk living in less fortunate circumstances beyond. It was hardly the sort of stuff of which revolution is made, yet the effect was instant. You'd have thought she was suggesting something perfectly outrageous – constructive dialogue with Monsieur Jacques Delors, for instance, or a cabinet job for Heath. The party faithful – people who, but a minute before, had been straining the vocal cords on hymns proclaiming glory and peace, smiling at all foes, and 'Streams of living waters/Springing from eternal love' – started to boo and hiss in a perfectly unecumenical fashion. It was odious, distasteful and made a complete mockery of the opening religious service. Clearly, the active citizens of 'Sion's city' do not welcome talk of the poor.

Seated next to me was a hanging-and-flogging QC, cheeks ruddily suffused with the tell-tale signs of boozer's spidernaevi. Somehow, in the space of three minutes, he had managed to invite me, a perfect stranger, to the Ian Smith Monday Club lecture, a Scottish whisky distillers' cocktail party, dinner that evening and Thursday night's Conference Ball. I declined all four suggestions on instinctive 'dirty old man' intuition. Heaven forfend, I mused, that such a creature should ever be appointed to the judiciary. For this was just the type to give a multiple rapist two weeks' suspended sentence, ('These women nowadays are always looking for it'), and ten years to a pensioner caught shop-lifting in Tesco's ('Such abject behaviour undermines the very fabric of our society'). From red to violet, to positively purple, his face changed through every colour of the spectrum as the mayor ploughed through her piece. 'Shame!' he shouted angrily. 'Shame!' His apoplectic features would have made a classic H. M. Bateman study, perhaps along the lines of 'The man who saw a lady opening her Filofax in the Garrick.' I escaped his impending coronary and attentions before the farming debate began.

Of course, with few exceptions, the Conservative Party Conference is a symphony of harmony and light. Rarely do the perfectly stage-managed proceedings deteriorate into anything even vaguely analogous to real debate. Just occasionally, however, self-back-patting motions such as 'This conference congratulates the government on its handling of the economy' will meet with one vehement opponent. We all hold our breath, as this lone, unrepentant Christian throws himself to the party lions. No, the young martyr will argue, thinking of future candidates' lists to be compiled at Central Office. He, for one, could not possibly accept such a motion. He has tried in his heart and soul, but no, he just cannot find it in himself to agree. Instead, throwing caution to the winds, he would beg to move another, bravely contentious motion: 'This conference congratulates the best government that this country – indeed, *any* country – has ever had, led by the best and most beloved woman, apart from Esther Rantzen, that this country has ever known, and continues to marvel at its unbelievably inspired – indeed, *sponditious* – handling of an unprecedented booming and brilliant economy.'

It is of such things, at the Tory Party Conference, that disagreement is usually made.

Up on the platform also, the illusion of unity has to be preserved at all costs. As with royal marriages clearly on the rocks, affectionate supporters still want to see appearances maintained whatever the personal cost. The strain of the Tories' hypocritical humbug was in stark contrast to Labour's cathartic conference. For if nothing else, at least Blackpool showed that stabbing in the back was no longer official Labour Party policy. Policy nowadays, as reworked by Ron Todd himself, is simply stabbing the leader in the front. But open recrimination plays no part in Conservative Party philosophy. Former chairman, Norman Tebbit, and his wife, Margaret (tragically paralysed after the Brighton bombing), were both welcomed to the platform with a standing ovation from the floor. The platform itself, on the contrary, was awash with conflicting emotions. For what was the point in pretending that Tebbit's recent book, *Upwardly Mobile*, had not caused absolute furore among certain members of the Tory hierarchy? For starters, it had reopened the wound of the Parkinson/Keays affair, something for which the even more upwardly mobile Parkinson might have been forgiven for cheerfully strangling the author. But Cecil – lips, as usual, quivering tremulously, ('Never trust a man with a weak mouth,' my dear mother used to tell me) – put on his bravest face. He recalled the happy Tebbit/Parkinson days, operating together in the Hemel Hempstead Conservative Association. The gesture was kind. The words were generous. But who will ever know what Cecil *really* had in mind?

The most spectacular kiss and make-up performance had been staged the previous day. As everybody knows, Norman Tebbit and Trade and Industry Secretary, Lord Young, have long loved each other as brothers: Cain and Abel-type brothers. For it was Lord Young whom the Prime Minister had brought in over Chairman Tebbit's head when the 1987 election campaign seemed to be going wrong. Young, so the rumours ran, would be seen entering Chequers secretly by the back door whilst the beleaguered Tebbit, having received his statutory earful, would be leaving disconsolately by the front. Neither did Mrs Thatcher make any secret of her desire to see the darling David in the position of Party Chairman, an idea then scotched by Lord Whitelaw in his infinite sagacity. So it was hardly surprising to see the few conference non-believers cringing visibly as Lord Young heaped praise on the 'architect of the 1987 election success', on the very man whose authority he had done so much to undermine! For all the veneer of polite urbanity, the Tories are a deceptively vicious crowd. Not so very long ago, Tebbit and the Prime Minister's Press Secretary, Bernard Ingham, could be counted on – to use a Healeyism – as Mrs Thatcher's 'hired assassins'. What exquisite irony, finally, for hired assassin Tebbit: to belong to a party so democratic that even the assassins get done in.

Of course, the conference is much poorer for want of its two star speaking attractions, Tebbit and Heseltine. Heseltine in particular, the Tory Party's answer to Charlton Heston without the toupee, was always the conference's most glamorous draw. For he, of all members of the cabinet, knew how to refresh the parts that other ministers dare not reach. 'Michael,' sighs one veteran conference watcher nostalgically. 'Ah, yes, Michael somehow found the clitoris of the Conservative Party.' Judging by the drooling masses of Tory shire matrons, collapsed ecstatic in the aisles, such a discovery was clearly just an annual event. The maestro would then sit down, bathed in sweat from his exertions, positively reeking of masculinity: a man's man; a woman's man; in fact, just about everybody's man. I watched his now-sidelined performance at a Tory Reform Group fringe meeting, as he called for increased public spending to improve the general quality of life. He was polished, professional, passionate even. But if practice makes perfect, then so he should be.

Denied the high-profile platform of a cabinet minister, he is currently wooing the support of all conceivable nonentity Conservative MPs by agreeing to speak in their far-flung constituencies. For unlike the Labour Party, as Heseltine knows, any leadership battle in the Tory Party is decided by MPs' votes alone. Heseltine's efforts during the wilderness years have made him an increasingly strong outside contender. Certainly, the pin-up boy of conference would be a popular choice with the rank and file. Myself, I never fully trust a politician who works so hard to create an image.

One evening, at a cocktail party, Michael Heseltine joined the group of guests with whom my husband was involved. The same day, as it happened, England had won a stunning Test Match victory. (Yes, it was as long ago as that.)

'Are you interested in cricket?' Phil asked Heseltine, trying amiably to draw the newcomer into the group's chosen topic of conversation.

'Not at all,' replied Heseltine rather sniffily. 'Are you interested in trees?' And with that he walked off.

Phil thought no more about it until about half an hour later. Having spoken to the assembled cricket-mad politicos, the man's man had realized he'd made the most terrible PR gaffe. For Tarzan, of all people, could not be seen so contemptuously to dismiss the nation's glorious summer game. It might be better, suggested Heseltine, sidling up to Edmonds with a totally disarming smile, if his deprecating comments were never mentioned again. Phil found the whole damage-limitation exercise hugely amusing. To him, it was merely another sign of our media-dominated times, a salutory lesson for our more inflated MPs. For whoever he is and be he never so glamorous, there was never a politician born to compete with the aura of a sportsman.

But Michael Heseltine was by no means the only pretender busily trying to convince the faithful of his leadership credentials. Everywhere, the ravening 'Me/Next' hoards were all too clearly in evidence. For the Conservative Party Conference has always been an ideal opportunity for cabinet ministers to overshoot the confines of their specific briefs, and to prove their wit and adversarial skills at an absent Opposition's expense. At the same time, it is imperative for such weighty contenders to convey their cosmic grasp of the wider issues at stake. And yet for all their laudable efforts that week, and despite the indiscriminate shoals of sycophantic applause which greeted them, most of the gods on offer were distinctly uninspiring. Indeed, for the first afternoon's transport, trade and industry and defence debates, the bars in the foyer had to be closed. It was the only way to force an unwilling and largely uninterested congregation back into the hall.

Of all the heirs-apparent, however, Social Security Secretary and yesterday's blue-eyed boy, John Moore, was without doubt the saddest casualty of the show. Despite assertions that, with funding of £50b., his was the largest budget in government, spending more than the Defence, Education and Energy departments put together, his personal stature is no longer commensurate with the amounts he claims to disburse. Naturally, the news that work-shirkers, cheats and fraudsters were in for a harder time went down extremely well. So did the revelation that people want self-reliance, independence, and personal responsibility – good news, indeed, particularly for the mentally handicapped. So did his rhetorical musing on whether the glorious prospect of a council flat and unearned income might be coutributing to the increase in pregnancies amongst unmarried teenagers. Perhaps this phenomenon was far better left unmentioned, for, if anything, such personal tragedies are merely a further, damaging index of the hopelessness of today's growing underclass. For what must be the aspirations, horizons and hopes of any young woman, who, in high moral ground parlance, is prepared to 'wreck her life' for the corner of a council high-rise block?

Despite mouthing all the right clichés to a heavily biased audience, Moore's saturnine contribution failed to rate the usual tumultuous standing ovation, a very bad sign indeed. At a Conservative Party Conference, even the floral arrangements come in for standing ovations. But the Secretary of State's delivery was that of a man in trouble, lacking in confidence and disturbingly wooden. Every day, his resemblance to the hapless Dan Quayle is becoming increasingly striking. The physical similarity has always been apparent. But latterly his actual performances have taken on the same forlorn edge. Unsure of himself, he now skids around, as one commentator put it, 'just like Bambi on ice'. How cruel the game of politics is: to think that only a year before, the same Mr John Moore was being tipped as Mrs Thatcher's most likely successor. But whatever his destiny, at least it will be kinder than that of the hopelessly inadequate Vice-President Quayle. For if anything happens to President Bush, they say, the security services are under orders to shoot poor Dan at once.

But the new, long-term 'man most likely to' was barely to be seen at all in the conference hall. The anonymous John Major, Chief Secretary to the Treasury, spent most of the week immured in his room, successfully conciliating the financial demands of all the various Secretaries of State. The son of a sometime circus performer, Mr Major is clearly the ideal man for dealing with clowns. Indeed, so effective were his efforts, that there was no subsequent need to convene the Star Chamber, the ultimate arbitration body to be chaired by Cecil Parkinson. No doubt this pleased the Chief Secretary's boss, Nigel Lawson, as much as it did Mr Major himself. For it is no secret that the Prime Minister would like to see the cherished and far more pliable Parkinson ensconced at Number 11. With the no-knee-bending Nigel out of the way, and with the favoured economist, Sir Alan Walters, back in the kitchen cabinet, her title of First Lord of the Treasury would then become a working reality. If nothing else, at least Major's triumph deprived Cecil of this particular opportunity to shine. But even more important for his own long-term prospects, it earned him the respect of those colleagues still more impressed by ability than smarm, and by effectiveness than flash.

Talking of smarm and flash, the Energy Secretary's contribution was of necessity full of both. British Coal too, he trumpeted, was now on the next Parliament's privatization agenda, a grandiose revelation designed to hit the headlines. By way of revelation, this 'historic pledge' had one distinct disadvantage. It had already been made before Parliament's summer recess. Privatization is a good thing, continued Parkinson, because it has enabled consumer choice. His little cheeks, like two soon-to-be-privatized blast furnaces, glowed red with radical enthusiasm. To our cabinet ministers' eternal credit, they all appear to have developed a highly sensitive switch-off-shame-and-reality-function. For at the very moment of Cecil's triumphant declamation, our newly privatized

British Gas was being found guilty by the Monopolies and Mergers Commission of a jolly cocktail of misconduct – discriminatory pricing, abuse of monopoly positions – and it did not look to most of us like a very good thing at all! Up and down the country, industries totally dependent on British Gas for their energy supplies were being unmercifully exploited and forced to pay exorbitant rates. Overnight, many had lost their competitive edge over their European trading partners.

And *this*, we are expected to believe, is *choice*! *This*, we are told to swallow, is *progress*! What arrant nonsense! Without the necessary adjunct of competition, the very factor in the privatization equation which is so often conspicuously missing, all the government has done is to replace *public* monopoly with *private* monopoly, the worst of all conceivable worlds. For instead of serving the interests of the consumer, such organizations merely serve the interests of an extremely limited group of shareholders. The customer is the last person to be considered. Just ask anyone who has had dealings with British Telecom of late. But why should any such operation give two hoots about customers' rights, when the poor old customer has nowhere else to go? And even that is not the worst of it. Privatization fever, serious at the moment, may soon turn out to be terminal. I, for instance, have yet to meet the person who does not believe that the privatization of our water supply will not be highly deleterious to the health of the nation. For how many health and safety corners will private suppliers feel obliged to cut in order to make an attractive profit for potential shareholders? And which of these operators, in the long term, will continue to cough up the billions needed in investment to restore our many dangerously antiquated sewers? For the good of us all, basic public utilities should remain precisely that: public. Over the years, Mrs Thatcher has been allowed to sell off the family silver. There is no doubt that it has made her housekeeping books look good. But who is going to stop her now, before she sells the family home as well?

Like the nation's assets, fossil fuels, argued Cecil, are all being wasted away. This is why, he concluded, we need more nuclear power, a resource without which the terrible Arthur Scargill would have beaten the government in 1985. It was therefore all the more surprising when, barely a week later, it was announced that

Britain's £25m.' research programme into the generation of energy from nuclear fusion (so-called 'clean' nuclear energy) would be virtually ended by 1992, an exhibition of short-termism astounding even by politicians' own inimitable standards. Few people seemed interested in the decision or, indeed, even aware of it. But I had good reason to be more specifically concerned. Since 1976, I have interpreted at meetings of the Joint European Torus (JET) international fusion project at Culham in Oxfordshire. Like any research undertaking, it has had its ups and downs. But in the main it has been a fascinating endeavour, embracing fourteen participating nations happy to pool their scientific and technological resources to one end: to obtain energy by forcing hydrogen atoms together – by 'fusing' their nuclei. The technique involves the heating of hydrogen to temperatures equivalent to that of the sun's surface, about 100 million degrees centigrade, and the most obvious problem is constructing a device (the Torus) capable of withstanding such temperatures and containing the resultant plasma. Now, I have never been one to get overexcited about white-hot technological revolutions, rolling back the frontiers of science, or constructing banisters on the stairway of life. Instead, during the twelve years I have worked at JET, I too have been known to wonder about the prospects of an organization which, whilst enthused by the challenge of a workable Torus, has never actually managed to make the ladies' lavatories flush. Nevertheless, although the technology of fusion has proved expensive and difficult, the scientists at Culham are now making momentous breakthroughs, one of the most significant, ironically, occurring during the Conservative Party Conference. There is no point pretending that nuclear fusion, as indeed every other form of energy, does not have its own inherent problems. But the beauty of nuclear fusion, above all others, is its cheap, freely available and unlimited supply of raw material: sea water. Considering the amounts of money involved compared to the enormous potential of the project, the government's decision to axe the research programme has failed egregiously to square with its new Green-*cum*-nuclear philosophy.

'Others talk, we do,' claimed Parkinson, slavishly echoing his mistress's voice – the Prime Ministerial one, that is.

Try telling that now, Cecil, to the UK Atomic Energy Authority!

The figure of Parkinson himself is only intriguing so far as it raises fundamental question-marks over the soundness of Mrs Thatcher's judgement of male horseflesh. It is odd that the leader of the high moral ground party, impervious on most fronts, should be so taken with his type. But perhaps, ironically, Parkinson is all the more the apple of the Prime Ministerial eye precisely *because* of his vacillating misbehaviour in the past. For as the Prime Minister is well aware, without her personal patronage the Energy Secretary has no constituency whatsoever within the party. He could never mount a serious leadership challenge to her authority. Similarly, Lord Young, the other court favourite, can pose no threat to her from the House of Lords. Other cabinet colleagues, each in his own way on the political make, must always be seen as opponents, and thus viewed with the deepest suspicion. Inexorably, as in Wilsonian days, a Thatcher kitchen cabinet has emerged which precludes all such potential vipers from its bosom. Such a trusted band of intimates wields more influence over the Prime Minister than the cabinet itself. With its confidants and cronies, its friends and advisers, this system owes nothing to the precepts of elected representation. Not for nothing has Charles Powell, Mrs Thatcher's brilliant Private Secretary and high-flying Foreign Office co-optee, been dubbed the 'Deputy-Prime Minister' by disregarded and disgruntled Tory MPs. It is little wonder that some of the Prime Minister's much snubbed cabinet colleagues have begun, now quite obviously, to chafe at the bit.

'If you are interested in cricket,' said Roy Hattersley on one occasion, 'then you should take care never to meet the cricketers.' I have news for the likable Lucullus of the Labour Party. Precisely the same precept also goes for politics. What a bitter disappointment the majority of our lacklusture leading politicians are. For precisely who, in effect, do we appear to be saddled with? We have a Defence Secretary (George Younger) who looks incapable of fighting his way out of a wet paper bag. We have an Energy Secretary (Cecil Parkinson) whose best-documented energies have been devoted to hammering the bedsprings. We have a Transport Secretary (Paul Channon) whose department thinks it a welcome sign of prosperity that traffic in the capital has virtually ground to a halt. We have a Foreign Secretary (Sir Geoffrey Howe) who is capable of addressing foreigners fluently in any language so long as it is English. We have a Health Secretary (Kenneth Clarke) who is an overweight smoker. We have a Home Secretary (Douglas Hurd) whose chairs don't always appear to be there. And we have an Environment Secretary (Nicholas Ridley) whose passion for the environment extends about as far as the preservation of his own Cotswolds back yard. So why, oh why, I wonder, do we have to have an Education Secretary with cultural and intellectual pretensions. Not that Mr Kenneth Baker has not done all the right things to enhance his credibility in this department. An anthology of poetry is a pleasantly effortless way of ensuring that a little of other people's collated genius may rub vicariously off on you. But I'm sorry. I still persist in the belief that a real intellectual is someone who reads Russian literature in the original and quietly assimilates the message. A pseudo-intellectual, on the contrary, is someone who reads Russian literature *in translation*, for goodness sake, and is proud to broadcast the fact. Our Education Secretary, I'm afraid to say, is of this second class of citizen.

Not that Mr Baker is ever likely to be rumbled by today's Conservative Party. If he sticks to simple concepts like reading, 'riting, 'rithmetic, times-tables off by heart, and Mister Men are good for you, then his stock should continue to remain high. Indeed, at three-to-one during the party conference, the Education Secretary was lying odds-on favourite as the Prime Minister's most likely 'short-term' successor. His advisers had duly been to work on him, trying to inject the man with a little more passion, to make him sound 'altogether more Heseltine'. The results of their endeavours, sadly, were none too promising. Rather stiffly, he wound one arm round one way and then the other one round the other, and generally looked like an ataxic traffic policeman in the throes of a sudden attack. Of course, it is difficult to generate mass hysteria with assaults on the state of the nation's spelling and punctuation. Far more rousing instead were Mr Baker's educational prescriptions for parents in the home. Children, he waxed, should be taught that it is wrong to lie, steal, cheat and bully. Obviously, his cabinet minister's 'switch-off-shame-and-reality' function had been flicked to overtime mode. For here is the government of Westland telling our children not to lie! This is the government which whips its recalcitrant backbenchers into submission over the poll tax, the Official Secrets Act, and eye and dental charges, now urging our children not to bully! Yes, and this is the same government which pumps public money into industries about to be hived off to the private sector busily exhorting our children not to steal or cheat! Well, children, are you listening carefully? I know it's difficult for you to understand. But lying, stealing, cheating and bullying, these are all games only politicians are allowed to play. And right and wrong? Yes, children. Of course you must learn to tell the difference. But perhaps one day, if you fail to cut the mustard in a respectable profession, you too may end up as a Member of Parliament. And then, of course, you must forget it all again.

But the core curriculum; tests for youngsters at the ages of seven, eleven, fourteen and sixteen, daily acts of collective Christian worship in schools; and so-called 'topping-up' loans for students – none of these issues, delivered Baker-style, was ever likely to set the conference ablaze. Certainly, watching the odds-on leadership contender, it was easy to understand how the Prime Minister can afford to feel so smug. Nevertheless, Mrs Thatcher herself has proved how an Education Secretary, and not even a conspicuously successful one at that, can succeed in making it right to the top. True, Lady Luck combined with her own Machiavellian machinations have ensured that she is now perceived as she wants to be perceived: on her own terms, as the only possible person to lead the party into the 1990s. 'Who else is there?' you hear the party faithful cry. And perhaps they are right. Nevertheless, it is worth thinking back to 1975, to the days when, for a lark, the Tory grandees thought they might give the filly a run. For that was a time when no one in his right mind would have given odds of 1,000–1 against this redoubtable warhouse battling on so far. At three-to-one on, if he turns out to be a stayer, perhaps Mister Education Secretary Man is still in there with a chance.

The health debate was a far more enthusiastic affair. A large woman, dressed in a fuchsia barrage balloon, came to the rostrum and informed us loudly that she was what they called 'a health watchdog'. She proved it by baring her teeth. How true Mr Baker's afternoon lecture on general ignorance would subsequently ring. For what better example could there possibly have been than this?

Health authorities, argued the balloon, were irresponsible spendthrifts, their constant whingeing ever ringing in her ears: 'We're like Oliver,' she shrilled, scratching around in the paucity of her Dickens for a suitable analogy. 'We want more.'

Let us hope that the benefits of Mr Baker's great education reforms may at least be visited on this lady's children. Then they, unlike their mother, may understand why Oliver asked for more: for the very simple reason that he was starving to begin with. Or perhaps the watchdog's imagery was just more apposite than it knew.

Of course, as everybody at the Conservative Party Conference will readily agree, we are lucky to have the best nurses and doctors in the entire world. With that traditional exercise in lip-service duly performed, everyone then feels wonderfully free to start slagging the medical profession off. Barely had two minutes elapsed before the usual jibes about golf-playing absentee consultants started up with gusto. It made me see quite red. For whilst I cannot answer for the situation in the more affluent Home Counties, I suspect that few Northern or Midlands inner-city consultants are proud to boast a single-figure handicap. Nurses, naturally, are sacrosanct. Publicly, at least, not even the Conservative lady watchdogs dare have a go at them. For nurses are angels of mercy which is why, as celestial beings, they are above such sordid considerations as a decent living wage and the idea of fighting to achieve it. But sadly, I noticed, no balloon saw fit to address the issue of junior hospital doctors, a prime example of NHS waste and extravagance if ever there was one. What with contracts of ninety-six hours maximum per week, the first forty hours paid at the correct rate, thereafter at one-third of that rate, making for an average of £1.20p per hour; with weekends on call stretching from 9a.m. on Friday to 5p.m. on Monday with no break, no recuperation, no holiday in lieu and effectively more hours worked in a weekend than most people work in a week; with all this and not even the prospect of a golf-playing consultancy job to accede to when you're fifty, it really is astounding that, like Oliver, these greedy wastrels have not also been after more!

The health service, I have no doubt, is awash with redundant administrators. They are the result of successive governments' stupid, ill-targeted, interventionist schemes. Even when Keith Joseph, that most radical of reformers, tried to rationalize the service, all he did, in the end, was to add an extra tier of bureaucracy to the system. Now, I dislike bureaucrats as much as Mrs Thatcher affects to dislike them. For, as everybody knows, when medical bureaucrats are told to make cuts, they will happily cut nurses' and doctors' jobs, essential services, hospital beds – anything and everything – but there is one thing they will never cut: themselves. Nowadays, the government is even offering top administrators huge cash incentives to 'keep within certain financial limits'. Keeping within the limits, that is the gospel for today. So just forget about the quality or the availability of patient care. If you want to get your bonus, just remember to keep within the limits. It is insane. A National Health Service worthy of the name cannot be run like a production line nor even a grocer's shop. Let the watchdogs weed out inefficiency by all means. Let them give the administrators a tough run for their money. But when it comes to deciding cuts in the service, let us all remember one fundamental principle. There was never a patient admitted to Intensive Care who asked to see a desk-man.

But the Health Secretary had what at least looked like good news to offer that week. The government, he claimed, would deliver the nursing profession's new pay and career structures *exactly as promised* the previous April. And the reason for this sudden surge of munificence? Let nobody think it had anything to do with naughty, striking unions like NUPE and COHSE, nor with the indefatigable stirring of Labour's Robin Cook, that 'bearded agitator who refuses to pay his community charge'. No, it was all down to the fact that this Conservative government genuinely does *care* about the Health Service. Let no one even suspect that anything else was involved, especially not opinion polls indicating national alarm over the state of the NHS. Arguments over the nurses' pay settlement, however, would still continue well into the winter, the often unfair and arbitrary regrading exercise causing much dissatisfaction. At the same time, justifiably cynical observers refused to be overwhelmed by promises of a £2b. injection into the NHS. On further scrutiny, the figure was found to include health authorities' land sales, income-generating schemes and efficiency savings, not to mention

£300m. to be plundered from a raid on employers' contributions to the NHS pension scheme – hardly the 'new money' from the Treasury it was all cracked up to be. But the real tragedy of the NHS is that no amount of money now can effectively stop the rot. You cannot plant a shrub, stubbornly refuse to water it for ten years and then imagine that a quick shot of Baby Bio will bring it sprouting back to life. Morale in the NHS is currently so low that it will take years of nurturing and naturing to revive it once more. All over the country, excellent and dedicated nurses have already left the service in droves, attracted by higher salaries in other, less demanding professions. Overworked and frustrated junior doctors are contemplating more lucrative and fulfilling careers in Canada, the United States, Australia – anywhere but here. Restoring confidence is an uphill task. As the polls are still showing, perhaps even a trifle unfairly, people no longer trust this government to follow its avowed road to the end.

The economy debate, by contrast, was less stridently triumphal than usual. With rises in inflation and wages, plus an unprecedented trade deficit, some of the faithful were even beginning to think the unthinkable. Was the gilt on Nigel Lawson's copious gingerbread finally starting to tarnish? For all that, I must still admit to a strange soft spot for the Chancellor of the Exchequer. In a sea of mediocre men, there are few senior politicians whose ability releases them from the need to court personal popularity amongst their party colleagues. Nigel Lawson is one such man. He seems genuinely not to care. He has even been prepared to risk open confrontation with the Prime Minister herself, confident in the knowledge that it was his stewardship of the economy which won her the last general election. Besides, there is something quite appealing about the one man in the cabinet who, on occasion, has actually mustered the guts to tell the boss to shut up. Mrs Thatcher and her government need more of Nigel Lawson and his ilk.

The Chancellor of the Exchequer is not a naturally brilliant speaker, though over the years he has gained greatly in confidence. He is often accused of arrogance, which is probably fair comment. But at least, unlike so many of his colleagues, it is arrogance based on high intelligence. I studied him throughout his Budget Speech in March 1988. Looking hot and expressionless but increasingly user-friendly, he reminded me of an overworked cash dispenser on a Saturday afternoon as, in short, sharp little rat-a-tat bursts, he generously returned to us the money that was always ours to start with. Despite the problems looming on his personal horizon, his performance at the party conference was equally self-assured. He had, after all, weathered the worst Stock Market crash since 1929, whilst simultaneously managing to balance the budget and continue repayments on the national debt. Higher interest rates, he argued, would teach those reprobate consumer boomers a salutary lesson in financial self-restraint. Besides, he continued, such rates were a welcome development for those many people dependent on savings: pensioners, for instance. No doubt, if the Chancellor's subsequent on-the-record/off-the-record/did-imply-it/didn't-imply-it remarks on senior citizen 'targeting' are to be believed, such increased savings may even result in a nice little drop in their pensions for them. It must be edifying, in old age, to be so charitably unshackled from the grasp of the dependency culture!

But Nigel's message was full of other good news. In the decade of Conservative government, he observed, the United Kingdom had moved from one of the highest taxed of major countries to one of the lowest. And, promised the Chancellor, meeting one of Labour's repeated criticisms full on, tax cuts would not be reversed. Well, I for one was very pleased to hear it. For, unlike so many people, I have never queried either the wisdom or morality of Mr Lawson's decision to cut top tax rates from 60p to 40p in the pound. On the contrary, I have always wondered why, with the increasing paucity and decreasing quality of public services on offer, we are currently expected to pay any income tax at all! Why, since we've come so far, shouldn't the Thatcherite revolution now be allowed to reach its logical conclusion? Why shouldn't government simply be encouraged to get off people's backs completely? If social welfare is to be left ever more to the nation's charitable instincts, then why not every other budgetary item also? An annual Wogan-fronted *Budgethon* could then be introduced as a far more democratic way of deciding the country's spending priorities. 'OK, then. All of you who want to pledge money for a government nuclear defence policy, please ring this number now ... And here we have a very generous offer, just come in. It's from a Mr K. Clarke of SW1 ... he has just promised all his worldly goods if a certain Ms E. Currie can be bound, gagged and kept totally *incomunicada* from now until Christmas. Wonderful. Just keep those pledges rolling in. And now then, all those of you who would like to fund a National Health Service ... And those of you who feel like picking up the champagne and caviar bill for the British embassy in Paris ... And anyone who wants to contribute to the Duchess of York's royal tour to Australia ...'

Yes, I could not agree with Mrs Thatcher more. I too am all in favour of giving people the 'freedom' to choose.

But of course, giving people the freedom to choose rarely produces the results that governments want to see. A quick straw poll, subversively slotted into the law and order debate by a young up-and-coming 'hang'em high' type, demonstrated overwhelming conference support for the reintroduction of capital punishment. Conversant with the general level of discussion in that lofty forum, Arthur Balfour once averred that he would rather take advice from his valet than from a Conservative Party Conference. Quite clearly, things have changed very little since Arthur Balfour's day. No longer, however, is it the apoplectic shire colonels or sexually repressed village curates screaming for physical retribution. Today, the hangers and floggers come from the inner-city areas of Liverpool and Glasgow, their thirst for vengeance from the darker side of Islamic fundamentalism. These are people whose influence on party thinking is not to be taken lightly. In future, only prospective candidates with 'sound' views on capital and corporal punishment should be selected, it was argued. Furthermore, those sitting MPs who disagreed with hanging should not be allowed to vote against a referendum on the issue. The final nails in the coffin of MPs' so-called independence are now being hammered home fast.

But with solutions ranging from hanging to tagging, with all the many and varied remedies in between, there was little convincing analysis of the roots of society's evil. 'Respect for the law begins at home,' resounded the oft-reiterated cliché, an interesting reflection on the domestic scene of the two cabinet ministers with daughters guilty of hard-drug abuse. Of course, there is never any real defence for crime of any sort. Whilst an environment of poverty and despair may explain the current epidemic of some fifteen-year-old children's delinquent behaviour, it can never completely excuse it. And yet it is naïve for any government to pretend that crime is simply a matter of good and evil, and to act as if vastly disparate social conditions have nothing to do with the problem. An honest government must accept the consequences of the society it creates.

The Home Secretary, a closet liberal who looks increasingly as if he is working from autocue even when he isn't, somehow managed to escape his ordeal intact. The conference did not even boo him. Cleverly, Douglas Hurd skated over the hanging issue, satisfying blue-rinse blood-lust with a welcome philippic on violent crime and 'waywardly lenient sentences'. Swiftly, he moved on to more banal topics, knives and alcohol, the very weapons and analgesic of life itself at Westminster. And neatly he rounded off with a clarion-call for 'responsible citizenship – the heart of the Conservative tradition', as if, by definition, only Labour, SDP, SLD and SNP voters were ever likely to be villains. I cannot explain why I always feel so sorry for Douglas Hurd. But it may be that, with his wiry, grey hair, his lugubrious demeanour and his unconvincing lines clearly concocted by Someone Else, he is starting to remind me of my other childhood hero, Harry Corbett's puppet Sweep.

Thus deprived of their statutory whipping-boy, the more rabid elements of the faithful were only too delighted when their former leader, Ted Heath, took the floor to speak on Europe. It was, as anticipated, the answer of the man who took Britain into Europe to the woman who, but weeks before in Bruges, had brought the scale of that commitment into serious doubt. As Heath's speeches go, it was one of Ted's more veiled criticisms of the Prime Minister. And yet, all the law and order 'respect for others' wash looked spurious indeed, as the roughneck element of today's Conservative Party made the nation's lager louts look sympathetic by comparison. What a pitiful state of affairs it is, when the party of so-called 'responsible citizens' cannot even find the common courtesy to listen to its own ex-Prime Minister without hissing, jeering and trying to interrupt. Heath, it was later claimed by Tory anti-marketeer, Jonathan Aitken, was 'a misguided voice' who had 'misjudged the mood of the conference'. Try as I might, I still cannot think of a higher accolade to bestow on any speaker at a Conservative Party beano.

Ted Heath, of course, does suffer from one major problem. He is a man imbued with the sort of idealism which has long since been forgotten in the Tory Party. Mrs Thatcher, naturally, was nowhere to be seen for the duration of his speech, a useful history lesson which exploded some of the myths and misinformation which anti-marketeers promulgate so merrily. How often do we hear, from Mrs Thatcher amongst others, about the dangers of our country being ruled by hoards of faceless bureaucrats in Brussels? And yet the truth of the matter, as Heath took pains to point out, is that the Commission in Brussels takes no decisions whatsoever. It merely makes proposals which are discussed, accepted or rejected by the Council of Ministers, a body in which British ministers, together with the ministers of the other eleven Community countries, are all represented. Of course, civil servants everywhere are adept at framing legislation which appears to preclude certain options whilst openly advocating others. There was never a clever Permanent Secretary born who could not 'predispose' the majority of ministers' thinking on any given issue. How else, for Heaven sake, would the average politician come by an idea to start with? And yet, despite the posturing of so many of our tin-pot emperors who still seem to think they have their clothes, it is bureaucracies everywhere which form the real power behind any throne. Of all, perhaps this is the silliest misapprehension under which Westminster's anti-marketeers continue to labour. For it is precisely those MPs who worry so feverishly about the influence of Brussels bureaucrats who still believe that it is they in their House of Commons hide-out, and not the mandarins of Whitehall, who call the policy shots in this country. Such naïveté might be touching if it were not merely misplaced self-importance.

There is another useful myth which anti-marketeers love to spin for the xenophobic element of British society: it is the very *vastness* of the bureaucracy in Brussels. And yet, as Heath explained, despite the barracking of those simply not interested in the facts, the Brussels Commission has a staff of 9,100 civil servants to deal with twelve countries and 320 million people. It is obliged to operate in nine official languages. In Edinburgh, by comparison, there are 11,900 civil servants dealing with one country, Scotland, and 5.5 million people. It just helps to put those tales of Brusselian 'vastness' in proper perspective. But the yobbo element of the conference simply did not want to understand. They did not want to know that European countries, operating in concert through the European Coal and Steel Community, have succeeded in making European steel the most efficient in the world. They did not want to believe that the United Kingdom is afforded far more status as part of a supranational European partnership than as a second-rate, forelock-tugging satellite of the USA. They did not want to hear that Mrs Thatcher's misgivings will not slow other European countries down, that they will simply forge ahead without us. Three times before in Europe – over the Coal and Steel Community, the Economic Community and the European Monetary System – the British have managed to absent themselves from crucial, embryonic, and policy-forming periods. In all, over twenty years of formative influence have been lost, thanks to Little Englanders' short-sighted chauvinism. The myopic must not be allowed to lead us into the same mistakes again.

But oh, how the Thatcher zealots howled at Heath. 'No to Ted!' their pre-orchestrated posters ran. 'No! No! No!' they shouted as he explained the inexorable consequences of the Single European Act, consequences which the Prime Minister herself has rather belatedly understood and now refuses to accept. But dare one make so bold as to suggest a degree of inconsistency in the leaderene's current Euro-behaviour? For the Single European Act, after all, was a piece of legislation *forced* through the Commons, *guillotined* through Parliament by Mrs Thatcher's government itself. But what did the hoodlums care about such minor technicalities. 'No! No! No!' they shouted to Ted's European vision, their impotent rage like that of miscreants sent down for long-term sentences. Old Ted, to his credit, remained aloof and unperturbed, positively statesmanlike in his stance. Let the anti-European hooligans holler, he seemed to imply. *Il est trop tard.* For it is *their* heroine who has enacted the very legislation which will make Ted's dream come true. And there is no point in anyone's whingeing about it now, except to complain (*plus ça change . . .*) that the British public was never properly informed at the time. Now the Euro-horse has bolted. And *les jeux sont faits.*

On a less political, more personal note, this somewhat spiteful exhibition of anti-Heathism spoke volumes for the vagaries of the collective Conservative psyche. For unlike Labour supporters, the average Tory's allegiance is focused heavily on the party leader, an index, no doubt, of that well-rehearsed Conservative monopoly on respect for authority and discipline. But allegiance to a figure-head, ironically, precludes eternal loyalty to any specific individual. Of necessity, the object of the party's adulation changes simultaneously with its leader. 'Two weeks after Heath went,' claimed one Conservative backbencher of many years' standing, 'you were hard pressed to find a Heathite in the party, or at least one who'd own up to the fact. And mark my words: a fortnight after Margaret goes, you'll be just as pushed to find a Thatcherite.' No doubt the Prime Minister, in her wisdom, took due note of the tenor of her predecessor's reception.

It was left to the natural diplomacy of the Foreign Secretary to smooth over the divisons. The conference organizers did not want the vulgarity of dissension spoiling the party's great unity display. A much underrated conciliator, Sir Geoffrey Howe found himself charting a very perilous course, somewhere between the Scylla of Thatcher's minimalist, free-trade-area Europe, and the Charybdis of Heath's all-out European integration. To his credit, the Foreign Secretary navigated his passage with distinction, though his position to this day remains as intriguing as invidious. For of the two visions of Europe on offer, it is the Heathite version which Sir Geoffrey and his Foreign Office boys would far more readily espouse, an interesting conundrum for them all, especially when the boss is on the rampage in places such as Bruges. Perhaps, after all, the Emperor Napoleon was right. Perhaps we are a nation of shopkeepers, led now by the mercilessly mercantile vision of that profession's most influential daughter. But unfortunately for Mrs Thatcher, the majority of Europeans see their future in less restrictive, less purely monetary terms. True, the Prime Minister's outburst in Bruges was influenced by Jacques Delors's rather hyperbolic assertion that 80 per cent of the Community's social and economic policies would shortly be decided in Brussels. Mrs Thatcher's vehement reaction, under the circumstances, was only to have been expected. Nor, in my view, was she wrong to demonstrate that Britain would always be prepared to fight for its national interests when resolving the substance of such legislation. At the same time, however, it is becoming increasingly obvious that British interests are not necessarily coterminous with the interests of Mrs Thatcher's government, that radical cabal where dogma and not common sense increasingly rules the roost.

But what, precisely, were the heinous Euro-suggestions that had so ruffled the Prime Ministerial feathers? Surely legislation to ensure minimum wages and fair treatment for part-time workers, female workers and guest workers cannot be so utterly obnoxious? And surely there is nothing so disgraceful in proposing that such employees should benefit from pension and employment rights as well? Perhaps the anti-worker pendulum has swung just a little too far in this country since 1979. Perhaps it is high time to concede some fair and equitable adjustments. Besides, with the centre-right majority currently prevailing in Europe, there is really no cause for Mrs Thatcher's alarm over the Community's future ideological prospects. Is there any real need to worry about a Community which, since its inception, has been vilified by its critics as nothing more than a charter for capitalists? No, despite the Prime Minister's near-hysterical protestations to the contrary, there is little danger of the dreaded bogey-man of Socialism returning overnight through her British back door. Certainly, it is useful for the purposes of her tabloid-targeted rhetoric that the current President of the Commission should indeed be both French and a Socialist to boot. But Herr Martin Bangemann, West Germany's ex-Economic Minister turned Commissioner and Mrs Thatcher's preferred candidate for the presidency, is after all a Liberal. And the West German Liberals, though closer to Mrs Thatcher from an economic point of view, are without doubt the most ferociously federalist Europeans of them all!

But the real motive for Mrs Thatcher's renewed Euro-offensive cannot be pinned on Jacques Delors's assertions alone. Her underlying antagonism has two quite different and far more fundamental roots. First, the Prime Minister dislikes any organization run by foreigners unless, of course, those foreigners happen to be American. Americans, in Mrs Thatcher's book, are quite different. Americans can do no wrong. Just ask their neighbours in Central and Latin America. And, secondly, Mrs Thatcher cannot understand a Community whose decisions and policies are based on that odd, old-fashioned concept of *consensus* – an archaism she personally expunged from the British political lexicon almost a decade ago. Herein lies the real reason for the PM's noisy exhibitions of British individuality, those well-publicized eruptions which are always followed, incidentally, by quiet periods of acquiescence in which Euro-legislation wends its inexorable, Tory-whipped way through the Houses of Parliament and on to the statute book. The tragedy for Mrs Thatcher, despite the undeniable kudos of her long-term service, is that she has missed her greatest opportunity to sparkle in an international firmament. That destiny never lay, as she still mistakenly believes, in her chosen second-string role as the American millionaire President's favourite Little Orphan Annie. Her true international prestige was always tied up with the far more inspirational and influential figure she might have been, had she ever cared to take the lead in a strong, united and economically first-rate Europe.

But such thoughts, in Brighton, were as remote as Nicholas Ridley. With the smell of her carefully applied greasepaint and the roar of her undiscriminating crowd, there was no one to touch the Conservatives' Number 1 performer as she moved centre-stage for a truly theatrical climax. The understudies' hopes were quickly dashed along with the *diva*'s immediate proclamation that 'We are all too young to put our feet up.' Poor darlings, waiting impatiently in the wings, they knew only too well what that meant. Yes, what her lines lacked in scansion, they made up for in thrust. How she played the part of elder statesperson to consummate perfection! The voice, interrupted every stanza by an irritating little cough, was pitched precisely right for the occasion. Somewhere between Fenella Fielding and the Archbishop of Canterbury, it amalgamated the breathily sexy and the resonantly sanctimonious so artfully into one.

The gag-writers ('The Labour leopard cannot change its spots – even if it dreams of a blue rinse'), should not have bothered. Humour, unfortunately, is just not the *diva*'s genre. She is best left to weave the spell of her own highly personalized brand of magic. To witness it, it is, indeed, an incredible performance. For the sleight-of-hand is so sure and swift that no one ever knows how the trick has been done. How is it, for example, that everything good, decent and admirable in our society becomes, with a wave of the

Thatcher wand, so exclusively Conservative? Prosperity, argued the *diva*, answering one repeated Labour criticism, has not created a selfish society but, on the contrary, an extremely generous one. Witness the fact that we are now giving more to charities than ever before. True enough. But the clever ploy is the PM's tacit implication that such benefactors are indubitably all Conservative. Next, the concept of patriotism is similarly hijacked. And yet no amount of Tory Union Jack waving will ever convince me that Labour, SDP, SLD, etc., supporters are not equally patriotic. Then, with a fleeting abracadabra, the concern for law and order becomes a Conservative monopoly too. And so it is that, gradually, imperceptibly, the grand illusion is created. Only the mean and the treacherous, we feel, only the traitors and the criminals could ever fail to vote for Maggie.

Bewitching though all this was, however, it failed to rank in the premier league of Prime Ministerial feats of wizardry. Leading up to the *pièce de résistance*, for example, came the great 'Environment' act, a daring performance of which Houdini himself would have been justifiably proud. Amazingly, a government which has consistently blocked European anti-pollution legislation, managed to wriggle free from the shackles of this incontrovertible fact, to proclaim, with the greatest of fanfares, that the 'Environment has *always* been a Conservative issue.' For sheer *chutzpah*, it was a breathtaking exhibition, though more sceptical members of the audience somehow spotted the flaw. In order to protect the environment from the effects of fossil fuels, the PM had stated, we now must rely more on the safe use of nuclear energy. 'Ah-ha,' chorused the few non-believers, this sudden shaft of light shattering the carefully created Green illusion. They saw it in a flash, the deception soon laid bare: if the greenhouse effect doesn't get us first, the radioactivity will.

But the most beguiling trick of all was saved fittingly for last: the inimitable, the exceptional, the unbelievable 'Euro-illusion'. As with all the most astute Magic Circle entertainers. Mrs Thatcher took great pains to divert her audience's attention from what was really going on. For months, red herrings had been strewn about and the usual Aunt Sallies carefully tried out. To begin with, the Prime Minister had roundly condemned the idea of 'identikit' Europeans, a notion never even on offer, and rejected just as vehemently by every other European country. Indeed, the very fact that Scottish Nationalists, Basques, Catalans and a host of other ethnic and linguistic minorities now see their very salvation in the European Community undermines that old 'identikit' ploy completely. Moreover, Mrs Thatcher's well-meant chauvinism really does imply a most extraordinary degree of arrogance. Of course, as a nation, we have much of which we ought to be proud, much we should cherish. But let us not be led into one very dangerous, nationalistic trap. We are not the only country in Europe which believes its specificity and heritage are treasures worth preserving.

Ironically, it is in her attitude to Europe that Mrs Thatcher is becoming most European – indeed, a veritable Don Quixote. For nowadays she excels at creating non-existent windmills at which to go and tilt. No European, for example, has ever suggested the suppression of nationhood, a menace recurrently perceived by Thatcher. Neither can the complexities of Europe be reduced to a simple choice between a free-trade area or a system of centralized Socialist control and regulation, that other Thatcher myth. Finally, it is Quixotic indeed for the Prime Minister whose government signed further national rights away with the Single European Act, to start pontificating now about independent sovereign states. It sounds like nothing so much as Mata Hari bewailing her lost virginity. President Mitterand, claimed Sir Geoffrey Howe earlier that week, had once said he found the Prime Minister's changes in attitude 'intriguing'. Even Howe professed some faint surprise at the President's choice of epithet. Quite frankly, so did I. For there is one niggling doubt about this story which continues to assail me. I was not, sad to say, an interpreter at that particular meeting. But I cannot help wondering whether *intrigante* was not the term the President actually used. *Intrigante* – in translation, not 'intriguing' at all, but rather 'meddlesome' and 'scheming'. Certainly, Mrs Thatcher's 'pick and choose' philosophy towards international treaty commitments would seem to bear this theory out.

But the faithful, as oblivious to reality as Nigel Lawson on the day of the Queen's Speech, were only too happy to have the wool pulled over their eyes again. Now they too had convinced themselves that the Community would allow its economic fruits to be plucked without care for its social and regional problems. It was odd behaviour, all told, especially since the entire week had been spent preaching the opposite sermon of prosperity's concomitant responsibilities. But nurtured into such a happy state of illusion, it was now time to hit the believers with the most fantastic wheeze of all. This was to be the grand finale. This was to be the rabbit out of the hat, the egg from behind the ear, the stream of handkerchiefs from out of the mouth, the doves from up the sleeve and the lady sawn into two, all rolled into one. In short, the entire episode would defy belief. It was all too improbable, too inconceivable, too altogether impossible. Why, if I hadn't seen it with my own eyes and heard it with my own ears, I wouldn't have believed it myself . . .

Our vision of Europe, claimed the *diva*, employing the now usual royal 'we', and bringing this surreal week to an entirely fitting climax, is the true vision of Europe, the Europe its founding fathers always wanted.

It was positively mind-boggling, the ultimate party trick. I reeled as I recalled my own fledgeling days at the European Community, days when I counted myself privileged to listen to men like Jean Monnet, to work for men like Jean Monnet, when Jean Monnet was a hero of mine. The rapturous applause continued unabated as one thought sped through my mind. Prime Minister, you are no Jean Monnet.

# 8 / *1992 and all that*

*"OÙ EST LE CRUISE-MISSILE DE MA TANTE?"*

Over the past few decades, there has been a gradual, almost imperceptible and yet very definite drift of sovereignty away from the Houses of Parliament and into European Community institutions. Whole spheres of policy-making, including a most sensitive area of indirect taxation, are now decided in Brussels and not at Westminster. For all that, mention the topic of Europe in this country, and still people's eyes glaze over with that look of infinite indifference. Go one further. Ring up the House of Commons information office and ask when the debate on the Single European Act was held. You may chance upon the same young lady I disturbed, presumably in the middle of her afternoon's nail-filing session, and who categorically assured me that there is not, nor has there ever been, any such thing. Then try dropping the figure '1992' into conversation at the pub and see what happens. In Paris, so they tell us, *quatre-vingts douze* is already part of pavement-café life. In beer gardens in Munich and pizzerias in Rome, excited patrons speak of little else. But here? In this country the British seem to have developed some kind of Euro-block. They genuinely do not care. Even by 1988, MORI statistics indicated that 88 per cent of the population knew nothing, or not enough about the European Parliament – an alarming revelation with their elections scheduled for the following year's summer! This resolute apathy towards the Community and its various institutions has already cost us dear. It could turn out to be even more expensive. For shortly, for the second time in history, the European boat is coming in. On past performance, we Brits shall all be at the airport.

The European Community, as everybody knows, was first established as a job-creation scheme for otherwise totally unemployable modern language graduates. And so it was that I joined the Commission of the European Communities as a trainee conference interpreter in 1973, the year the United Kingdom acceded to the EC, and subsequently spent many happy hours in Brussels as the highly paid conduit of much well-meant, multilingual drivel. They were heady times back at the beginning, stumbling in the thickets of Bretton Woods, grappling with 'snakes in tunnels' and wrestling with the intellectual conundrum of fixed yet moveable exchange rates. Suddenly, we were overnight experts on matters as abstruse as 'multivariate regression analysis' in German, and 'double-entry methods' in French. Within weeks we could talk about the 'Norwegian pout box' in Italian, and discourse knowledgeably in all languages on the Common Customs Tariff of 'knickers, gussetless', and 'undershorts, whether or not Y-fronted'. Admittedly, at times, it was difficult to see the grander, overall European design, but we were a small band then, worked all hours, and if on occasion we grumbled, we still felt the thrill and enthusiasm of belonging to a new generation of *peaceful* Europeans. Besides, interpreters of English mother tongue were at an absolute premium in those days. The British have always been notoriously bad at languages and we were heavily in demand.

Yet despite our tireless efforts on their behalf, visiting emissaries from Whitehall were still fair game for clever, continental polyglots long since familiar with the arcane Common Market ropes. We would watch those poor, etiolated creatures from the Ministry of Agriculture, Fisheries and Food, unshackled from their linear-growth graphs for the first time in years, all hopelessly lost in the labyrinths of the Commission's Berlaymont building, and grasping their government-issue briefcases tightly to them like white sticks inviting understanding and help. Or in the Council of Ministers conference rooms, where the complications of headphones, microphones, simultaneous interpretation and free but unopenable bottles of Looza orange juice would often prove just that trifle too much. Most of them would spend the first few hours twiddling with the interpretation system's bakelite knobs, listening to incomprehensible Danish translations of speeches in Dutch, and quite genuinely believing in some dastardly Euro-conspiracy to keep them permanently in the dark.

All the same, the whole business was clearly a novelty for them. Now the perks of overseas travel, unintelligible menus, obnoxious Belgian taxi drivers, bovine Sabena air hostesses and the rare delights of Zaventem airport duty-free shop were no longer the exclusive preserve of their flashier Foreign Office colleagues. Not that the FO chaps were much hotter than they on the language front. As late as 1980, a survey of the British Embassy in Paris revealed that, *even there*, fewer than half the staff spoke anything vaguely corresponding to the language of Racine, and those who could were mainly in the telephonist/receptionist/minor clerk categories. But perhaps that was not quite so ridiculous as it might have seemed. Perhaps it was even the result of a positive policy decision. In the light of events, it was probably less dangerous for our senior diplomats to remain completely incapable of communicating with the locals under any circumstances. Why, in earlier years in Paris, so the story ran, one highly placed francophone diplomat, had created quite a stir after the failed assassination attempt on President de Gaulle's life. 'Pity they missed,' he allegedly commented in flawless French, hardly the sort of sentiment designed to foster mutual Anglo–French goodwill and understanding!

But during the 1970s there was no overwhelming danger of too many of 'Our Men in Brussels' dealing direct with the natives. Lengthy sessions spent interpreting the Committee of Permanent Representatives (the equivalent of ambassadors to the EC), seemed to indicate that a fairly healthy proportion of our high-flyers still hailed from the '*deux* gin and tonics, *trois* no trumps, and *où est le Cruise missile de ma tante?*' school of languages. It was hardly surprising, therefore, when you come to think of it, that the UK had joined the Euro-club on quite the wrong conditions, and that for many years these fiendish foreigners continued to run rings around us . . .

But back in 1973, the British government was only too delighted to be in Europe at last, almost irrespective of terms, and our entry was regarded as a great personal triumph for Tory Prime Minister, Ted Heath. Frustrated by negotiating deadlock, Heath had by-passed all the usual channels and decided instead to appeal directly to the French President Pompidou. Reporting back to the House of Commons in May 1971, Mr Heath confirmed the substance of these bilateral conversations: that 'Britain looked forward whole-heartedly to joining in the economic and monetary development of the Community' and that he had been able 'to dispel any reservations which the French might have felt about the British government's willingness to accept the consequences of this development for its own policies'. After almost twenty years of British bleating about the European Community's goal-post moving capacity, it is worth bearing those original promises and protestations in mind.

Even so, Heath's valiant efforts were always liable to be thwarted by a sizeable Tory rebellion in the Commons and, in the end, it was Labour's pro-market renegades led by Roy Jenkins who ensured the PM's ultimate success. This may have been, to paraphrase one Labour wag, the only time Roy had ever fought for anything in his life, apart from a table for two at the Mirabelle. His due reward came later, when he was appointed to the lucrative position of President of the Commission from 1977 to 1981. On his triumphant return, flushed with Economat claret and ideas on proportional representation, Roy Jenkins joined the Gang of Four to found the SDP. And the rest, of course, is oblivion . . .

The British people had been led to expect great things of the Community, but they were soon to be disappointed. Anti-marketeers and constitutionalists, opponents who had rightly warned against the loss of British economic sovereignty, were quick to demonstrate how the compensatory benefits of membership failed to accrue. But if we were suffering from sudden hikes in our cost of living, the original six members (France, Germany, Italy, Belgium, the Netherlands, and Luxembourg) were also feeling the pinch. The year 1973 heralded major economic recession for all industrialized countries as the OPEC-generated oil crisis began to take its toll. In the UK, however, the Community soon became a convenient scapegoat for all our ills. If the 52 bus was late again, if the Safeways check-out girl seemed *even* more vacuous than usual, if we lost a Test Match, it was all somehow down to membership of that dastardly Common Market. British politicians found – indeed, still continue to find – the catch-all Euro-excuse a marvellous godsend. For it is always far easier for them to blame problems on some nebulous Brussels bureaucrats than admit to their own sheer impotence in controlling events. British industry too, grown flabby on years of a Commonwealth-preference diet, preferred the easy option of an EC whipping-boy to any admission of their own inability to compete. In short, the Little Englanders were not happy, and Brussels was soon to be flooded with our most plentiful commodity, that most unattractive of British exports – the Whingeing Pom. Grouse as we might, however, the European ground rules had been fixed by the Treaty of Rome way back in 1957. Almost two decades later, the original six member states found it rather impertinent when some Johnny-come-latelies started trying to change them to suit themselves. Indeed, as irritated Frenchmen were only too keen to point out to our public-school and Oxbridge officials, the sort of chaps who had invented the ethic in the first place, joining any club means abiding by its rules. Either that, or getting out. But after such protracted efforts to join the Community in the first place, the idea of British withdrawal was never *seriously* on the cards . . .

There is one apocryphal story which describes the plight of an American tourist doing the usual London sights. Confused and utterly lost in Whitehall, he stops one of our 'wonderful English policemen', and asks him which side the Foreign Office is on. 'Well,' answers the bobby after a moment's thought, 'it's supposed to be on our side. But sometimes I wonder.' The average British citizen has always viewed the judgement and efficacy of all those faceless 'men from the ministry' with healthy scepticism. And often rightly so. There can be little doubt, for instance, that our entry into Europe, late and thus on quite the wrong terms, was due almost entirely to a chain of major FO blunders. Fortunately, civil servants remain unaccountable for their balls-ups – indeed, tradition generally dictates a mention for them in the Honours List. But these anonymous characters must shoulder much of the blame for the growing disillusion with which many people view the European Community today. For the Foreign Office's Euro-soap is a sorry tale, not so much high tragedy as bad bedroom farce. It kicks off with a series of missed opportunities and misread situations at the beginning, moves on to a period of complete policy reversals in the middle, and winds up with an almost obsessional devotion at the end. Not that our diplomats were alone in their original dismissal of the European movement. Most of our post-war politicians (Winston Churchill was an eminent exception) believed that the UK could manage quite nicely outside Europe, despite the disintegration of its empire. Politicians, however, are paid to be daft and blinkered, the best and the brightest of the Civil Service most certainly are not. Neither did it help that successive governments, including today's, continued to believe in some mystical 'special relationship' with our American allies. Even after 1956, when Eisenhower refused to support an Anglo–French invasion of Suez, the bitter truth still refused to percolate home. Britannia would never accept it. But her love affair with Uncle Sam had somehow fizzled out . . .

So where did all this leave us when the cold and realistic light of day finally dawned? Somewhere mid-Atlantic without a paddle and with no one to blame but ourselves. Certainly, we had managed to miss the Euro-boat quite comprehensively, though from the European side, there had been no want of encouragement for us to leap on board at the outset. Even as the pan-European vision was beginning to take shape after the Second World War, French Foreign Minister, Robert Schuman, and Finance Minister, Jean Monnet, Europe's 'founding fathers', had been counting on Britain to play the protagonist's role. Still cauterizing the wounds of war, the French saw British involvement as the best way of offsetting the possibility of any renewed German dominance. Italy's De Gasperi and Germany's Adenauer were equally happy to see Britain as the major contributor to a new, peaceful, political order. For their part, the smaller Benelux countries wanted Britain in to guard against an excessively powerful Franco–German axis. And the Americans too took a very positive view of British involvement in a new and united Europe, an added bulwark to the dreaded threat of Communism. But after all the lobbying, what did we do in 1955 when the invitation arrived for the Common Market launch party in Messina? Not unnaturally, the first thing we did was consult our British ambassadors in Europe. That, after all, is why we keep such people there. But their Excellencies, presumably, were far too busy with the Linguaphones to grasp the full significance of what was going on. It was not a 'serious' sort of thrash, they declared; certainly not the sort of 'do' respectable diplomats would care to be seen dead at; besides, it had possibilities of degenerating into something vaguely sordid – commerce and the like. Best do the right thing, though, and send *one* chappie along from the Board of Trade, but really couldn't see that it would ever amount to anything much . . .

Nor was this the first time a Euro-invitation had been so fatefully ignored. Already in the early 1950s, Britain had refused to join the European Coal and Steel Community so that nice Messrs Monnet and Schuman were beginning to despair of our ever joining in. But what could they do? At Westminster, all political parties continued to demonstrate a sentimental commitment to a Commonwealth of guaranteed markets and never-ending supplies of cheap raw materials. Or at least that was the theory. Newly independent colonies could be forgiven of flexing their economic muscles, and acting and thinking otherwise. Nothing, however, could dispel that quaint British notion of ourselves as a major world power, still calling all the shots. When the treaty establishing the European Economic Community was signed in Rome in 1957, no one was really surprised when the signature of the 'designated plenipotentiary of Her Majesty the Queen of the United Kingdom of Great Britain and Northern Ireland' was missing. Britain wished her European neighbours well, but still proclaimed a greater affinity to places as far flung as India, New Zealand, Australia and the West Indies. We continued to feel our greater interest lay with folk with whom we could feel historically comfortable, the sort of people who readily understood the finer nuances of our English language and, more important, of our glorious summer game.

Gradually, however, under the Conservative government of Harold Macmillan, attitudes started to change. Until then, European Community issues, perceived as simple trade questions, had been left almost exclusively for the Treasury to deal with. It was not until the early 1960s that anyone began to take the Euro-phenomenon at all seriously. Rather late in the day, the significance of British industries' decimated share in world markets began to ring warning bells even in places as remote as the Houses of Parliament. Enviously, we peered across the Channel and contemplated the living standards of our European neighbours, especially the West Germans, all awash with affluence, consumer durables, state-of-the-art BMWs, expensive, murky-green Loden coats, and silly felt hats accessorized with shaving brushes. In influential circles, the feeling that a Britain outside Europe could no longer prosper began to gain currency, and overtures were made with a view to EC membership. The man on the Clapham omnibus, of course, was still far from convinced, but Whitehall policy-makers have yet to lose sleep over the views of the sort of people who take buses in Clapham. Besides, the Foreign Office was now completely besotted with the idea, an overnight *volte-face* if ever there was one. True, the Labour Party and a fair proportion of Tories, not to mention Mr Average British Citizen, remained antagonistic. Certainly, as far as Mr Average was concerned, he simply did not care to be tied up, however loosely, with a pile of continental garlic-eaters. Even the less xenophobic and the more high-minded felt that the potential loss of sovereignty could never be compensated by vague promises of short-term economic gains. 'It does mean if this is the idea,' Hugh Gaitskell had argued at Brighton during the Labour Party Conference of October 1962, 'the end of Britain as an independent European state – it means the end of a thousand years of history.' Mr Gaitskell need not have worried. For years the British anti-marketeers would have the most formidable of allies on their side. It came embodied in the person of none other than President de Gaulle.

The President of France, General de Gaulle, was, of course, quite familiar with England and the English. He had, after all, spent a glorious and heroic war secreted over a jewellery shop in London's New Bond Street. No one would deny that the situation then was bleak. *Sacre bleu!* By the time the General arrived, they were clean out of diamonds of any sort and even passable aquamarine was impossible to come by. Nevertheless, what little we had we were glad to share with a man whose country was temporarily relegated to the second division of Thomson's holiday brochure. Sad to relate, however, our generous hospitality somehow failed to impress a guest who yearned desperately to be back home in *la patrie*. There, in gay Paris, jolly, thigh-slapping troops of German tourists would have been more than happy to organize alternative accommodation in the prestigious SS bed-and-breakfast hostel on the avenue Kleber. Alas, it's all so long ago. Who now could ever really understand the reasons why the good General took so violently against us? Perhaps it was the restricted number of English soft cheeses which aroused his undying antipathy. Or perhaps he felt Cartier's was never really good enough for a man of his stature. Maybe he was suffering from the familiar abreaction of many a rehabilitated loser: that of biting the hand that fed him.

Whatever his reasons, in 1963, President de Gaulle vetoed Britain's first serious effort to join the Community. The official justification, naturally, was rather more laudable than any of the above. Neither General de Gaulle nor *la France* (by this stage, like Mrs Thatcher and Great Britain, the two had become virtually indistinguishable) was prepared to risk a British Trojan Horse dragging the Americans into Europe. British dependence on her Transatlantic ally, whether real or perceived, was seen as positively inimical to the European cause. As far as the French were concerned, VE Day was very much a thing of the past. It was now they who held the pivotal position in Europe, and that they were loath to relinquish.

Undaunted, Harold Wilson's Labour government tried again in 1967. By that time, over a decade had elapsed since the country had first been subjected to the full asperities of life without the umbilical cord of empire, and few viable alternatives to Europe appeared to be on offer. Britain, at this late stage, was in an emasculated bargaining position, far too willing to accept poor conditions tempered by a few minor and mostly interim concessions. Even so, de Gaulle vetoed the deal, leaving only one possible conclusion. Until the great man was either off the political scene or, preferably, two metres under, there was little hope of the United Kingdom's ever joining this particular comity of nations. Sure enough, it was left to his successor, President Pompidou, to witness the United Kingdom's signature on the Treaty of Accession in December 1972. Ted Heath and the believers (sounds like a bad

1960s rock group) were thrilled, and earnestly extolled the benefits of membership as they promised the British people a Golden Age of increased trade, employment and productivity. As for the cost of joining the club, they would, like Scarlett O'Hara, think about that tomorrow . . .

We were still no more than half-hearted Europeans, however, and acceptance of Community membership was far from universal. Returned to power, Wilson's government was obliged to redeem its election promise to renegotiate terms of entry, and in 1975 called a referendum on the far from successful outcome. The whole business was something of a pantomine. Wilson was hardly vehemently anti-Community, having tried to join himself in 1967. Yet again, the more constitutional issues were never really aired amongst the broader public. Attention was focused instead on more jobs and higher pay, and the weight of the media was distinctly behind the 'Yes to Europe' lobby.

I often wonder how many Honourable Members actually took the trouble to study the conditions of the European Communities Act (1972) they were called upon to endorse. Very few, I would guess. For how else could they have swallowed the blanket provision governing the implementation of the Community Treaties? This condition states that

all such rights, powers, liabilities, obligations and restrictions from time to time created or arising by or under the Treaties, and all such remedies and procedures from time to time provided by or under the Treaties, as in accordance with the Treaties are *without further enactment* [my italics] to be given legal effect or used in the United Kingdom, shall be recognised and available in law, and be enforced, allowed and followed accordingly [Chapter 68, Part I.2(1)].

All right. So on the clarity stakes it is hardly translucent. But hack your way through that little lot of legalese, and even an MP might realize that a major constitutional change was being agreed. But isn't that the most disturbing hallmark of so many of our politicians? So busy are they clambering up the greasy pole, watching their backs, and racing round and round the Division Lobbies, that they rarely notice what they are legislating until the result is on the statute book. Then, of course, the bitching starts in earnest, but only when it is all far too late. At the time, few MPs fully understood and fewer still managed to warn against the far-reaching economic and political consequences of what they had accepted. And anyone who did could be conveniently dismissed as either Loony Left or Rabid Right. When I interviewed him early in 1988, Tony Benn gave me a copy of a pamphlet he had published way back in 1974, just before the referendum. It is entitled 'Loss of Self-government', and almost fifteen years later proves uncannily prophetic:

British membership of the community subjects us all to laws and taxes which your Members of Parliament do not enact, such laws and taxes being enacted by Authorities you do not elect, and cannot dismiss, through the ballot box. British membership of the Community means that Community laws and taxes cannot be changed or repealed by the British Parliament, but only by the Community Authorities not directly elected by the British people . . . I am not, of course, here addressing myself to the general or political arguments for or against entry, nor commenting on the view that the advantages of membership might outweigh the loss of democratic rights that I have described. But no one who votes in the ballot box should be in any doubt as to the effect that British membership has had, and *will increasingly continue to have*, in removing the power the British people once enjoyed to *govern themselves*.

At the other end of the political spectrum, Enoch Powell, that Cassandra of the Tory Party, was warning darkly against blank, signed cheques to finance an uncontrollable European Common Agricultural Policy.

It was all to no avail. The sovereign British people, heedless of the admonitions of those voices crying in the wilderness, decided overwhelmingly to sell Gaitskell's 'thousand years of history' for a mess of Euro-potage. The Australian aboriginals, so the historians relate, once parted with the city of Melbourne for a bag of beads. (Sydney folk, incidentally, still believe they were overcharged, but that is another story.) How we love to laugh at the commercial stupidity of such primitive people! As transactions go, however, our deal turned out to be little better.

Like some hapless insect negotiating a spider's web, only when the United Kingdom was well and truly in did she belatedly start to struggle. The oil crisis had, of course, put paid to any hopes of an economic boom, but there again nobody could be blamed for failing to foresee the oil crisis. The effects of the Common Agricultural Policy (CAP), on the contrary, were eminently predictable in the form of those blank, signed cheques of which Enoch Powell had so presciently served notice. Virtually severed by now from her cheap Commonwealth food supplies, the British housewife soon realized the full cost of being European. Yet while she battled to pay twice the price for everything, she kept on hearing stories of the Euroland of plenty; of wine-lakes, skimmed-milk-powder mountains, intervention stocks agogo, not to mention cheap butter sales to the Russians. Who was to blame for bringing her into this topsy-turvy universe? Who on earth had subjected her to the wild, wacky world of the CAP? Having failed originally to explain the consequences of their decisions, it was so much easier for British politicians just to blame Europe for the lot.

But British disillusionment with the EC has not been one-way traffic. Far from it. Great Britain has proved a major disappointment to its European partners too. For if, in the early days of membership, our industry failed to exploit access to a vast new market, a market of some 250 million consumers, then it had no one to blame but itself. It had no right to whinge. In fact, it was just such failures which made the cost of the CAP and our net payments to the Community budget seem so disproportionately large. Mrs Thatcher, as everybody knows, is not the sort of woman to throw good money after bad. But her hectoring 'I want my money back' negotiating tactics, whilst going down well with the more chauvinistic elements of the British press, only tended to exacerbate long-standing intra-Community frictions. Not that it has ever been the function of British Prime Ministers to be nice to foreigners. Perish the thought. And not that the British tax payer should have been expected eternally to shoulder an unjustly onerous share of Common Agricultural lunacy. Granted, Mrs Thatcher's success in achieving a ceiling on Britain's budgetary payments in the early 1980s was a credit to her determination as a negotiator. But it was also an index of our European partners' sense of 'fair play'. It is true the Prime

Minister can be a stubborn and daunting adversary. She also knows how to use that added ace of femininity to full advantage. Of all the many male opponents she has encountered, only the former French Prime Minister Jacques Chirac has ever been known to have the 'balls' to say as much to her. But rightly or wrongly, it is Mrs Thatcher's 'good housekeeping' philosophy which continues to deny the Community the funds it now needs to meet increasing regional, social, industrial and technological problems – all issues best dealt with at a supranational level. For despite chronic attacks of wind and gripe, and despite concerted attempts to smother it on occasion, the monstrous Euro-baby has survived to toddle. The question is, are we now prepared to let this peculiar hybrid thrive to full maturity?

In 1988, after three successive election defeats, the Labour Party decided it was perhaps, after all, high time to 'listen'. Now 'listening' is not a condition which readily affects your average politician, and everybody knows it. So back at HQ in Walworth Road, the admen dreamt up a snappy new campaign – 'Labour Listens', a strategy based almost entirely on the well-known marketing premise that any slogan with enough alliteration is bound to convince us. It might have been enlightening, just to establish where they had all been going wrong for so long, if the lads had kicked off by listening to a couple of London taxi drivers. You know the sort: ' 'Ere in this cab is the pulse, luv, an' I've got me finger on it. Know warra mean? Too many blacks/poofters/women at work/bloody foreigners in the country/private cars in Central London/trendy lefties on the telly. Not enough hangin'/floggin'/entrayprenewers like me/page-three pull-outs.' More profitably, of course, they might have tried listening to their own market researchers, MORI, the pollsters who have predicted the last three election results with such remarkable accuracy. In early 1988, their chairman, Bob Worcester, had some revealing statistics hot off the word processor. For whilst the results of the 1975 Euro-referendum had shown 67 per cent of the British population in favour of the EC, with 33 per cent in favour of withdrawal, by 1988 the polls demonstrated a hefty 12 per cent swing against membership: 55 per cent in favour of Europe and 45 per cent against. Interesting figures, indeed, and all the more interesting in light of a letter sent the previous month by Neil

Kinnock to one Enrique Baron, Member of the European Parliament, and Chair of the Manifesto Committee for the Confederation of the Socialist Parties of the EC. Here, for the first time in history, a British Labour leader made a positive contribution to the forthcoming Euro-elections. He expressed the hope that the comrades might 'avoid the necessity for the British Labour Party to produce a separate manifesto to that agreed collectively by the confederation'. He made an unprecedented Labour commitment to working constructively within the Community rather than threatening to pull out of it at the earliest opportunity. And he even suggested common Socialist policies 'to overcome public disenchantment with the Community's institutions'.

How about that as a turn-up for the books? Of course, Kinnock was chancing his arm by announcing this complete policy *volte-face* without waiting for any formal decision from the National Executive Committee. But considering the subsequent defence débâcle, this was only small potatoes. All the same, it did seem vaguely ironic that the Labour leadership's conversion to Europe should come at the very time when almost half the electorate was shown to be so heartily disenchanted with it. Nevertheless, Kinnock's courageous, pragmatic, if somewhat ill-timed, U-turn did leave one message clear. Growing in numbers though the polls may suggest the Little Englanders to be, not even the Labour Party is listening to them now. For better or for worse, for richer or for poorer, and even if it was all the most terrible mistake at the outset, we are now irrevocably committed to the European Community. It is high time we started exploiting the fact.

My own personal survey, conducted throughout the spring of 1988, and without a trace of objectivity in wine bars everywhere, proved equally revealing. The Single European Act, according to half the people polled, was no doubt an unfortunate one-night stand in Torremolinos. That would be it, together with the usual nasty consequences of such European union. All this, however, was before Lord Young decided to take the new Euro-challenge in hand. Overnight, his Department of Trade and Industry was transformed into the new-look government Department for Enterprise – as if, like military intelligence, the concepts of government and enterprise weren't mutually exclusive. A multimillion pound promotional budget was swiftly earmarked to explain to British industry about the creation of a 'single internal market' by 1992. The much hyped 'Europe Open for Business' campaign was soon well and truly under way. In fact, so well and truly under way that, after the first six months, an executive from the advertising agency concerned was obliged to phone a chum of mine at the London Business School. Would he come out to lunch, the adman enquired, and explain what 'all this European mumbo-jumbo stuff' was really about? Well, what can you expect for a mere £5m.? Nowadays, that kind of money wouldn't buy you a John Hurt voice-over on an anti-perspirant commercial! Poor chap had probably had a career in biological stain removal before this account came along.

Nevertheless, despite the problems of active public apathy, Lord Young and the boys are still pushing ahead, concentrating their efforts on the positive side. A single European market of 320 million consumers, a market larger than either that of the USA or Japan, an area where goods, capital, services, persons, Mr Alan Sugar's Amstrads and Mr Bruce Oldfield's frocks may all move freely without let or hindrance, a frontier-free Europe – that, they suggest, is the ticket. It is the only ticket, in fact, that Mrs Thatcher wants to see. But in Europe, as she ought to have realized by now, nothing is ever quite that simple.

The Single European Act came on to the British statute book in 1986. It was framed originally to give a new impetus to European integration, a process which had become paralysed over the years due to rules on unanimity voting in the Council of Ministers. In effect, the whole thing was really only a very watered-down version of a Treaty for European Union, the brainchild of Italian, Communist Euro-MP, Altiero Spinelli, a wonderful old character, now sadly deceased. Signor Spinelli, who looked like God the Father whilst steadfastly refusing to believe in Him, had a boundless enthusiasm for matters European. It was a fervour which people in general, and interpreters in particular, often found difficult to follow. For, as if to compensate for being only semi-intelligible in his own language, he soon became wholly unintelligible in another four besides. Not that any of this would have mattered, really, were it not for his constant insistence on operating in a scrambled amalgam of all five simultaneously. Yes, indeed, there were many sweated interpreter-hours spent trying to disentangle Altiero's high-powered cerebral spaghetti, most of them happily to no avail. Nevertheless, despite – or perhaps even because of – this remarkable inability to communicate clearly, Spinelli was universally admired and loved. He was, like Schuman and Monnet before him, a man of great vision, a remarkable European, and a politician of stature. What he was doing in the European Parliament, of course, was one of the mysteries we could never quite fathom.

If all now goes according to plan – and there is absolutely nothing in recent European history to suggest that it will – the first objective of the Single European Act should be achieved by the end of 1992: a frontier-free Europe where brain surgeons from Birmingham may set up shop in Bari, where sausages from Scunthorpe will pass the fitness test in Seville. Unfortunately, however, it is not every Euro-Thomas, Ricardo and Henri who finds himself involved in such elevated matters. His concerns are often far more mundane. What the average Brit would rather know, for instance, is whether he will be able to fall off the Malaga special at Gatwick, pick up the four-feet stuffed donkey the wife bought in that moment of excess-Rioja aberration from the Saturday street market in Marbella, march straight through Customs and Excise and Passport Control wearing a ridiculous sombrero, radiating third-degree burns, and singing 'Viva España', and all without being stopped and asked for his papers. Well, the answer to this modest aspiration, as far as the British Home Secretary is concerned, is: no way. As an island race, Mr Douglas Hurd maintains, we do not want to be invaded by hoards of drug-trafficking fraudsters and international criminals. We already have enough such people running both the City and rings around the Department of Trade and Industry. Even when the Channel tunnel is ready, continues Mr Hurd, border controls of some sort will be maintained between Us and the Continent. And with that go any hopes of persons and goods circulating freely over here!

But the odd passport and document check will be the least of our problems. Even the worst hypothesis means simply a continuation of the status quo. On the other hand, even a superficial scrutiny of the Single European Act reveals that further crucial developments of wide-ranging political significance have again been nodded through by our Westminster windbags. Even the act's preamble kicks off with a commitment 'to transform relations as a whole among the member states into a *European union* [my italics]'. And Article I continues with its stated aim of 'concrete progress towards *European unity*' [my italics]. Once again, the nation wakes up to find that major changes have been made to its constitutional arrangements without any genuine or informed public debate. The transformation of the Community into a political and constitutional union, combined with an increase in the application of majority as opposed to unanimity voting in the Council of Ministers, means yet another usurpation of British sovereignty. Speeches at Bruges are all very well. But it is too late now for the Prime Minister, a lawyer when all is said and done, to start quibbling over the terms of the international treaty which her own government has signed. So much for the depth of scrutiny at Westminster! Yet again, MPs have approved profound constitutional changes as if they hardly mattered.

Is it that our MPs do not *mind* or is it simply that they do not *know* what they're doing when it really counts? It is not even as if the Single European Act were a lone instance of their ineptitude. In 1972, too, politicians were shown to be ignorant of the ramifications of the European Communities Act. They failed egregiously to explain the issue to a trusting electorate. Yet again, in 1974, when a slice of the European Community budget was placed within the competence of the European Parliament (an institution which at that time was not even elected, but merely appointed), only two MPs in the entire House – the ever-vigilant Nigel Spearing, chairman of the Select Committee on European Legislation, and the implacably anti-EC Enoch Powell – had the slightest idea of what was going on. True, the European Parliament was given authority only over so-called 'Non-compulsory Expenditure', that part of the budget left over when the Community has forked out for agricultural expenditure. In a good year this usually amounts to something over a fiver, but the principle remains the same. The House of Commons should have thought rather harder before placing funds within the jurisdiction of a non-elected body. It is precisely this Euro-story which brings us to one sorry conclusion: if our MPs cannot be bothered to monitor legislation properly, if they are content to be mindless rubber-stampers, then the blame is theirs when such legislation robs them of the few rights they retain. For almost two decades now, MPs have allowed and accepted this gradual erosion of British sovereignty, this transfer of legislative power to Brussels. There are those who believe, considering the average calibre of Westminster Man, that this is no bad thing. I happen to be one of them. But there is one wee democratic problem. Who may we rely upon now to control that non-elected executive, the European Commission?

Up on the thirteenth floor of the Brussels Berlaymont building live the European Commissioners. They were, so received opinion would once have had us believe, a merry band of has-beens, never-weres, or, having accepted this stint of five-star political exile, never-will-be's-again. The same is certainly no longer true today. For any Commissioner worth his salt may wield far more power, will end up far more high-profile than ever he could as a minister back home. Even for the dwindling 'surplus to domestic requirements and put out to grass' contingent, the job still carries enormous kudos and compensations: a large salary, generous expenses, a suite of flash offices, and guaranteed, well-pensioned comfort for the rest of your life. Naturally, there are certain rules by which this Euro-college is obliged to abide. In assuming office, all Commissioners pledge to forgo the specific interests of their own nation, and to act and think 'European', whatever that may mean. Although a political appointee, a Commissioner must never be subjected to pressure by his own particular government. Indeed, governments are clearly instructed not to try and interfere. But sadly, two of our British Commissioners took their Euro-oath too seriously for the liking of Mrs T. First Labour's Ivor Richard, then Conservative Lord Cockfield went so far as to 'go native'. Unhappily for them, they even began to see the broader picture. For such integrity and effort, both were very swiftly axed.

Ensconced on the thirteenth floor from 1986 to 1988, and shouldering specific responsibility for the internal market, sat ex-Tory minister, Lord Cockfield. Francis Arthur to friends, he would always remain 'Sweet F.A.' to officials from his previous incarnation at the Department of Trade and Industry. Now, Lord Cockfield is a man of many fine qualities, not least of which is the remarkably soporific quality of his voice. Even at his most animated, the noble Lord makes Sir Geoffrey Howe sound like Tina Turner in concert. For a woman of the Prime Minister's Euro-devotion, this was just the man to bore those Europeans into total catalepsy. Unfortunately for the PM, however, no sooner was the mild-mannered Sweet F.A. out of the country, than he too contracted the dreaded Berlaymontitis. Within months, like the previous victim, Ivor Richard, Lord Cockfield had started thinking and behaving 'European'. The condition, which for British politicians is invariably terminal, is easily contracted up there on the thirteenth floor. Divorced from the domestic realities of everyday political expediency, and quietly contemplating the battalions of beastly Belgians doing battle down rue de la Loi, even the strongest of minds has been known to succumb. Lord Cockfield, poor dear, soon surrendered to a bad dose of 'harmonization hallucinations'. So serious were they, they even involved telling Mrs Thatcher to bring British indirect taxation into line with European norms. Obviously, it was only a matter of time before Lord Cockfield was on his way . . .

Cast your minds back, for a moment, to January 1988. Try and recall the original SDP/Liberal merger manifesto, 'Voices and Choices for All' – a piece of political ineptitude, stunning even by Mr David Steel's own inimitable standards. Why, the commitment to Trident alone would have sufficed to curdle any good Liberal's organic yoghurt and make the mohair on the back of his Fair Isle polo-neck stand up on end. But even that wasn't good enough. No, they had to go one further, and suggest the imposition of VAT on children's clothing. *VAT on children's clothing?* Where on earth, everyone wondered, could these people have found such an idea? What could have generated such manifest mental aberration? Perhaps, before going any further, they really ought to go and consult a good doctor, although on second thoughts . . . But apart from proposing a luxury tax on Zimmer-frames, no one could have tried harder to commit political suicide at birth. Reaction came swiftly and the beleaguered Mr Steel had a very bad time trying to bury this still-born charter as soon as possible. But where was the genesis of this loopy idea? Where else, indeed, but the European Commission.

In an internal market, Lord Cockfield and the Euro-mandarins argue, rates of indirect taxation such as VAT must be harmonized in order to avoid distortions of trade. But the right to levy taxes – or, indeed, for social reasons, the right *not* to levy taxes – is a crucial area of government, and an area which the British government is now fighting a losing battle to retain. Mrs Thatcher has always pledged her opposition to the imposition of VAT on traditionally zero-rated items such as children's clothing, food and fuel. But a controversial ruling from the European Court of Justice in early 1988, insisting that VAT be applied to a number of hitherto zero-rated products, came as the first whiff of grapeshot. It was, as veteran Tory anti-marketeer Teddy Taylor put it, 'the first time since the Ship Tax in the seventeenth century that a body outside Parliament has told Parliament what taxes it can levy.' This might have sounded a trifle excessive, particularly as the ruling in question only related to spectacle frames. But where, you may well ask, will it all end? Will attempts to harmonize indirect taxation be followed by efforts to co-ordinate direct taxation also? Will Westminster degenerate into more of an ineffectual talk-shop than it already is? And, frankly, would anybody give two hoots even if it did? Well, one man who doesn't appear to care – at least, not from listening to him – is our admirable Trade and Industry Secretary.

'The trouble with politicians,' maintains Tony Benn, 'is that they mystify or oversimplify when really they ought to clarify.' I contemplated these wise words as I listened to Lord Young launching his 1992 Euro-awareness campaign. 'It does not matter,' claimed the good Lord on that occasion, 'whether we all have the same rates of VAT or tax. The priority is having similar products, like an electric plug that can be used in any of the European countries.' Of course! The apogee of the European founding fathers' aspirations! The Euro-plug! Why get bogged down in explaining mere details like European union and unity? Why get upset over who'll be dictating taxation strategy in the future? No – let's concentrate instead on the really important problems, issues like plugs. Not that I, of all people, am not utterly convinced of the importance of the harmonized plug in the grand European fresco. After all, as staff at that excellent establishment will readily testify, the whole of Strasbourg's Holiday Inn can still be brought to its knees by one woman stuffing a Luxembourg hair-dryer into an incompatible French power point. Of course it would be desirable to have such anomalies sorted out. But even at this late stage, I'm afraid the British government's fobbing-off really will not do. Lord Young, with his regional breakfasts, the odd snappy ad, and sod-the-sovereignty-let's-pilot-a-new-plug stratagems, is no substitute for a proper public-information campaign. After more than fifteen years in the European Community, it is time the British people were fully informed of deals already struck on their behalf. Only then, perhaps, will certain politicians be forced to stop their specious patriotic public posturing, and finally accept the responsibility for what they themselves have done.

For an intelligent woman, Mrs Thatcher often seems remarkably slow at learning her historical lessons. It seems strange, for example, that someone so implacably opposed to the dependency culture should have tried so slavishly to hitch her wagon to an American (B-movie) star. Perhaps the Hollywood glitz surrounding her friendship with former President Reagan simply blinded her to reality. But the uncomfortable truth behind all American foreign policy is that it is based, has always been based, and always will be based, on American self-interest, on that and on that alone. In bartering away US nuclear weapons at Reykjavik, for instance, did good old Ronnie give a second thought as to how this would undermine the security of Western Europe? Of course not. He was only too happy to negotiate right above his European allies' heads. There is no doubt that Mrs T.'s deeply meaningful relationship with the old cowboy was her finest PR coup. But their schmaltzy farewells prior to Reagan's departure obscured a far more pertinent point, the real sign of who's who in the international arena. For the first European leader whom President-elect Bush chose to meet was not the British Prime Minister at all. It was the West German Chancellor, Herr Helmut Kohl. President Gorbachev, too, has been courting the European Community assiduously. For if there is one thing that Russians, of all politicians, can be expected to understand, it is the intrinsic power of blocs. With the Euro-writing now clearly on the wall, Gorbachev is at pains to ensure that a post-1992 'Fortress Europe' will not damage the future prospects of his own economic revival. Both world superpowers have finally woken up to the importance of the European phenomenon. But thanks to Mrs Thatcher, the guidance of the Euro-dynamic has been ceded to the Germans and the French.

But even today the Prime Minister refuses to accept the inevitable. Still she maintains her 'pick and choose' attitude to Euro-deals long since signed, sealed and delivered. Try as she may, her shameful and premature recall of dedicated British Commissioners will not slow the integration process down one jot. Indeed, the choice of Sir Leon Brittan as Lord Cockfield's successor may prove merely another unexpected rod to beat the Prime Ministerial back. To many it seemed an odd appointment and raised many questions. For Brittan, a ministerial casualty of the Westland 'leaked letter' scandal, is a politician who must fit into one of two categories. Either he was guilty of some impropriety in relation to the leak, in which case others would be far more worthy of the plum Euro-job. Alternatively, he was not guilty of any misconduct in relation to the leak, in which case he must have played the fall-guy for Someone Higher Up. Who will ever know the full truth of the matter? At all events, the affair prompted old parliamentary hands to recall that popular (even if not wholly appropriate) ditty from Profumo days;

> To lie in the nude
> Is not at all rude,
> But to lie to the House
> Is obscene.

It is a tragedy for the country, and for Mrs Thatcher herself, that the Prime Minister has stubbornly refused to take this most golden opportunity to shine. It is time the British and their *fin de siècle* Westminster Men finally understood the way the winds of change have been blowing for years. For today, it is only as an active and positive partner in a strong, independent and prosperous European Community that the United Kingdom can ever hope to survive. Popular disillusion with the Community has been nurtured disgracefully by successive governments' failure to explain the issues. The British media, too, must accept part of the blame. Granted, the situation has improved. But even today, our so-called quality papers carry far less European news than their continental counterparts. Ignorance and indifference have been allowed to thrive.

Yet one development remains certain, whether people have understood it or not. Membership of the Euro-club has left Westminster a weaker institution. The transfer of sovereignty over important areas of policy-making and taxation has invested new and important responsibilities in the Commission. Perhaps at some future date, a stronger European Parliament will manage to assert a more democratic form of control over all those areas wrested from national parliaments' purview. 'The European Parliament!' I can hear the critics exclaim. 'But they're nothing but a bunch of second-rate no-hopers.' I used to think so too, incidentally, until I discovered Westminster . . .

# 9 / The next steps: a Thatcherite solution to the Houses of Parliament

**QUESTION OF POLITICS**

MARGARET THATCHER   IAN BOTHAM   CECIL P

"OH NO, NOT A 'HOME' QUESTION!
I ALWAYS GET THOSE WRONG."

The most intriguing phenomenon about the Houses of Parliament is how the institution has managed to survive at all in third-term Thatcherland. For if ever an assembly failed to do its appointed task efficiently; if ever an organization fell short of its consumers' expectations and requirements; if ever an outfit was run for the benefit of its inmates rather than that of the public, then that institution is the Houses of Parliament today. In accordance with every tenet of Thatcherite philosophy, this incompetent establishment must now be a prime candidate for privatization. It is surely only a matter of time before a new-look governing body, Big Ben Promotions plc, will be set up in its place. Of course, the belated process of rationalization will mean heavy casualties. But never has radical surgery been more necessary than on this particular heap of dead wood.

Certainly, the Upper House could be sacked overnight without anybody's even noticing. Its status as a revising chamber is vastly overrated. And its proven unwillingness and inability to act as a brake on the immoderation of elected government has left it devoid of any purpose. More outstanding members could still commit their wisdom to the opinion columns of the papers, a more appropriate forum for the cosmic nature of their thoughts. But in a society based exclusively on merit, and economic merit at that, this bastion of orchestrated privilege has no further *raison d'être*. In a nation where everything must justify its cost, it is high time the Lords was axed.

The fate of our 650 elected representatives is equally open to debate. For, under the new regime, there is no sound economic reason for MPs' continued monopoly of 8 acres of prime SW1 real estate. With property prices ranging from £120–90 per square metre, the Palace of Westminster has become far too valuable an asset to be wasted on MPs' inefficient work stations. Indeed, MPs should be thrilled at the prospect of their relocation. They do nothing, in any event, but whinge about the paucity of Westminster's facilities. The palace could then be leased out far more profitably, possibly to a hotel or restaurant group. With a wonderful hint of irony, the name of Trust House Forte springs to mind. Never fully accepted by the Old Establishment, how happy Lord Forte would be to have the opportunity to run it.

Rehousing MPs should present no problems whatsoever. Let them join Whitehall's newly 'hived-off' executive agencies in their travels up to Runcorn. Only in such places can they enjoy all the office space they require at the far more realistic rate of £30 per square metre. Besides, the move would be a salutary sociology lesson for the majority of MPs. Perhaps those green-belt Tories, currently hysterical at the prospect of a high-speed rail link from Folkestone to London, might take a good look at the countryside as they make their journey north. Since the industrial revolution, the new environmentalists might then realize, this country's prosperity has been bought with the pock-marks of Midlands coal mines, with the scars of slagheaps and chimney-stacks all over the industrial North. But no one, of course, ever gave a damn about that. It was only when the oast-house vote of Kent starting whining that the concept of 'progress' was finally called into question. For too long, the general interests of this country have suffered from governmental South-centricity. As the new seat of government, Runcorn would prove as fair a crossroads as the Commons could hope to find.

The insidious dependency culture of Westminster must also be rooted out. It has gone on far too long. No longer is there the slightest justification for the universal payment of MPs' salaries. A means test must be introduced immediately. Far too many millionaires, even Tory millionaires, even *nouveau riche* Thatcher-genre millionaires, are shamelessly grabbing the cash along with all the paupers. It is as if they had never heard the Gospel according to St Margaret. Comfortable in the security of their affluence, these folk become MPs simply to indulge their hobby of politics. It is, after all, a pleasant post-prandial exercise to watch the party protagonists at play. Such dilettantes hanker to join the Westminster Club as do cricket lovers the MCC, though the MCC, I must hasten to add, is more discerning in its choices.

The question of overmanning comes next on the privatization agenda. Big Ben Promotions plc has no room on its books for mere interested dabblers. Shareholders are bound to ask what sort of job the present 650 employees are actually doing. The question is a tough one. I've been asking it now for over a year, and I still don't know the answer. For on what precise business are our MPs so busily engaged? They are no longer educators. That role has been taken over by the media. They are not policy-makers or legislators. Civil servants in Whitehall and Brussels have seen to that. They are not scrutinizers, as issues ranging from Zircon to the Single European Act have so blatantly exposed. And neither are they gutsy, free-thinking individuals keeping a curb on government, as the success of the party whipping system has amply demonstrated. Some, it is true, have turned themselves into decent welfare officers. But that is a job more effectively consigned to appropriate full-time agencies. No, self-justify though they will, the organization is clearly chock-a-block with supernumerary staff. In the new, lean and keen Big Ben Promotions plc, we are talking mass redundancies.

We must be radical. We must be brutal. We must be 100 per cent pure Thatcher. Today we live in a TV age. The winning combination is the party leader's image plus a flashy policy-marketing campaign. MPs, if the truth be told, are now completely surplus to requirements. For years, they have striven to keep the press, radio and television out of their hermetically sealed environment. They wanted to keep their club both elusive and exclusive. Their grudging, eleventh-

### The next steps: a Thatcherite solution to the Houses of Parliament | 229

hour agreement to allow the TV cameras in 'on trial' has come too late. So elusive and exclusive have they become, that now they are simply irrelevant. At last we have the technology to make true democracy work. Technical advances mean that the nation's wishes can be reflected most accurately through a system of direct polls. The predominantly white, middle-aged, middle-class, male MP, that unrepresentative filter which has created the gross distortions of the past, must now be removed from the equation.

In future, television – deregulated television – will provide us with the ultimate in democratic government: government by *genuinely* popular consensus. A weekly panel game, *A Question of Politics*, featuring the party leaders and their chosen PR men (Mrs T. with Tim Bell, Mr K. with Peter Mandelson, etc.) is all we really need. Panelists will be encouraged to explain the party's policy on any given issue without hesitation, repetition or deviation. David Coleman will act as Speaker. A few guest celebrities – Ian Botham and Bill Beaumont, perhaps – may be invited along occasionally to help with the *What Happens Next?* quiz. 'What happens next when taxes are cut, consumer spending booms, the trade deficit widens and interest rates rocket?' I. T. Botham's guess, as events have shown, would be as helpful as Nigel Lawson's. At the end of the show, the viewing public will be asked to ring in and vote for their preferred policies. No waste, no inefficiency, no nonsense, a government at last directly answerable to its consumers – surely this must be the apogee of third-term Thatcherism? Mark my words and pay attention to Her Majesty's next Queen's Speech . . .